NATURE IS YOUR GUIDE

This unusual book by a great Australian navigator explains how to find your way by land or sea anywhere in the world simply by observing the signs of nature. By reading and interpreting these signs correctly primitive man could travel great distances across the oceans or through harsh bush country without the aid of map or compass. Modern man, on the other hand, has become so dependent on mechanical gadgets and scientific aids that he is in danger of losing the powers of observation and deduction which were a matter of life and death to our ancestors. Here is how to develop those powers and sharpen your senses.

With this book you need never be lost.

Other Works

THE RAFT BOOK

AROUND THE WORLD
IN EIGHT DAYS
(*with Wiley Post*)

HAROLD GATTY

NATURE IS
YOUR GUIDE

*How to Find your Way
on Land & Sea*

WITH A FOREWORD BY
LIEUTENANT GENERAL
J. H. DOOLITTLE

*52 Illustrations by Francis Lee Jaques
Douglas Woodall & Others*

FONTANA
Collins Australia

ACKNOWLEDGMENTS

I wish to extend my grateful thanks to Dr. Robert Cushman Murphy, eminent ornithologist and leading authority on oceanic birds, whose advice and assistance in the chapter on the habits of sea birds have been most valuable; and also to James Fisher, the distinguished English naturalist, for his valuable editorial assistance in this chapter and elsewhere in the book, and for contributing a number of original facts, useful criticism and suggestion. I owe much also to my wife, without whose aid in the translating of research materials from other languages, and in the testing of methods and theories of path-finding in the field in various parts of the world, this book would not have been possible. For all her help and encouragement over the years I am deeply grateful. Plate I is taken from a photograph in *Coming Events in Britain* and is reproduced by kind permission of the British Travel and Holidays Association.

The paintings of Sea Birds are by Francis Lee Jaques

First published 1958 by William Collins Sons & Co. Ltd.
First issued in Fontana Books 1977 by
William Collins Publishers Pty. Ltd., Sydney
Printed at The Dominion Press, Nth. Blackburn, Victoria.

ISBN 0 00 634510 7

CONTENTS

6 CONTENTS

PLATES

7

FOREWORD

By

LIEUTENANT GENERAL J. H. DOOLITTLE

FUTURE generations will have reason to be grateful that Harold Gatty, during the latter years of his life, recorded with painstaking care his immense and unique fund of knowledge in the realm of pathfinding by natural methods on sea and land. Even in these days of highly advanced technical aids, situations can arise when it is vital for us to be able to find our way by observing the signs of nature. In this field Harold Gatty was uniquely qualified. During World War II, *The Raft Book*, his first work on the subject, was standard equipment in U.S. Army Air Force life rafts. Written to help men who were adrift at sea, it proved of great value. In *Nature Is Your Guide*, Harold Gatty has vastly expanded his treatment of the topic. The present book covers much of the marine material in the earlier work, and also deals with pathfinding on land—in the wilderness, in the desert, in snow-covered areas, and under other conditions, in most parts of the world. Drawing on years of study and observation, the author has provided illuminating accounts of the methods by which early explorers and primitive peoples found their way on their long journeys by observing nature. In fascinating detail, he records ways in which we also can profit from their methods simply through greater knowledge and observation of such phenomena as birds, animal life, weather, vegetation, the shifting of sands and patterns of snow fields, and of course the position of the sun, moon and stars.

Harold Gatty was born at Campbelltown, Tasmania, on January 5th, 1903, and educated at the Royal Australian Naval College. Thereafter he served for several years as a ship's officer in the merchant marine, and undertook special research in air navigation. My own friendship with him started in 1931 when he won world-wide fame as an air navigator through his record-breaking eight-day flight around the world with Wiley Post in the *Winnie Mae*. For this achievement, our country, by special Act of Congress, awarded him the Distinguished Flying Cross.

That same year, the U.S. Army Air Corps embarked on its first specialised courses in air navigation, and Harold Gatty was placed in charge of Air Navigation Research and Training. The military regulation normally restricting such a post with our armed forces to American citizens was waived in his case to enable him, as an Australian, to accept this position, which he filled with distinction for several years. Among his students were many officers who have since held prominent commands in our Air Force.

During World War II, he served with the rank of Group Captain in the Royal Australian Air Force. In this capacity, his excellent work as Director of Air Transport for the Allied Air Forces, first in Java and later at General MacArthur's headquarters in Australia and New Guinea, contributed to the final victory.

After the war Harold Gatty settled in the Fiji Islands, where he established and operated the Fiji Airways. He also conducted a coconut plantation on his beautiful island, Katafanga, in the South Pacific.

In the course of my own early experiments in instrument flying, I learned that there is, among humans, no such thing as an innate or intuitive sense of direction or balance, and that maintaining altitude and course depends upon observation, either of instruments or of natural things.

Through long and patient research which led him on special journeys to many parts of the world, Harold Gatty gathered and tested in the field the wealth of pathfinding secrets presented in the following pages. His book is a treasury of practical and little known lore, most of it given in no other volume. Clearly and graphically, it tells exactly what natural indications to look for in finding your way, and how to interpret them.

Shortly after finishing this book, Harold Gatty died suddenly at his home in the Fiji Islands. It is fortunate that this work will remain as a monument to his boundless interest in the natural world around us and to the precision of observation and thought which made him the foremost navigator of his time. To many readers everywhere it will be a rare and valuable experience to share in this life work of research and observation, which included also a great love of nature and all outdoor life. To a unique degree, Harold Gatty has given us a work which can serve as a companion, illuminating and expanding our pleasure in the outdoors, and at the same time minimise its dangers. The reader will not only gain confidence; he will also discover a more intimate appreciation and understanding of the world of nature. And I feel sure that that is what Harold Gatty, himself, hoped to accomplish in writing this book.

J. H. DOOLITTLE
Lieutenant General
U.S. Air Force Reserve

PREFACE

THIS IS a new sort of outdoor book. In it I have attempted to bring together in a single volume the natural methods which can be used as practical aids in pathfinding. The book's aim is to enable the reader to find his way, on land or at sea, if necessary without map or compass, by using his own powers of observation and knowing how to interpret the signs of nature.

The countless clues and guide-posts which nature places at our disposal as aids in natural navigation are for the most part little recognised or known to-day. With the invention of such technical devices as the chronometer and gyro-compass, radar and the automatic pilot, modern man tends to forget that earlier and more primitive peoples have had little difficulty in finding their routes through the wilderness and across the wide deserts and oceans completely without the aid of any such devices. My hope is that this book may help to revive this all but vanished art, and that it will enable the reader to acquire a practical and dependable knowledge of pathfinding by natural means.

In the course of my regular work I have been engaged for the past thirty-five years in research in navigation, including not only modern methods but also those used by early and primitive peoples. This latter phase of the work soon made it clear to me that the early explorers, lacking modern aids in navigation, relied in large part on observing and interpreting the natural things around them. This has been true not only of Occidental explorers but also of pioneers of other races such as the Polynesians, the American Indians, and the aborigines of Australia. These and many other peoples unversed in modern science have amply demonstrated their remarkable skill in traversing long distances through the wilderness or across the oceans, aided only by natural signs and their own skill in observing and interpreting them. To-day, these same methods of pathfinding can be used equally effectively by those who know what to look for and how to read the signs correctly.

In the course of my own work as a navigator, and on other occasions, the methods described in this book have been tested and found practical. The various chapters have been designed to cover the many differing types of conditions encountered over a large part of the world. Most of the methods described will not be found in the usual outdoor books, and it is hoped that they will be useful to readers engaged in many different outdoor pursuits.

In order to use the book most effectively, a few general considerations should be borne in mind. Although it embraces many diverse parts of the world, it is obvious that no one book could possibly hope to cover every locality in detail. The examples given apply in some cases to particular areas, but are also meant to illustrate the type of thing which every reader can learn about his own locality. Many of the general suggestions given in the book can thus be adapted to local conditions and applied in your own region.

In using these methods of observing and interpreting the evidence of the natural things about us, it is important to remember that under difficult conditions, too much reliance should never be placed on any one observation, since it may perhaps be an exception to the general rule. It is the combined evidence of a number of different indications which strengthens and confirms the conclusions to be drawn from them individually.

It should also be emphasised that the methods of pathfinding described in this book are intended not to replace the use of map and compass, if these are available, but rather to supplement them. Map and compass techniques are dealt with in many readily available outdoor books and manuals and are beyond the scope of the present volume. Nor is the book intended to cover methods of obtaining food, water and shelter in order to sustain life in the wilderness, or in case of distress at sea, subjects which have already been adequately covered by publications of the armed forces.

Compact tables for telling directions from the sun, at all times of year and in all latitudes from the Equator to 60 degrees North and 50 degrees South, will be found at the back of the book. These tables have been especially prepared for the book, to fill the need for such data in compact form, practical for the use of the average outdoorsman. The professional sun tables hitherto in print are so detailed and voluminous that only a trained navigator or surveyor has the specialised knowledge needed to use them.

May I add that this book is not only intended to help the traveller who is seriously concerned with finding his way in the outdoors. In my own experience, a knowledge of natural methods of pathfinding and orientation adds a great deal to the pleasure of even an otherwise uneventful walk in the country or cruise on waters near home or in the world's far places. Whatever the reader's individual circumstances in this respect, therefore, it is my hope that this book will add to his enjoyment by helping him to understand and interpret the natural world around him.

HAROLD GATTY

KATAFANGA ISLAND

FIJI ISLANDS

August, 1957

CHAPTER I

NATURE IS YOUR GUIDE

"HE MUST have a wonderful sense of direction"—I must have heard this expression in everyday use by honest people hundreds perhaps even thousands of times—used by them, in all innocence and sincerity to convey the idea of a mysterious ability, somewhat vague and quite indefinable in its nature and operation. Some people, with a knowing nod, will even go farther, and imply that the sense of direction is a sixth sense, a quite special sense to be added to the five senses with which the ordinary man or woman (and many another animal) is born.

I do not believe that there is any such sixth sense. A man with a good sense of direction, is, to me, quite simply an able pathfinder—a natural navigator—somebody who can find his way by the use of the five senses (sight, hearing, taste, smell and touch—the senses he was born with) developed by the blessing of experience and the use of intelligence. All that the pathfinder needs is his senses and knowledge of how to interpret nature's signs.

There is a whole world of these natural signs and guide-posts for us to observe and interpret. By means of them we can find our way in remote and lonely places, on land or sea, if need be without map or compass. Nature always has a reason, and the chief purpose of this book is to help you interpret those reasons and apply them in pathfinding.

A good pathfinder can become so proficient that he can amaze the average person. If he likes to be mysterious he can easily persuade his friends that he has a sixth sense; but if he wants to be honest he must admit that he has nothing of the kind.

Nearly everybody is born with eyes, ears, a nose, taste-buds and a sensitive skin. Some, of course, are born with sense-organs more sensitive than those of others. All of us use our sense-organs instinctively; that is, we do not have to be taught to use them, but inherit the ability to do so along with the organs themselves. But some use them better than others; and all of us are given the power of improving the use of our senses, by experience, by practice. Much of the use that we make of our senses depends on our early environment. Many city dwellers cannot seriously have to consider the necessity of pathfinding once they have learned to talk and read, but for their own self-preservation the country dweller, the forester, the fisherman, the sailor and many others of us have to become thoroughly familiar with the natural things around them.

In our increasingly urban civilisation the necessity of observing and interpreting nature's signs is, I suppose, slowly disappearing. By this I mean it is no longer often a matter of life and death: but because it is no longer a vital necessity there is no reason why it should decay, any more than music, painting, bird watching, tobogganing or any other forms of pure art, science or sport should decay. I think that the interpretation of the signs of nature can and should be taught to children in schools at the same level as geography, mathematics. I think it is still tremendously important for anybody to be able to find his way by the use of nature's signs; and I think it is even more important that, trained in the use of nature's signs, all should be able to gain a wide appreciation of the natural things around them even if they are not likely to have to navigate. The habit of natural observation, of noticing natural details, natural features, is one that can easily be developed with proper training and practice— developed to such a pitch that astonishing feats can be performed without conscious mental effort.

There is something which all the greatest artists and writers, naturalists and scientists, voyagers and explorers, poets and pioneers, share. It is an interest in the external world and the ability to contribute something creative to human life in this world by means of taking parts of the world to pieces and putting them all together again. The ability to observe, and the ability to see the little things that seem trivial at first, may become amazingly important and meaningful. Out of little observations huge ideas may grow; and if a mind, made receptive by training in the use of the senses, can store away a mass of observations, the time will come when the whole collection can be unrolled, connected together as a great novel is planned, in a compelling pattern that tells us something *new*. Many of our greatest naturalists, like Gilbert White and Charles Darwin, spent many years of their youth pottering around, in activities which must have seemed aimless to many of their friends. Darwin's parents and teachers, indeed, got very anxious because they thought he was lazy, when all the time he was quietly storing up observations which many years later came spinning forth, all welded together as the greatest scientific idea of the nineteenth century. Not all of us can be Darwins, but all of us can be constructive potterers, all of us can go for walks with no purpose in view but that of watching, of observation, of developing the use of the senses we are born with, of arousing thought and stimulating the imagination, of awakening the creative faculties. Everything becomes more meaningful to him who watches and listens without too much thought to the value of his time.

One man, Lord Baden Powell, the first Chief Scout, built a whole movement on watching and listening. He called it " Scouting " and the movement swept the world. I have met many natural scouts in a life of much travel and in a long search for material for this book. I have rubbed my own theories and knowledge of pathfinding against those of others, and often I have come across many surprising examples of people who have developed keen faculties of observation. I have only space to devote to three of them here, three very different people. What they can do shows how striking are the results of training, of natural interest, of long experience and practice.

In the summer of 1949, I was visited in Fiji by Dr. Robert Cushman Murphy, the eminent American ornithologist. He is certainly the world's greatest authority on seabirds: but my first taste of his ornithological ability came when he and his charming wife motored four miles with me, mainly through the town of Suva, from their ship to my Fiji home. Now Fiji has not got a very large variety of birds. There is no recent published list of the birds of Fiji but if you study Dr. Ernst Mayr's *Birds of the South-West Pacific* you will find that you could spend a whole season in the gardens and country around Suva without seeing more than about thirty-three different kinds of birds, although you will pick up a few more if you go farther inland into the dense forests or up to the hills. On our way to my house we talked, quite busily, but when we arrived there Dr. Murphy remarked, " I've seen eleven different kinds of birds since we left the ship." That was about a third of all those he could have seen if he'd stayed there a year. This great scientist had so trained himself that he could observe birds and identify the species all the while talking of other things.

My second example shows what an interest in nature can unveil to the untrained observer. My wife was brought up in Holland and has lived in cities all her life, and in them has had no very great need to navigate by nature's ways. She travelled with me all over Europe and North America to further the research for this book, and took such a great interest in the subject I was working on at the time—directions from plants and trees—that when we reached San Francisco after a tour of two months she could tell North, South, East and West just by looking out of her hotel window.

This window looked out on to Union Square. In this square there was a tree, surrounded on four sides by a border of pansies. My wife had quickly noticed that the yellow pansies were in bloom on the east, south and west sides, but were not yet out on the north side—which was sheltered from the sun by the tree.

And now for the results of practice. Colonel Richard I. Dodge, the well-known author and authority on the American Indian, wrote a passage in his book *Our Wild Indians* which well shows the peak of practice that necessity brings to the pathfinder.

" Ask an Indian how to go to a point at a distance, one mile or a hundred miles, and he will simply point out the direction. Press him closely and if he has been to that point, he will by his minute description disclose another of his remarkable traits, his wonderful memory of landmarks.

" Similar and monotonous as they appear to the uneducated eye, each hill and valley, each rock and clump of bushes, has for him its distinguishing features, which, once seen, he knows for ever after and careless as he appears when travelling, not one of these distinguishing features escapes him. . . . If going on a journey into a country unknown to him, he consults with some warrior who has visited it; and it is simply astonishing how clearly the one describes and the other comprehends all that is necessary to make the journey a success."

I should explain at this early stage of my book that I have had thirty-five years experience, first as a marine navigator and later as an air navigator. For many of these years I had my own Navigation School in Los Angeles and for many others I taught navigation to the United States Air Force. During all my teaching I stressed to my students the importance of natural navigation—the kind of navigation that they did not then, and do not now, find in their text books. Conventional air navigation is performed, of course, by all kinds of instruments and mechanical devices, and by maps. I tried to show my students that they needed to use their eyes for registering the details of the country below them in addition to all the modern mechanical aids.

After our world flight in 1931, the late Wiley Post and I spent five months on a goodwill tour, during which the *Winnie Mae* travelled in a criss-cross pattern across the United States, averaging a town per day. Wiley Post was pilot, I was navigator; and while we were in the air I used to familiarise myself with the country below, especially with those aspects of it that were not marked on any conventional maps or charts. Such things were the type of vegetation, the kinds of crops, the layout of farms and farm buildings, the architecture of the houses and barns, the shape of the haystacks and grain stacks, the type of fencing and field boundaries.

Many things told me which way the wind was blowing on the

ground, the smoke of houses, the bending of trees, the silvery undersides of their leaves. I found that it was much easier to tell the wind direction on Mondays than on any other day by watching the clothes-lines, for Monday is wash day the world over. And by watching for the odd details I discovered that certain regions had their own peculiarities, almost their signatures. Throughout the farming areas of Ohio, for instance, almost every little barn and building had an elaborate lightning conductor, there was an amazing number of these rods bristling on buildings throughout the State. Now, compared with any of the other neighbouring States, Ohio is not more subject to lightning: it seemed to me that the enterprise of some persuasive salesman had left its mark.

Of course, not everybody is lucky enough to be able to see the country from the air and follow its changing personality over a great continent. Certainly my early North American flights taught me much of the value of exercising my awareness, indeed, after practising observations such as those I have described, I found that in quite a short time I had become able to recognise a locality almost anywhere in the United States without consulting my map.

To read the personality of a countryside like this, it is not invariably necessary to leave the comfort of one's own home. If you cannot, for the time being, study scenery from the air, from a railway train or car, you must study photographs. It is great fun to observe the details in a scenic illustration whose caption is covered up. After some practice, the careful observer of detail can often tell a great deal from a photograph of an area with which he is personally completely unfamiliar. The amateur indoor nature detective can occupy himself for many profitable hours with a collection of air photographs, such as is published (under the auspices of the British Institute of Sociology) in E. A. Gutkind's *Our World from the Air*. The drawing facing page 96 depicts a scene somewhere in the British Isles. Supposing that we know no more than this, what can we further deduce by studying it closely?

From the general nature of the hillside country it is clear that the picture cannot have been taken anywhere in Central, Southern or Eastern England.

From the architecture of the building it seems very likely that the place is in Northern England. From the state of the vegetation, the season appears to be early spring. The main part of the house probably faces south to get the greatest warmth in the living-rooms; from this we can make a first deduction of the orientation of the picture.

From the length and direction of the shadows, we can further deduce that the picture was taken around noon and that the shadows point towards the north. Thus the road must run roughly east and west with its eastern end in the foreground. The shape of the trees confirms the north-south direction of the shadows and of the south-facing building, for the southern branches of trees tend to be more horizontal because they secure full sunlight, whereas the northern branches tend to be more vertical as they reach out to obtain more light. There is also a greater branch foliage on the southern side.

Needless to say, the presence of Shetland ponies is no indicator of place. There are far more Shetland ponies outside Shetland than in it, and the picture could not possibly have been made in Shetland, where few trees grow and those seldom more than twenty or thirty feet high, and where the architecture and general physiognomy of the countryside are quite different.

I often play the photograph analysis game: it is amazing how much the problem of identifying a photograph without captions adds to its interest and improves one's own powers of perception and deduction. The photograph ceases to be a photograph and becomes, instead, a story.

We may play the photo-navigation game in fun and may make a sport out of pathfinding. Sometimes we may forget that to our own ancestors these affairs were no game but a dire necessity. Actually, the primitive ancestors of most humans in our western civilisation, though pretty good navigators, were by no means the best of all the primitives. Undoubtedly those primitives who have made history as pathfinders, by living with and by nature, were the Polynesians, the Australian aborigines and the

American Indians. More often than others, these races have been accredited with the mysterious sixth sense I wrote of earlier in this chapter, with a mysterious " bump of locality," with a magical " sense of direction." At the risk of making a point more than once (and I shall make it again) I must repeat that these primitives, or indeed any human navigators, and as far as we know any animal navigators, have used and use no more than the five senses of conventional literature and philosophy, namely, sight, hearing, smell, taste and touch. If they use a sixth sense, which may be different from or at least partly independent of any of the conventional five, then that sense is a time sense, an ability to perceive accurately the passage of time which *may* be dependent on " internal rhythm " and at least partly independent of the observation of the movement of the sun. I shall have more to say of time sense later.

The great primitive navigators, then, simply used nature as their guide: and no better example of their keenly developed powers of observation can be given than that of their ancient art of tracking. Of course tracking does not consist of navigation and orienting oneself. It consists of the reconstruction of a journey made by man or beast from the marks and signs left behind on that journey's path. It is universally acknowledged that of all the primitives the most skilled native trackers are Australian aborigines. An " abo " tracker's ability is not simply due to his great personal acuity of vision and other senses. Undoubtedly the instinctive senses of the aborigine are very highly developed; but his incredible skill lies as much in his training and in his intelligence and reasoning capacity. A good aboriginal tracker has a thorough knowledge of bush craft, animal lore and the habits of human beings; and a brilliant faculty of putting a mosaic of observations together and making deductions therefrom. He can locate his quarry with the least possible effort and with an almost unerring success. The following account of the re-markable training process of the aborigines was given in a paper by A. T. Magarey in 1897.

" No sooner does the dusky child of the sparse wilds of Australia begin to leave his mother's head-borne cradle, than he is set to chase and capture some living thing. Step by step the youngster rises in proficiency until beetles, spiders, ants and such-like fairy track-makers are followed over the tell-tale ground. Such training is continued until manhood is reached; until of gliding snake, bounding wallaby or the crafty dangerous lurking foeman, all the earth signs are seen, noted, interpreted, followed or avoided as the circumstances may demand. To his vigilant eye the fresh sharp-cut imprint, the up-springing grass blade, but newly bent by the swiftly passing foot tread, each tells in its own way its own story."

It is true to say that all the aboriginal natives of those vast, arid regions in the continent of Australia can follow tracks imperceptible to the average European. But even though each aborigine is trained from childhood and is constantly practising his art, there is always a difference between the ability of one individual and another. Only a few aborigines of fantastic skill know how to follow really obscure tracks.

This difference in navigating and tracking ability between individuals is, of course, just as likely to occur among any group of humans as it is among the aborigines, but among the humans of a Western civilisation, pathfinding and natural tracking are so little developed (except perhaps in some well-trained fighting services and the Boy Scout movement), that notwithstanding all differences of innate ability, the man who has learned the simplest drill in reading nature's signs is bound to outstrip the inexperienced observer, however intelligent he may be, and can not only outstrip him, but frequently amaze him. To the averagely intelligent Western man, nature's signs can be read with a little practice just as clearly as if they were street signs.

The drill for proficiency is fairly simple; the beginner must walk, and preferably walk alone, for talk distracts the beginner who must concentrate; the seasoned pathfinder thinks of nothing but the job on hand. He must think purely of the external world. The man who walks to solve an internal problem on his mind, or to daydream, is going to learn nothing about natural navigation. I would never advise any beginner to overstrain his memory in the early stages of improving his powers of observation by practice.

The quick tracker and fine natural navigator has developed his powers of memory through years of practice; the beginner has to carry a pencil and notebook to list features, landmarks, associations, etc. It is extraordinary how the novice forgets colours. I would almost go so far as to say that most people have a black and white mind, unless they have seriously cultivated painting or colour photography. The average person is much more sensitive to shape than to colour. He is more inclined to note a misshapen rock, or a twisted tree-trunk, than a tree of a distinctive colour, and as often as not the beginner, too, will rely more purely on sight than on any other of his senses, forgetting that places have their own characteristic sounds and their own characteristic smells. Oddly enough (at least as far as my own experience is concerned), sounds and smells often stick faster in the unconscious memory than in the conscious memory.

Often the beginner in natural navigation fails to see his journey in reverse, as he must do if he is successfully to retrace his steps. I would advise him to practise sketch maps and sketches of the relative positions of landmarks seen from time to time " over his shoulder " on the outward journey. I call this exploring with one eye on the return journey, " maintaining the thread." All primitive pathfinders and trackers use the method, which largely accounts for their success. To them, it is quite natural to remember detours round obstructions, zigzags and turns, and file them away in their memory in such a way that they can be followed in reverse.

The primitive natural navigator almost invariably measures his distance between landmarks by time rather than by space. So accustomed is the Western man, however, to judging distances and measuring spaces on maps, and so greatly has he lost his natural sense of time, that he chooses to think in terms of distance. Navigating by nature, the Western traveller chooses, if he can, a high point near his starting place and looks all around the horizon, estimating the distance to the natural features, taking in the detailed picture in each cardinal direction, noting, re-membering (and if he cannot remember, sketching) the general outline and profile of mountains or any other silhouettes on the horizon, then switching his attention to the foreground in each of the cardinal directions, north, south, east and west, noting the type of country, the dominant vegetation, the configuration of hills, the direction of valleys and streams, the architecture of buildings and the relationship of all these features to each other and to the point of observation. The habit of mental map-making thus developed tends, as it improves, to become progressively free of the notebook. Eventually small hills, stones, trees, bushes, are mentally recalled with very great ease, and in their proper succession, and become bound in the observer's memory as the links of a chain.

To conclude my remarks on the use of powers of observation, here is a remarkable example of a person finding his way in extreme circumstances.

About fifty years ago, Enos Mills, a mountain guide, became snowblind and found himself lost when he was on the summit of the Continental Divide in the Rocky Mountains of the United States, 12,000 feet above sea-level with the nearest house many miles across ridges of rough mountains. His factual story of how he successfully found his way by the intelligent application and observation of natural things is recounted in his book, *Adventures of a Nature Guide*, written some 36 years ago.

It is an excellent illustration of how the practice of noticing nature's signs can be developed by learning to interpret them. Mills was an unusually keen observer of nature and he managed to remain calm and confident of finding his way back when he found himself lost. He said of the incident: " My faculties were intensely awake. The possibility of a fatal ending never occurred to me." His matter-of-fact attitude coupled with his ability to interpret the natural signs of that particular region enabled him to survive; *e.g.* certain pine trees growing on a slope, the bark of trees, trail blaze marks on trees, echoes and aspen smoke.

Mills was confident of his ability to get out of the predicament in which he found himself. He could not use trails because of the extreme depth of snow, but in his mind he had a clear mental map of the slope down which he had to travel. It was made up of the impressions he had gathered before the darkness of snow-blindness settled over him.

Carrying a long staff, he set out on snowshoes to find the blaze marks on the trees which he had made on his forward journey. Making his way from tree to tree he thrust an arm into the snow feeling the bark of the trees until he discovered the mark of the blaze. He resorted to the trees for the points of the compass. In his study of tree distribution he had learned that, in this locality, canyons running east and west carried limber pines on the wall that faced south and Engelmann Spruce on the wall that faced north. With limber pines on his left and Engelmann Spruces on his right he was now satisfied that he was travelling eastward and should be on the eastern side of the range. To check this, he examined the lichen growth of low-lying boulders and the moss which encircled the trunk of trees, concluding that the surrounding area must be such as to admit light freely from all quarters.

To get an idea of the topography of the canyon he shouted, noting from which direction the echoes came, their intensity and the cross replies—concluding from these that he was going into the head of a deep forest-walled canyon.

In the night a snowslide almost smothered him as he made his way and progress was made more difficult by the enormous rock masses and entanglements of fallen branches and leaves.

Suddenly he caught the scent of smoke, which he recognised as that of aspen, a wood burned in the cook-stoves of the mountain people. Under favourable conditions, a person with a keen sense of smell can detect aspen wood smoke for a distance of two or three miles. Going forward in the direction from which the wind was blowing, he emerged from the woods where the smoke was strongest and knew that human habitation was near. In fear of passing it, he stopped to use his ears. As he stood listening a little girl gently, curiously asked: " Are you going to stay here to-night? "

CHAPTER II

HOW EARLY MAN FOUND HIS WAY

"FOR TWENTY-FOUR hours there have passed by the ship a great many pieces of wood and fruits that we do not know; the sea is calmed down in spite of the strong wind from the south-east and these circumstances combine to convince us that there is land close by to the south-east of us."

In those words Louis de Bougainville told, nearly two hundred years ago, how he knew that he was near the coast of Australia (although it was out of sight) on his famous voyage round the world. De Bougainville, like all great early explorers, kept a log; and, like nearly all the logs of his contemporaries, his account often shows how necessity forced him to use his powers of observation, to use natural navigation in the absence of the full repertoire of mechanical aids and charts that the navigators of to-day enjoy.

Nowadays navigators rely so closely on technical aids that they find it much harder than the Western explorers of a couple of centuries ago to believe in primitive navigation. It is the very technical advancement in scientific navigation which has made the scientific navigators of to-day only too prone to build a wall of mystery, fable and myth around the natural navigations of the past. So used are we to navigating by the compass, the chronometer, the sextant, the radio, radar and echo sounder, that some of us just cannot believe that early peoples could make long journeys in unknown areas, and find their way through unexplored wilds and across uncharted seas with only their normal senses and traditional wisdom to guide them. It is an interesting fact that the whole myth of the mysterious sixth sense of direction of the primitive human or animal navigator has come into prominence only in this latest era of scientific and electronic navigation. With these fantastic devices around us, many of us have lost sight of the truth, that the native, the perceptive savage, the " uncivilised " primitive, has, or had, keener perceptions and more highly developed powers of observation than most of us, and used these powers to perform almost incredible feats of pathfinding on land, and land finding at sea.

One of the greatest barriers to a public understanding of the navigating abilities of primitive races is the conventional history book, which gives us a picture of the world inhabited by " natives." These natives, in the islands and countries where they lived, were " discovered " by the great explorers of the West. Somehow the fact that the " natives " had in nearly every case " discovered " their homes by their own much earlier and unaided exploration gets left out of the books. The books forget to make a point of the astounding fact that at the time of the first great Western opening of the undiscovered world, practically every part of the land surface, including such remotest oceanic islands as were habitable, was already occupied by humans, usually by dark-skinned humans.

These people themselves had made long migrations overland or overseas from their original homelands. Unblessed with the written record, they left but verbal legend or traditional tale to explain how they got there. Such legends, such tales, are often garbled and unreliable. It is only when we look into the methods of navigation, which were found to be still in use by some of these primitive but undoubtedly civilised peoples in fairly recent times, that we get some idea of the ways in which the ancient human migrants navigated.

One thing becomes immediately clear if we study the navigation of primitives and early Western man—exploration was seldom, if ever, at random. Few, if any, primitive explorers appear to have led a voyage or expedition haphazardly into the unknown. Almost invariably they had some goal, even if that goal was a fabled goal and not an actual one. The history and folklore of Western Europe, especially Ireland and Portugal, is full of mythical islands which supposedly lay to the west in the

Atlantic Ocean and which were the cause of many voyages of search. My own belief is that the visible tracks of bird migration were also a powerful influence in the opening up of the world. Some of even the greatest of our Western naturalists were arguing as late as the eighteenth century whether birds migrated or no; but for thousands of years the primitives have certainly known better than this. They knew that birds migrated all right. They saw the land birds setting off across the seas on their annual migration. They surmised that these birds could not survive if they alighted on the ocean and they concluded, by the simplest common sense, that another land lay in the direction of their flight.

Most people may think that bird migrations occur only in a north and south direction; but this is by no means universally the case. Ornithologists are beginning to map us a clear network of migratory routes or, as they are called, " flyways " over the surface of the earth. Not all birds migrate on restricted flyways; many species pass on their journeys across land and even across great oceans on what is known as a broad front: but perhaps the majority of species and individuals of all migrant birds, use flyways. By no means all of these flyways run simply north and south; some run east and west, others up and down river valleys, others along coasts; some skirt mountain ranges or find their way through them by well-marked through passes; others (and particularly birds of prey) choose migratory routes where abundant thermals provide risings of hot air on which they can soar their way to their goal without using up muscular energy; many of these thermal flyways pass or skirt sun-warmed deserts. Some of the spring flyways differ from the autumn flyways, mostly because of prevailing winds; thus several species of birds from South Greenland may cross direct to Europe in the autumn on the prevalent westerlies but island-hop *via* Britain, the Faeroes and Iceland on their way back in spring, assisted by more prevalent southerlies. The migratory routes of birds are probably very ancient; though some may well have been modified, even in historical times, with the changes in the distribution of the species and in climatic conditions.

A score or more species of birds use, in spring, the Scotland-Faeroes-Iceland stepping-stone migration route, with sufficient predictability to assist the Scandinavian ships which, sailing westwards from Norway, could pick up the avian pilots. The first settlers in Iceland were probably Culdee priests from Ireland and they probably found their way there in their open curraghs in the spring by the route Ireland-Hebrides-perhaps Shetland-Faeroes-Iceland; which is a route used by many species of ducks that nest all over Iceland, especially in that wild-fowl oasis, Lake Mývatn in the north-central part of that great island, and by at least one Irish goose, the yellow-billed race of the white-fronted goose that summers and nests in West Greenland and that almost certainly flies back to Greenland in spring by the Iceland route.

Some of the migratory routes of birds should probably be described as emergency routes. It would seem, for instance, that the bulk of the spring and autumn passage of Western European migratory birds runs along the Continental coast of Norway and the North Sea; but when easterly winds prevail (as they often do because of the standing anti-cyclone over Scandinavia) many birds get deflected from this route and use instead the eastern coast of the British Isles, joining up with the Continental coastal route again by the shortest sea gap between Scotland and mainland Europe, which lies between Shetland and the westernmost point of Norway. Although this may be a secondary route and is not used by quite such a dense or regular stream of birds as the Continental coastal route, it is probably sufficiently reliable to have helped a human passage across this same sea gap. In any case, once the help of migrant birds has demonstrated to humans that a route is possible, future navigators on the same route can to a certain extent dispense with the birds' guidance—particularly if a group of vessels sail in company with the ships arranged on an extended front after the habit of the old-time Polynesian voyagers.

It seems certain that the Polynesian voyagers (who seem to have been greater and even more daring explorers of the sea than the early Irish and the early Vikings) must, like the Irish and the

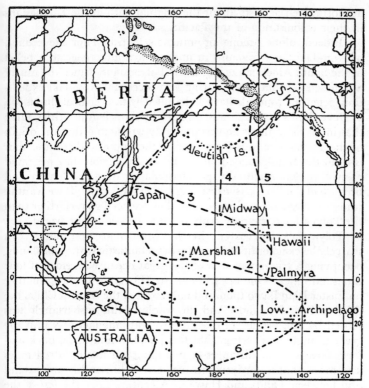

Bird migration routes in the Pacific

Vikings, have been assisted by the visible migration of birds. Above is a chart derived from a paper written by Wells W. Cooke illustrating the probable pattern of bird migration flyways in the Pacific Ocean. The interesting thing about this chart is that it was prepared by someone who was concerned only with the problems of bird migration and was (unlike myself) not particularly interested in the movements of the Polynesians through the area. But if we study Cooke's map, we find that the route marked 1 coincides with the conclusions of nearly all authoritative scientists about the original path of the Polynesians in their colonisation of the Pacific.

Indeed, alone among prominent scientists Thor Heyerdahl, of Kon-Tiki fame, remains in unequivocal adherence to a belief in the South American origin of the Polynesians. Since the much publicised account of the daring and successful Kon-Tiki expedition, scientific journals have been filled with a critical discussion of Heyerdahl's theories; and universally the scientific critics agree that in his main thesis he was probably wrong and that the origin of the Polynesians was from exactly the opposite direction, that is from the Indo-Malayan area. From this region they migrated eastwards and eventually peopled islands over the length and breadth of the Pacific (see drawing facing page 99). If we want to study the navigation of early man, then we need go no farther than the Polynesians, the only truly oceanic people in the world.

Polynesia's vast extent in the world's greatest ocean can scarcely be exaggerated. It comprises a fantastic scatter of islands, occupying a triangular area of the great ocean with sides of four thousand miles. One apex lies at the Hawaiian Islands, another on Easter Island, two thousand miles west of the coast of Chile, the third at New Zealand. And the whole of this vast triangle was settled by one people, of one culture and language. Within the great triangle it is certain that this people could make back and forth voyages over distances of two thousand five hundred miles and more, that is, for instance, between Tahiti and New Zealand and between Tahiti and Hawaii. A century after the *last* of the great Polynesian colonising migrations, Western Europeans were still afraid to venture out beyond the Pillars of Hercules into the green sea of darkness, the Atlantic. The Pacific Ocean islands had been discovered and happily settled long before the birth of Christopher Columbus.

The Polynesians were the greatest pathfinders in history. Who knows why they first started to explore? Pressure, perhaps, of over-population in South-East Asia, tribal differences and wars, maybe. Whatever the cause of the start of their great wanderings, they were the first of the world's peoples truly to become seafaring. Colonising, trading in semi-precious greenstone, or simply visiting friends and relations, they maintained frequent intercourse between groups of islands thousands of miles apart, in an ocean that belies its name.

The Pacific Ocean, of course, is far from calm, and the Polynesians never sailed great distances upon it in vessels which could reasonably be described as " canoes," although they often have been so described. In fact, when Captain Cook sailed into the Pacific in the 98-foot *Endeavour*, he was surprised to find that these ingenious islanders traversed the vast and often rough stretches of the Pacific Ocean in double-hulled vessels—catamarans —110 feet long with two masts and mat sails, and with a small cabin on deck, and capable of carrying one hundred and forty people. Once the Polynesians reached Tahiti, it became an important headquarters and dispersal point for these people; for from Tahiti they colonised north to the Hawaiian Islands and south to New Zealand. Their voyage from Tahiti to the Hawaiian Islands was on the same track as is used every year in spring by the Pacific golden plover, *Pluvialis dominica*, and the rare bristle-thighed curlew, *Numenius tahitiensis*. Both these species to this day fly between Alaska and the Hawaiian Islands, Tahiti and other islands of the South-West Pacific each year.

The second Polynesian migratory track is considered to be partly along the route marked 2 in Cooke's map. I have added to this map a route 6 which is the well-established track of the long-tailed cuckoo, *Eudynamis taitensis*, a brown and rufous bird spotted with white, with white under parts streaked with black, which breeds in New Zealand and on migration is found throughout Polynesia. In September this migrant cuckoo flies south to New Zealand; and it seems more than a coincidence that its flyway is the route used by the Maori fleet which colonised New Zealand from Tahiti in about A.D. 1350. The Maoris, of course, were not the first colonists in New Zealand. My own belief is that the original Polynesian inhabitants of New Zealand came from settlements in the vicinity of the Solomon Islands, also following the migratory track of birds, in this case probably the shining cuckoo, *Chalcites lucidus*, which is much commoner in the Solomon Islands than the long-tailed cuckoo and which also flies to New Zealand for the breeding season. Another bird which may have helped the first New Zealanders is the Pacific race of the bar-tailed godwit, *Limosa lapponica*, which breeds in North-Eastern Siberia and Alaska and winters throughout the South-West Pacific as far as New Zealand. Unlike the cuckoos, this godwit is a non-breeder (i.e. a winterer) in the South, but its migratory flight takes place at about the same time and in the same direction.

There is no doubt whatever that, season after season, the Polynesians watched the bird migrations; and when they were confident that they had found a consistent flyway they set out to follow it. A study of their old chants and their old legends shows most clearly the importance they attached to the direction of the flight of birds. I know of nothing else that could have led these seafaring people from Tahiti to New Zealand but the repeatedly observed migration of the long-tailed cuckoo between these two places. In such migration flights the long-tailed cuckoos do not all set out at once, but straggle over a period of two or three weeks. Once *en route*, the cuckoos never fly very high over the sea and to the following voyager some part of the migratory flock could doubtless be seen nearly every day and perhaps heard at night.

On setting out to follow a flyway, the Polynesians took careful departure by lining up range marks on the shore sighted on the observed bird flights. Some of these range marks, pointing to distant lands, are still known in the Pacific. The Polynesians had no compass; they had no charts of any kind—charts of the kind that we know. As I shall presently discuss, they navigated, at least when in the open sea, by the stars. It would have been possible, of course, for the Polynesians to establish or check their shore marks by the stars, but it is a much more economical hypothesis that these landmarks were a line on bird flyways, bird flight-lines.

When Christopher Columbus made his famous voyage in 1492, he remembered that the Portuguese had already discovered the Azores by noting the directional flight of migratory birds; and it was because he kept a sharp lookout himself that he discovered the North American avifauna before he discovered the

New World. Columbus made his first landfall in America in the Bahamas—by his decision to alter course to the south-west because of the great number of small land-birds which he saw flying in that direction.

The use of captive birds as an auxiliary aid to navigation is almost as old as civilised man: indeed, the method is first mentioned in the Gilgamesh epic written several thousand years B.C. This Babylonian version of the Flood describes how Noah's prototype sent forth a dove; on the first occasion it found no resting-place, and returned. Next to be released was a swallow, which also returned to the vessel. Finally, a third bird, a raven, was sent out; it flew away and, seeing trees emerging from the waters, did not return.

A Hindu legend of the fifth century B.C. tells how Hindu merchants, when sailing on overseas voyages, carried with them several shore-sighting birds to locate the nearest land when the ship's position was in doubt. The same custom is mentioned by Pliny as being practised in his time—the first century A.D.—by the seamen of Ceylon on ocean voyages: they did not know how to steer by the stars.

Not unexpectedly, the captive bird method was known to the Polynesians. Most commonly they took with them one of the most agile and skilful of all the seabird fliers, the frigate-bird or man-o'-war bird. Frigate-birds are plentiful in the Polynesian region and, although patrollers of the open sea, do not normally land on water—their plumage gets waterlogged if they do. With a huge wing span and large wing area the frigate-bird has a vast operational range, and even in recent times has been used as a message carrier between the islands. When released, the birds fly to a height which gives them a far more distant vision than that of the crew on the deck of a ship; and if and when they sight land they immediately fly in that direction. Since frigate-birds are particularly disinclined to land on any water, they almost invariably return to the vessel if they do not see land.

Like other early voyagers, the Vikings used shore-sighting birds to show the direction of land. The saga tells that when Floki, the Norse navigator, left Shetland for Iceland he carried a number of birds called sea-ravens, which were probably shags or cormorants. When he was a few days out from Shetland he released a bird: it circled for altitude and, seeing land astern, flew towards it, thus giving Floki a back bearing on his point of departure. Several days later Floki released a second bird, and this one took a forward course to Iceland, showing him the direction to follow.

It is probable that those hardy sea kings the Vikings were never able to obtain much precision in their navigation, because of the weather conditions in the North Atlantic Ocean. The skies of the North Atlantic are almost chronically overcast; and it is natural that the Vikings were never able to develop a system of navigation by the stars. They were able to make return voyages between Europe and Iceland with reasonable certainty, but navigated to and fro from Iceland to Greenland only with the greatest difficulty. Their basic directions were obtained only by the flight of birds, the direction of the wind and waves, and the sun.

It was the Polynesians—whose ocean has more stable weather —who first developed natural navigation by the stars to a fine art. But it is possible that they may have inherited certain principles of star navigation from the early Arab navigators.

We know that the Arabians in the Indian Ocean—in addition to the use of birds—navigated by the Pole Star in a very simple manner. They used the fingers of the outstretched hand to measure the height of this star above the horizon; and this angle gave them their latitude. Later, they developed a better method of obtaining latitude with a piece of string and a short stick; and from this was evolved the cross-staff, a forerunner of the sextant used by modern navigators. In their long voyages across the Indian Ocean, they also used, often as a principal method, the known direction of chronic seasonal winds such as monsoons.

On these trips they noticed that the stars rose at the same points of the sky all the year round and set on the opposite horizon. Although they had no magnet, they divided the horizon into thirty-two points. These points were derived from fifteen stars which rose at approximately equally spaced points on the eastern horizon. The setting points of these stars on the western horizon gave them another fifteen points and north and south brought the total to thirty-two. The Arabs made a dial of wood with thirty-two spikes placed around its circumference representing the points. Checking the well-established prevailing wind with a star or some other sign, they steered by this device, which was in fact what is known to-day as a pelorus, or dummy compass —a compass dial without a magnet.

It was in about the second century A.D. that the Arabs brought the magnetic needle from China. At once they combined it with their thirty-two point division of the circle. This division of the horizon, coupled with the magnet, was introduced into Europe at the time of the Crusades; and it is still found on many of to-day's marine compasses.

The first European explorers in the Pacific were amazed to find that although the Polynesians did not know the magnet, many of the peoples in the Pacific used the thirty-two point dummy compass. From my studies I consider this further proof of the Indo-Malayan origin of the Polynesians: evidence that they explored and colonised into the Pacific from the coast of India *before* the introduction of the magnet, that is, before the second century A.D.—but *after* they had learned from the early Arabs the thirty-two point dummy compass.

With this dummy compass (but without the magnet) the Polynesians, when out at sea, were able to navigate by the stars with remarkable accuracy and simplicity. They saw the heavens as the inside of a dome, across which the stars traced their courses. Each could be regarded as a moving band of light; and the Polynesians knew the stars or bands which passed over the islands in which they were interested.

These accomplished navigators had names for one hundred and fifty stars. They knew the point on the horizon where each of these rose, and the time at which it did so. They knew the islands which each passed over. Watching the heavens, night after night, they saw that the stars stayed in the same relation to one another and rotated around an imaginary axis. Month after month the same stars passed over the same islands. They saw that the stars kept to the same path; but that each night they appeared slightly earlier—earlier by about four minutes by our way of measuring time. The Polynesians had no watches or clocks, but like all sensitive primitives and many wild animals they had an amazingly accurate time-sense. These island mariners could thus sail towards the star that they knew was over their destination at that particular time. Their system was amazingly simple; and needed no instruments whatsoever.

To clarify this method, let us imagine the stars stationary for a moment. Each star in the heavens will be exactly overhead at some place on the surface of the earth. If we can identify the star which at our moment is over the island of Hawaii, we have a shining beacon leading to it which can be seen thousands of miles away. Moreover, if we steer for this star, we actually follow the shortest possible course—the course which modern navigators allude to as a " great circle." Indeed, we are thus following a system more perfect in principle than our modern methods of compass navigation, for if the distance involved is fairly great the compass course is different from and necessarily longer than the great circle course to a given destination.

Not only does this star give us the direction and shortest course to our island, but tells us when we can expect to reach it, for when we do so the star will be overhead.

Now let us start the heavens (or, more accurately, the earth) rotating again. Our star is now moving on a definite track westwards. It is no longer stationary over Hawaii; but other stars which are the same distance north of the Equator will follow on exactly the same track. We can use the next one which passes over Hawaii to steer by, and then yet another in the same band, and another and another. This succession of guiding stars will continue until we make our landfall at Hawaii underneath the star which at that time of year and at that time of night is directly overhead.

If we disregard time entirely we can reach our destination from east or from west, simply by sailing along underneath this narrow band of stars that rotate year after year over our destination. From any other direction we can also steer to our island if we possess a sufficiently accurate time sense, and accept a certain margin of error—which must be corrected, in order to make the final landfall, by all the other natural means that we describe elsewhere in this book. The native navigators use this star method to bring them within a distance of, say, fifty to seventy-five miles of their island destinations. I have practised this method myself and have by turning myself around been able to judge that a star was overhead within an accuracy of one degree which is equivalent to an error of sixty miles at sea.

Although primitive peoples had no mechanical means of telling the time during the day or night, they had an excellent concept of time. In these days " civilised " man thinks of distance in terms of miles; our whole habit of geographical thinking is concerned with space. Nevertheless, though civilised man has very little use for his innate time sense, and takes little opportunity to improve it with practice, the presence of an innate time sense has been proved beyond question. MacLeod and Roff, for instance, confined two people in a soundproof room in which there was no possible external aid to the appreciation of the passage of time. The estimated time given by one of the subjects, who was released after eighty-six hours, was correct to within forty minutes; and that of the other, released after sixty-six hours, correct to within twenty-six minutes. The cumulative error of each subject was thus about ten minutes a day. Unquestionably the Polynesian must have added constant practice to this innate time sense and could get even better results—results as good as those attained by many different kinds of domestic and wild animals, of which there is an excellent collection in Frank W. Lane's *Animal Wonderland*. Mr. Lane shows that a sharp time sense, usually involving an accuracy at any time of day of within less than five minutes, is possessed by members of nearly all the principal orders of mammals and birds, by some fish and by a number of invertebrates, from sea-anemones and worms to ants and bees. Bees not only have a time sense remarkably developed, but can communicate information about time to each other.

The Polynesian had no word for distance, no use for space. He thought only of time. Between one place and another were so many canoe-days (not so many miles); and it is clear that he thought in terms not just of canoe-days but the equivalent of canoe-hours, even of canoe-minutes. The Polynesian had the innate time sense that all animals appear to have; and this he improved with constant use and checked with precision by his stars.

When Captain Cook first encountered the Polynesians he had as navigator the advantage over them of compass, sextant and chronometer. He also had the chart, though in the parts of the Pacific that he was exploring the western chart was not of much use to him. He found that the Polynesians also had mental charts based partly on time interval rather than space difference. A chart made by Cook and one of his assistants, Lieutenant Pickersgill, from information supplied by a native navigator led them to many islands which Cook would otherwise have overlooked. Tupaia, the famous Polynesian navigator, supplied the information for a chart to be drawn, which encompassed nearly eighty islands, an amazing exhibition of the outstanding geographical knowledge of these early oceanic peoples. This chart made from Tupaia's information marked Tahiti and the Fiji Islands, which are more than 2500 miles from each other! But Cook and his companions did not know Tupaia's language well, and mistook the native's directions of north and south, and thus reversed many islands on the chart. Nevertheless, half of the islands on the chart were unknown to Cook and this led him officially to " discover " many of them.

The only known cartographers of sea movement were the Micronesians of the Caroline and the Marshall Islands, who made, as an aid to their memory, wave charts and swell charts which showed a navigational technique which existed among no other native race. When the early explorers encountered these charts or wave maps they simply could not interpret them. Only later, and quite difficult, ethnological research has unlocked the secret of the Micronesian chart.

The part played by the primitive navigator in the opening up of the world is much misunderstood. In most of our books on exploration it is scarcely credited at all. Yet Captain Cook was not the only European explorer who received geographical advice from the natives of the lands which he " discovered." Nearly every western explorer and voyager in the unmapped and uncharted (and thus, he fondly imagined, " unexplored ") parts of the world encountered the native in his role of natural navigator, accurate chart and map maker—found, in fact, that the resident explorers had been there before him. Many of the early voyagers to Greenland encountered the Eskimos, who made maps for them depicting the coastline and outlying islands in a remarkably accurate manner. Often the Eskimos carved these maps on driftwood, realistically representing the natural features in three dimensions.

In the records of Beechey's voyage to the Bering Straits is clear evidence of the outstanding memory of the North Pacific Eskimo. Beechey tells how at Kotzebue Sound the Eskimos drew him a map of the countryside in the sand. " In the first place," he writes, " they drew the coastal line with a stick and measured it according to day voyages. After this they erected the mountain-chains with sand and stones and they represented the islands, with attention to their size and form, with heaps of gravel." After some time, when the mountains and islands were correctly placed, " they then showed the villages and fishing stations by means of a number of sticks which were placed in the ground, so that an imitation of the reality appeared." This chart, indeed, was almost a facsimile of the western relief map.

Of course the secret of primitive chart-making is the habit of making *mental* maps—maps of the outline and general shape of the homeland, of prominent landmarks and the relative positions of other people's homelands with the home village as the focal point. So keenly were these maps printed in the mind of many natives that they could at any time reproduce them from memory.

James Fisher tells me that, in 1953, when he and the American ornithologist Roger Peterson spent some days in the Yukon-Kuskokwim tundras of Western Alaska they found themselves in one of the few parts of North America not yet fully surveyed from the air. The combined delta of the two great rivers is a vast wilderness of flat alluvial lands and water, in which pathfinding in the absence of large-scale maps is a matter of maze threading a mosaic of meandering lakes and rivers of fantastic complexity. To reach the present Eskimo village at New Chevak from the now deserted old village at Old Chevak, a distance of not more than eight or ten miles as the crane flies, means a day's journey along winding rivers of nearer thirty miles than twenty miles. Every bend of the river, every landmark on this journey, every warning of blind alley or dead end was carefully sketched for Peterson and Fisher on the back of an odd piece of writing-paper by the young Eskimo, Jack Paniyak, in a couple of minutes. His map was far more precise than the existing small-scale published map, which contained at least one misleading and imaginary water channel which, had they attempted to follow it, would have cost them a day's journey.

Everywhere, then, and until the present day, skilful native pathfinders can lead the explorers of the west; and can better, from their natural powers of navigation, their skill with compass, sextant and timepiece. The Australian aborigines often aided white explorers from their capacity to draw sketches and maps from memory. In the same way, the eastern Siberian tribes reproduced their mental maps in the form of drawings on wood, with the outline and detailed features painted with reindeer blood. These charts were accurate enough to lead explorers on to new discoveries.

Often members of native races passed geographical knowledge in this way, not to white explorers, but to each other. An extract from *Our Wild Indians* by Colonel Richard A. Dodge illustrates this point:

" The old guide Espinosa, from whom I learned the rudiments of plains craft, told me that when he was a boy-prisoner among the Comanches, and the youngsters wished to go on a raid into a country unknown to them, it was customary for the older men to assemble the boys for instruction a few days before the time fixed for starting.

All being seated in a circle, a bundle of sticks was produced, marked with notches to represent the days. Commencing with the stick with one notch, an old man drew on the ground with his finger, a rude map illustrating the journey of the first day. The rivers, streams, hills, valleys, ravines, hidden water-holes, were all indicated with reference to prominent and carefully described landmarks. When this was thoroughly understood, the stick representing the next day's march was illustrated in the same way, and so on to the end. He further stated that he had known one party of young men and boys, the eldest not over nineteen, none of whom had ever been in Mexico, to start from the main camp on Brady's Creek in Texas, and make a raid into Mexico as far as the city of Monterey (a distance of over 380 miles as the crow flies), solely by memory of information represented and fixed in their minds by these sticks."

Of course the mental map, and the picture map based on it, could not solve all the problems of travel facing the native or " primitive." They could not guide him in unknown regions. When he wished to explore (and the " primitive " was as great an explorer as any hero of the west) early man devised a means of orientation which insured him against losing his way. This method seems to have been used by all primitive races alike. Its systematic nature alone is proof, if proof now be needed, that no primitive was under the illusion that he had an instinctive power, a " sixth sense " for pathfinding.

In the myths of the Greeks is the story of Thèseus, to whom Ariadne gave a thread which enabled him to find his way out of the maze-like cave after he slew the monster. Theseus carried the physical means of returning to his starting point, his place of refuge in known country. It is this " home-centre " system that the primitive employs. Only, in his case, the thread is an imaginary one. There can be no doubt that birds and other wild animals also employ this home-centre system to an important extent, though it is certainly not the only method which they use for " homing."

As early peoples ventured forth in search of food, they maintained a constant anxiety about their home and would often look back to see where they were in relation to their point of

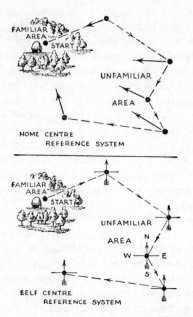

Home centre system and self centre reference system

departure. Each time they went out more territory would become familiar to them; and they would proceed farther and farther into the mysterious unknown, never once losing the thread.

An Australian aborigine described his method of orientating himself in unknown areas in the following way: " I don't go far in the beginning; I go some distance and come back again, then, in another direction, and come back, and then again in another direction. Gradually I know how everything is, and then I can go out far without losing my way."

Compare this simple and practical method of orientation with our much more complicated " self-centre system." Modern man, using this system, considers himself (wherever he is) as the centre. He divides the horizon into north, south, east and west, or even into the 360 degrees of the full circle of the modern compass.

He involves himself in an intricate network of calculations and, even with the aid of a compass, often loses his way. At each point when he stops to refer to the points of the compass, he may sever his connection with the previous place at which he did the same thing. All too easily, in this way, can he lose the thread which tied him to his original place of departure.

A better system than the " self-centre system " combines it with the home-centre system. We may call it the " local reference system." Under this system directions are related to some local prominent feature—a range of hills, a river, a coastline, a lake front. Some primitives have used this system: it is the basis of very accurate maps by Greenland Eskimos discovered by European explorers. Rather interestingly, it is also used by New York taxi drivers when they refer to " uptown," " downtown " and " crosstown."

From this we might conclude that the white man, the " civilised " traveller, can easily transfer to himself the " primitive's " remarkable pathfinding powers, by the simple adoption of the methods of mental map-making and the use of the home-centre system. But this is not so, because in the process of evolution of our civilisation we have lost something which was a matter of life and death to the primitive; that is, his highly developed powers of observation. These powers were common to all early men; and I do not hesitate to repeat myself by saying that they were due not to any innate keenness of the senses of sight, smell, hearing or touch different in any essential from that which we possess ourselves; but rather to the development by practice of the use of these faculties. The primitive traveller reached a state of awareness that only a few of the civilised have ever attained. He reached it because his survival depended upon it. Present-day man can reach a similar state of keen perception only by special and unusual efforts.

There are, of course, examples of intelligent Europeans who have applied primitive systems to finding their way, and have thus become excellent pathfinders. In the journal *Nature* in 1873, A. W. Howitt expressed his opinion, based upon many years' experience among the Australian aborigines:

" I have not met with aboriginal natives either as savages or as ' tame black', who possessed any power of finding their way from place to place differing in its nature, though perhaps its degree, from that to be found in every good ' bushman ' among the whites. Their knowledge of country is entirely local—special as regards the district belonging to their tribes or family—general as regards the country of the neighbouring tribes. They know it thoroughly because they have been born in it and have roamed over it ever since."

As Howitt claims, the white man can equal, if not better, the primitive at his own pathfinding. It is my hope that I may rid the reader of any illusion he may have of the existence of a " sense of direction "—a mysterious sixth sense—and to this subject I devote the next chapter.

CHAPTER III

IS THERE A SIXTH SENSE?

I F WE delve into the preserved and written records of antiquity, we discover that older civilisations than our own had no special idea of a " mysterious sense of direction." They were not prone, as only too many of us are to-day, to attribute magical powers to humans or even to animals. On the contrary, in the ancient writings of the orient and the west, there is a most realistic appreciation of the ease with which man can get lost on both land and sea.

It seems that the prevalent misconception about the path-finding ability of native peoples only began in the middle of the last century, and it appears to derive very largely from the loose testimony of a few explorers and missionaries. Not all such travellers are to blame, of course: for instance, the Jesuit missionary Père Joseph Lafitau, in 1724, gave a clear account of how the Iroquois Indians found their way through dense country entirely by visual means. But others who were less inquiring credited them with a mysterious ability.

Another French missionary, Père François Xavier de Charle-voix, was responsible for gross exaggerations of, and absurd theories about the instinctive abilities of the Indians in finding their way. De Charlevoix spent only five months among the Indians; but his statements, published in Paris in 1744, disregard the clear explanations given earlier by Lafitau, and indeed actually distort the facts given by him.

Other explorers added to the fable by similar claims about the pathfinding abilities of native peoples in many different parts of the world. Sir H. Bartle Frere, who had been Governor of the region of Sind in India before the mutinies of 1857, read a paper in London in 1870 to the Royal Geographical Society, of which he was Vice-President. Frere actually gave the key to the problem of how the native inhabitants of Sind kept their direction, when he described the interminable succession of sand dunes which were all aligned with the direction of the prevailing wind of the south-west monsoon. But as if not content with the most economical explanation, he sought to make a mystery of it by stating as follows:

" In the flat country of Sind, and especially in the great *Runn* of Cutch, where one finds neither natural landmarks nor tracks, the best guides seem to count entirely on a kind of instinct. They do not affect any mysterious science but are generally altogether incapable of giving the least reason in favour of their conclusion, which seems to be the result of an instinct similar to that of dogs, horses and other animals; an infallible instinct. . . ."

Clearly Bartle Frere was ignorant of the discussions of the evolutionists of the time; for already Charles Darwin and his school had exposed the error. But Darwin *was* personally to blame for some confusion by his misquotation from memory of the account of von Wrangel's expedition to Siberia. In 1873 the English scientific journal *Nature* invited correspondence on the mysterious sense of direction of men and animals. Like Bartle Frere, von Wrangel mentioned the true method of navigation that he had experienced, only to " throw it away." He described the parallel ridges of snow which were aligned with the dominant winds, and praised his Cossack driver's ability to maintain his direction—an ability which was shared by the other Siberians in his party; but he then wrote: " They appeared to be guided by a kind of unerring instinct." Darwin's misquotation was that they *were* guided by a kind of instinct. Later writers took up the testimony of de Charlevoix and Bartle Frere and the supposed testimony of von Wrangel and enlarged upon them—to the extent that, quite widely and generally, through Western thought during the latter part of the nineteenth century and much of the present century, some native peoples and even some Europeans were endowed with the ability of instinctive direction finding.

Many people still believe in this, though I am certain that the theory can stand up to no well-designed, scientific test.

Many believers in the sixth sense, of course, also believe in natural navigation. They hold that the " homing instinct " comes to the fore only under extreme circumstances. Let us see, then, what that famous antarctic explorer, Sir Douglas Mawson, writes about navigation under extreme circumstances:

" Thick drift and a fifty-mile wind on January 12 [1913] kept us confined for thirty-six hours. It was clear enough after noon on the 13th, and five miles were covered in four hours through thick surface drift. What the course was we did not care as we steered by the sastrugi [parallel ridges of snow]. If ever a man had any " homing instinct " it would surely show itself on such an occasion as this."

Yes, Mawson steered not by his sixth sense but by the sastrugi.

Many adherents of the sixth sense theory believe implicitly that it is possessed by blind people. This delusion persists in spite of the fact that not one sightless person has been able to come forward and demonstrate this supposed ability. Yet if there was even one among all the blind, who could prove that he was guided by a sixth sense and did not use normal senses, the whole world would know about it.

It is, of course, hard to realise that, without the use of his eyes, a man can avoid obstacles in his path and find his way. This problem has puzzled scientists whose experiments go back, at least, to 1749. It was in that year that D. Diderot was curious about " the amazing ability of a blind acquaintance not only to perceive the presence of objects, but to judge accurately their distance from him." Diderot's conclusion was that his subject judged the proximity of objects by the increased sensitivity of his facial nerves. This seemed to satisfy early writers; and Diderot was supported by other investigators for the next century. One of these investigators claimed that sightless people used their cheeks as " feelers," and another put a name to this ability— " Perceptio Facialis."

In 1905, Emile Jarval was responsible for introducing the term " sixth sense." He applied it to the blind, and supposed that it was akin to touch and was aroused by " ether waves." Others sought to explain it in terms of magnetism, electricity, vibration and the subconscious. Confusion reigned. Those who favoured the mysterious sense battled with the supporters of the normal senses, and among the investigators on both sides there was also internal disagreement. Each arguer thought that he could produce experiments which proved his theory. Theories dominated, almost directed, investigations. Only when investigations direct theories can interpretations be unprejudiced. Most interpretations remained prejudiced.

From this controversy of a half-century ago emerged a few who were on the right track. In 1904 T. Heller concluded from experiments that " sensations of approach do not depend upon a special touch quality nor upon a stimulation of a certain part of the skin," and he noted that " the perception of changes in the sound of his [the blind's] footsteps leads to careful attention for sensation of pressure in the forehead. If these characteristic sensations then arise he is sure that an obstacle is in his path and he turns aside in good time."

F. B. Dresslar conducted further experiments with those deprived of sight which qualified Heller's theories, stating that " the basis for judgment was due to differences in sound." Although the work of these two men did not entirely reveal the truth, their conclusions were the basis for further work which provided the logical answer to the question. In 1907, L. Truschel noted that as a man approaches an obstacle, the sounds of his footsteps rise steadily in pitch. Pierre Villey also paid attention to hearing. One of his observations involved the questioning of blinded soldiers and of these (he found) twenty-five per cent thought they detected obstacles by ear and twenty-five per cent by touch, and fifty per cent by a combination of the two senses. Villey concluded that both hearing and touch were used and that a combination of the two would, indeed, increase the ability to avoid obstacles. This was the real answer; but other investigators were not prepared to believe it; and many continued experiments and produced highly fanciful and illogical theories which served to lead people away from the truth. The problem was made no easier by the difficulty that the blind themselves found in explaining what sense they used.

It was not until 1944 that three American investigators, Michael Supa, Milton Cotzin and Karl M. Dallenbach of Cornell University published the results of many experiments in *The American Journal of Psychology*. These experiments, which were very thorough and too numerous to detail here, were designed to " resolve the contradictions between theory and experimental results " in a study of the perception of obstacles by the blind. The conclusions from them have completely clarified the question and calmed the confusion.

These three scientists tested a number of completely blind students in a large hall and observed their reactions when they came to obstacles placed in their path. They also questioned the students to determine exactly at what distance they felt the presence of the objects.

In the final summary of their conclusions, they eliminated the former theories of air- and sound-waves and the pressure theory of " obstacle sense " as applying to the exposed areas of the skin. They confirmed the use of hearing by the simple method of blocking the ears of the students, who then invariably bumped into the obstructions. One student had previously maintained that his judgments were based on " facial pressures " and that sound was not important. But when his ears were blocked, he lost his confidence completely, and reported that he was " not getting any sensations at all." He walked forwards with his hands held apprehensively in front of him. Another student said " the curtains of facial pressures that I once reported were pure fancy."

Supa, Cotzin and Dallenbach noted that one of the students, who was particularly good in his perception of the obstruction, obtained his cues from the increased tautness of the carpet in the immediate vicinity of the obstacle; but in general they observed that touch played a small rôle in the avoidance of obstacles by the blind. At the end of the series of experiments, the blind students and the investigating scientists were in complete agreement. They defined the perception of obstacles by the blind as the use of the sense of hearing aided at times by touch: and their experiments, or others very similar to them, have been repeated and confirmed many times over by scientists throughout the world.

The realisation that the blind have no instinctive powers, but highly developed natural senses, has been of immense benefit to the blind themselves—for work has gone ahead on aids to help them locate obstructions. Such inventions had been long delayed by the useless controversy. In England and the United States, research workers have been recently busy developing devices that send out ultra-sonic waves ahead of the persons carrying them. Another device, made in the United States, involves a reflected light beam which is transformed into a whistling noise which sounds every second in the user's ear and relays information about the distance of the obstacle. All of these inventions are in their early stages, and will undoubtedly be perfected for everyday practical use. They are tangible proof that the blind are not guided by a " sixth sense."

CHAPTER IV

WALKING IN CIRCLES

ANY THEORIES have been put forward to explain why lost people travel in circles. Some, less logical than others, favour a mysterious influence. There need be no mystery. There are several separate reasons why we walk in circles (whether we are lost or not) each of which is quite simple.

To understand the main reason we need only study the classic statue of the Venus de Milo. This traditional example of perfect human beauty is asymmetrical. She has the left half of her head more developed than the other—a characteristic she shares with nearly all right-handed people. Her right eye is lower than her left, and the dividing membrane of her nostrils is to the left of the centre line of her face. There was no mistake in the sculpting of the Venus de Milo. Every human body is lopsided. Ninety-eight people out of a hundred are born right-handed; and their right arms usually become longer than their left, with greater circumference, volume and weight, and their right shoulders become from half an inch to nearly one inch lower than their left. The directing impulses for the right hand come from the left brain, and it is a rule that the left brain of right-handed people is larger than the right brain and that the left cranial cavity is consequently also larger.

With regard to our anatomy, we are all of us unbalanced.

Right- or left-handedness has a decided effect on a person's rowing or swimming. Right-armed swimmers veer to the left when they are without visual clues to guide them, for their right arm is longer and stronger. A right-armed rower when facing aft will tend to pull his boat to the right of its forward course. Right-armed people normally have their right hands bigger than their left, as any glove manufacturer's records will show.

It is unlikely that anybody is born truly ambidextrous, although a popular theory would have it so. Ambidexterity is acquired and not innate. Many people—especially those who pursue sports and games—develop by practice the inferior arm until its dexterity almost approaches that of the dominant arm; but they still retain a preference for the use of the dominant arm —a preference which is doubtless inherited. Incidentally, apes form an exception to this rule, close though they are to humans in other physical aspects. They appear to be born ambidextrous, and can use either hand or foot with equal ease without training.

Psychologists tell us that while it is wise to encourage the naturally left-handed individual to develop the use of his or her right hand, it is unwise to compel this to the exclusion of the preferred hand, as this may even cause conflict which in some instances results in stuttering—possibly because the development of that part of the brain which directs movement may affect the speech centre which lies adjacent to it.

The effects of right- or left-handedness appear to be confined entirely to the arms, shoulders and head; and are not linked, as far as we know, in any way with the lack of symmetry of the rest of the body. But that the rest of the body is asymmetrical is unquestionable, and few persons can exist who have not at least a slight difference in the length of their two legs. This difference, is, of course, of great importance in determining the direction in which the person will veer in walking; and generally we find that for each individual there is a constant error in the same direction. Moreover, this error may be quite independent of the person's right- or left-handedness.

The famous originator of the scout movement, Baden Powell, warned his scouts of the dangers of walking in circles in fog. Once, in the mountains of Scotland, the Chief Scout was with a mountaineer in whom he placed considerable trust. After a time Baden Powell advised him that the wind had changed; it was on their left side when they set out: now it blew from the right. The mountaineer insisted that they were going in the correct direction, although the wind was then blowing on their backs. They soon found themselves back where they started, having gone in a complete circle. Although Baden Powell was aware of this tendency to walk in circles, he did not seem to realise the cause of it, nor the consistency with which the tendency applies to each individual one of us. This consistency appears to have been overlooked even by military authorities in field training—even though, as long ago as 1897, a German researcher, Mach, pointed out that when large numbers of troops marched at night or in a snowstorm they walked in circles and could end up at their starting point. Yet in the armed services' field training it would be quite practical to test each man to find the constant direction of his deviation, and its extent. Any man who knows his own deviation through his early training in manœuvres knows something really valuable when, in actual warfare, he is overtaken by darkness or obscurity.

A swerve pattern test is comparatively easy to make. Walk blindfold in a large open area, such as a field covered by snow, or a sandy beach on which there are no obstacles, even minor ones. The swerve pattern of your footprints will be there for you to see, measure, assess and compensate for in future. A swerve test is even possible in a large hall, with the aid of a friend who can observe the extent and direction of your veering and prevent you from walking into obstacles.

As far as I know the first recorded tests on the constancy of circular movement were made by the Norwegian scientist F. O. Guldberg in 1896; he reported that deviation was greater when the pace was faster, and found a correlation with uneven body structure, not only among humans but among animals.

It is curious how some scientists have passed over the natural reasons for veering, and have attached importance to the most unlikely sources and causes instead of taking into consideration the most probable hypothesis, namely, the difference in leg length of the veering individual. A much quoted authority, Professor L. Schaeffer of the University of Kansas (author of *Spiral Movement in Man*), believed that there was a spiralling influence centred in the brain of all living creatures and that this, and not a structural difference, was the cause of veering. He stuck to this theory even though the relationship between the clear difference in leg lengths and veering should have been evident to him.

It was Professor Frederick H. Lund of Bucknell University who put the whole question to the most exhaustive tests. In 3542 trials of 125 students he found that the greater the difference in leg length in each individual, the greater was the degree of deflection. A good fit between the difference in leg length on the one hand, and the direction and extent of veering in walking on the other, was noted in eighty per cent of a group of students. His tests also showed the consistency of veering in a number of trials of the same students; and the consistency of the reversal of veering when the same students walked backwards. The twenty per cent of cases which did not fit involved students who deliberately gave great impetus to the short leg, which resulted in compensating changes in their direction of deviation. Perhaps the most interesting of Lund's discoveries was that approximately fifty-five per cent of his students consistently veered to the right and forty-five per cent to the left; a sure sign that veering may have little or nothing to do with right- or left-handedness, since only two per cent of people are left-handed.

Further evidence showed that the greater the actual difference in leg length, the greater the amount of veering. Curiously, we learn from many tests conducted in 1913 on blindfold boys and girls that the extent of deviation was 5.7 degrees for boys as against 10.8 degrees for girls. This has been confirmed by the work of Carl Sandstrom in 1951.

Practically everybody deviates. Among the majority of people, the full blindfold deviation circle is formed in about half an hour. Others become displaced more slowly and may take from one to six hours to complete a circle. Practically nobody continues in a straight line. Deviation is increased when the subject's head is bent forward. If the subject walks forward and turns his head to one side, he will deviate to the opposite side. If he walks backwards with his head turned to one side, he will deviate to the same side. If the subject leans his head towards one shoulder, he will deviate in the direction in which he leans his head.

'The physical difference in leg length is in most cases the

primary cause of deviation from a straight path; but there are at least two other causes, one physical the other psychological. To appreciate the second physical cause a simple test can be made.

Keep both your eyes open and hold a forefinger upright at arm's length so that it is centred on some object ahead of you. Close your left eye. If your finger is still in line with the object your right eye is your dominant and sighting eye (though not necessarily your " better " eye). Now close your right eye. Your finger will appear to jump to the right of the object, if you are right-eyed; but will remain aligned with it, if you are left-eyed.

Everyone has a dominant eye, though few people realise it. In the field you may line up two nearby objects in order to preserve a straight path, but although you keep both eyes open the two objects will only be aligned with one of them. This produces another—though minor—source of error in preserving a straight path.

Among other minor sources of error can be the wrong balance of a haversack, a heavy weight or even a pick or rope held in the same hand for any length of time, and other physical factors which tend to pull an individual out of his normal balance.

A person tends to edge away from what I term the " irritant direction." Wind, rain, snow or dust storms can cause a man to deviate from his path. Of course he will lean his head away from the force and his steps will constantly deviate. Even a strong sun to the right of his path will cause a person to ease unconsciously to the left. A walker intending to take a level path along a hill may subconsciously follow the line of least resistance and gradually walk down hill.

But beyond these errors, due to structure and balance and " irritant forces " we must consider some undoubtedly due to a powerful mental influence which should not be underrated. When a subject meets an irritant force head on he will still tend to deviate, and his deviation will then be governed by what can only be identified as a psychological preference. Man has developed a preference for the right-hand side which is deep-rooted: it has been handed down to us either by inheritance or by age-old tradition (or both) and has become an influence of which few of us are aware. This preference is most clearly shown when a traveller meets a simple obstacle in his path. Each deviation then tends to be in the same direction and can result in an accumulation of edgings to the right which can reach substantial proportions on a long journey.

So powerful is this preference for right over left that, when given an otherwise uninfluenced selection, people almost invariably choose the right. Even the word " right " itself strengthens the prejudice. The right hand is the happy hand, the strong hand, the agile hand, the clever hand. Nearly all the people of the world, in their religions, beliefs, superstitions, laws, administrations, armies and tools have imposed the rule of the dominant " right." The honoured guest is placed on the host's right as a mark of distinction, and the other guests arranged on right or left according to the rank they hold in the social scale. In ancient battles the right hand held the lance and the weaker left the defensive shield; the right became the side of honour, the left its poorer cousin. The right hand is the hand of good faith, legally qualified to take oaths, to effect treaties. The joining of right hands makes marriage sacred.

One investigator, R. Hertz, sums this influence up as follows:

" So from one end of the world to the other, in the holy places where the faithful meet their god, as in the accursed places where diabolical pacts are made, on the throne as at the witness box, on the battlefield and in the peaceful work-room of the weaver, everywhere there is a fixed law governing the attributes of both hands. As the profane cannot mingle with the sacred the left cannot encroach on the right. The predominant activity of the bad hand can only be illegal or exceptional because it would be the end of man and of everything if the profane could ever surpass the sacred, and death over life. The supremacy of the right hand is both an effect and a necessary condition to order which rules and preserves good creation."

This preference for right over left has been particularly noted in the Swiss Alps. Here the most important of the old mountain passes are almost invariably to the right of the mountains: the St. Gotthard, the Old Grimsel, the Furka, Bernhardin, Splügen,

Julier, Abula, Brenner and others. Moreover, each of the old paths on the surrounding flat country shows the same right-handed inclination, and the smaller mountain tracks also run where possible over right-handed slopes.

Charles Widmer, who wrote an interesting article in a Swiss alpine journal on this question of the selection of right over left, went so far as to state that when a person is alone and has to make a sudden decision, he will never turn left when he has a completely open choice. Widmer confirmed this peculiarity in an interesting and most practical way by the study of thousands of pictures of skiers at ski-resorts. But it does not need the spectacle of a skier presented with a sudden obstacle to demonstrate this rule. Most of us can see it in operation much closer to our homes —indeed in any public place where there is an option of two entrances. So important is the operation of the rule, indeed, that its study has led to special arrangements in the design of display sequences in museum halls. At the entrance to any display chamber or art gallery the public chooses to turn right rather than left. For instance, when thousands of people were observed at the New York World's Fair, the majority were found to turn right when they had the alternative of two directions.

The moral to the traveller of this clear tendency to deviate to the right when irritated by some force or obstacle in his direct path is a simple one. Consciously he should keep this influence in mind and deliberately should he alternate to the right and to the left in passing obstacles.

To sum up then, in trying to follow a straight line without landmarks, the following principal sources of deviation must be guarded against, and the consequent errors anticipated and corrected:

1. In swimming right-handed people veer to the left, in rowing to the right, because of the different length and strength of their dominant arm.
2. In walking almost every person tends to veer in one direction or another in a consistent way. The chances of the deviation being to the right or to the left are approxi-

mately equal (fifty-five per cent tend to veer to the right, forty-five per cent to the left). This error is due in most cases to the difference in length of any individual's two legs. The tendency can only be measured, and therefore corrected, after personal experiment.

3. Irritant forces, such as wind, rain, or even sunlight, tend to deflect a person from his intended path.

4. In meeting obstacles, or irritant forces head on, on the intended path, the traveller nearly always prefers to pass on the right side.

CHAPTER V

WALKING IN A STRAIGHT LINE

THE DEFINITION of a straight line is the shortest distance between two points. It is true enough in terms of space: but there must be few cross-country journeys (except in some plains and deserts) on which the shortest distance between two points is the quickest or the easiest. Seldom does the desired path run in a direct line between starting place and objective. Normally the economical path involves detours which must be appraised and coldly calculated. Each detour must be estimated in length, and related in direction to both origin and objective; and these calculations must be committed to paper if the mind is not trained enough to store them. Each intentional detour should be kept as much as possible on a straight line. As every marine navigator knows, and every land navigator soon learns, curves are very hard to record.

Every region has its own anatomy and topography. Snow-covered mountainous country has its own constant natural signs of direction just as has a dense forest or an alluvial flood plain. A stranger with keen powers of observation and particular experience in the *sort* of country he is travelling through can do much to help himself in maintaining a straight line when walking. He must be careful not to generalise from a particular tree, a particular rock, a particular hillside or stream course. It is the average (or, if you like, the consensus) of the local characteristics which enables him to sense the " grain " of the country, to plan his detours to find his way to his goal.

First of course—and this specially goes for treeless open country

—the traveller must pick out distant landmarks and work to them or by them. It is elementary practice to find two landmarks ahead and line them up, and to do the same thing looking back. Back marks are just as important as, if not more important than, fore marks; and, in the absence of natural back marks, you can make your own. During Scott's expedition to the South Pole, T. Griffith Taylor, in a difficult country where there were few natural landmarks, resorted to the broken end of a signal pole. He tied a piece of sealskin to the top for a flag and painted it with blubber soot. His resourcefulness was rewarded; he could see this artificial landmark for miles back and could line it up with a natural one, a large crack in a granite cliff. This proved most helpful on his return journey, when he found it an excellent landmark, the stake lying directly in line with a crack in the cliff five miles off across the bay.

Less easy is it to make long-distance landmarks in forests; but all primitive woodsmen follow the old and tried method of trail blazing, breaking branches and hacking marks on trees with hatchet or knife. The best blaze mark for a forest trail is one gash on the front of a tree and two on the back. The back marks again are the most important, if the traveller intends to return home by the same route. The fore marks help the rescue party if you become lost; and their job will be the easier if the traveller practises the old dodge of breaking a branch in the direction of a turn.

The Indians of the eastern United States devised a very practical method of marking their trails, by deforming the trees in the direction of the trail. By one method they pulled a branch away from a sapling for a few feet in a horizontal position and tied it down with vines. In time the branch grew vertically from the place where it was tied. By another method they bent the top of a sapling over until it was buried in the ground, when a new shoot from it would sprout up vertically. Many of these permanent living road-signs, marking nodal positions and important detours on the Indians' regular routes, exist to this day. In Highland Park, Illinois; in the Mississippi Valley; and at Kregeville in Pennsylvania they are preserved as historic landmarks.

Forest trail blazing should of course be used with discretion. Nobody wants to inflict unnecessary scarring or permanent damage to trees. It would certainly be wrong to use this form of marking in national parks; but in dense forests where route finding may be a matter of life and death accurate blazing is very necessary. Often the trail blazer in really dense forest must check his blaze line from time to time by climbing a high tree to pick up the distant landmarks.

Two types of Indian trail markers

A method of trail blazing which damages no living thing is the method of the paper chase. When I was a boy in Tasmania the cross-country trail was a popular sport. The boy who was hare carried a sack of paper over his shoulder, and dropped a handful here and there along his tracks for the hounds to follow. On serious travel it is of course as often as not the hare who wants to follow his own trail home. Travellers in difficult country where few landmarks could be used or trees blazed, have used pebbles and red paper on snow, pebbles and black paper on sand. The paper chase method even works on calm waters; in the sheltered inlets of the coast of British Columbia the Indians on fishing trips used cedar chips dropped from their boat to mark their route in times of thick fog.

There is scope for much originality and invention with self-made trail marks. In Australia the aborigines light fires of Spinifex plant in open country and keep the smoke from these fires in line. As they progress beyond the fires they take a back line now and then to check their course. Spinifex, which will burn when it is green, is found in the sparse open country of central Australia. It must be used with circumspection and never if there is danger of fires spreading. The traveller wants smoke and not flames; and no one wants to destroy cover in semi-arid country.

One of the simplest of trail markers and back liners is the cairn. The traveller must survey the surrounding country and take care to heap his rocks up in a pattern sufficiently distinctive from any local natural formation. There are parts of the world where a cairn is the only means of establishing direction, and very few parts where it is not of some use. Cairns, of course, can be made of snow or ice; and in the vast expanses of the Antarctic, where monotonous weeks' journeys can be devoid of any land-mark, such cairns have been indispensable to history-making explorers. In the journal of his last tragic expedition to the South Pole, Captain Scott writes: " Had we been dependent on land-marks we should have fared ill. Evidently a good system of cairns is the best possible travelling arrangement on this great snow plain."

And Scott's further accounts relate how the sight of these man-made markers, piled up on the outward trip, gave heart to the whole party during their attempted return from the Pole.

" Thursday, Feb. 23, 1912. The data was so meagre that it seemed a great responsibility to march out and we were none of us happy about it. But just as we decided to have lunch, Bowers's wonderful sharp eyes detected an old double lunch cairn [large snow cairn built on the outward trip], the theodolite telescope confirmed it, and our spirits rose accordingly. This afternoon we marched on and picked up another cairn; then on and camped

Camel caravan in Australia keeping smoke from three fires in line

only $2\frac{1}{2}$ miles from the depôt. We cannot see it, but, given fine weather we cannot miss it. We are therefore extraordinarily relieved. Covered 8.2 miles in 7 hours showing we can do 10 to 12 miles on this surface. Things are again looking up, as we are on the regular line of cairns, with no gaps right home, I hope."

On a later expedition to the Antarctic a similar system of lining up artificial marks was used by Rear Admiral Richard E. Byrd. In place of snow cairns Byrd's expedition used orange-coloured flags tied to stakes; and they marked their trail with a line of these spaced at quarter-mile intervals to the east and west of their depots of food and fuel. Of the flags thus set out, every fourth one was numbered, beginning with the number of one and mounting away from the depot on either side. Flags to the east had a capital E. A flag stick marked W2 would be eight flags or two miles west of the depot. Byrd's ground party, on its 200-mile trip southward, used this system of marking the trail and depots.

A party of several travellers in open landmark-less country can become themselves landmarks, or rather direction marks, by proceeding in what has become known as Indian file. No such party follows its leader blindly, nor should any party do so, for all must remember that any leader is subject to the same physical and mental influences as can make his followers deviate from the straight line. In extended Indian file the last man of a line can readily see the veering of the leader.

In the Alps, where this method is often used, it is seldom found that even the most experienced guide leading a roped party in a human chain can keep a straight line. It is that last man who guides him—who checks the natural transgressions of the moving column. Such a check of course is not always infallible, and itself must be checked periodically by compass; but it does put the compass where it belongs—as an instrument for intermittent and not continuous consultation. It works almost as well in a snow-storm as in good conditions. When you are walking, the compass oscillates, so the whole party has to halt while it is read, whereas the method just described does not hinder the speed of the party.

R. H. Kahn had a personal experience of the technique of a

party walking in Indian file. He related, in a scientific journal, how he joined a group of mountain guides who used this system in bad weather when they could not see very far ahead. The group was travelling on the ice fields of the Pasterz Glacier on the Gross Glockner, that fine mountain in western Austria. An old drill among the mountain guides of this district, for snowstorm or misty travel, was the human rope-linked chain. The first guide took what he calculated was the march direction, and tried to keep to it. The last guide took sight over the slowly moving column of people, to control any deviations from the straight. All the guides knew that the front man could not perform this task alone, as indeed he knew himself. Kahn himself could easily see that the leader constantly showed a tendency to veer to the right in a circular path. Constantly did the last guide call out corrections to the front man. Aware though the leader himself was, of his tendency to swerve to the right, he could only partly correct himself and he still required—indeed relied on—the man in the rear to watch that he kept in a straight line.

In the Arctic or Antarctic the dog team and sledge, one of the most extensively used methods of travel, itself forms a line sufficiently long to be aimed and checked by the traveller. From leading dog to trailing sledge is fifty feet, a yardstick which can be kept aimed at a distant landmark, or oriented at a constant angle with the local grain of the wind-moulded snowdrifts. Only in the thickest mist or blizzard is visibility down to below fifty feet; and under such circumstances the polar traveller usually stops and digs in until the weather lifts. But on the fells or mountains a party of three or more overtaken by mist or bad light may seldom carry their food or shelter with them. They must push on, their file extended to the limit of visibility and their visibility aided by white cloths or handkerchiefs pinned at the back of the head or on the back. In the dark or fog shouts are preferable to visual signs, and a good penetrating whistle is more audible than shouts. Every member of every climbing party should carry a whistle.

This chapter is concerned with the methods of keeping a straight line, rather than with finding a straight line to keep: but it is important, of course, intermittently to check the party's general orientation, not only with the compass (as I have already indicated) but with the wind direction as given by clouds (and the higher the clouds the better), by the sun and shadows, by the moon and stars. All these fundamental navigational methods are of course discussed in later chapters. But apart from these fundamental methods there is an additional means of straight-line navigating that is worthy of discussion here—the method of the intentional error, the method of aiming (when the conditions of the journey permit) somewhat askew of the final target.

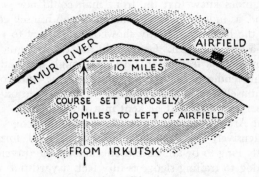

Amur River

I can recall from my flying days a successful use of this simple trick. I employed it on my world flight with Wiley Post in 1931, when we were in an area in which there were no distinguishable features to relate to the map. The area was eastern Siberia; and we left Irkutsk for a " leg " of some 1100 miles with the intention of refuelling at a small airfield on the bank of the Amur river. The last several hundred miles of this leg were over northern Manchuria—over high grass country with no towns, no roads— indeed precious few distinctive features of any sort. We knew that we were unlikely to land much before dusk and that the airfield was not lighted. We could not afford to waste any time looking for it. I purposely set a course to hit the Amur river ten miles to the left of our destination. When we reached the river I told

Wiley Post to turn right. We rounded a bend and there lay the airport. We made our landing with just enough light. Wiley Post could not understand why I was so definite about turning to the right until I later explained it to him. There had been no check points for the last part of our route; and our maps were very questionable. If we had set a course directly to the field and had missed it when we reached the Amur river, we could have used up all our daylight by turning in the wrong direction.

Of course this method can be adopted by the pathfinder only when certain circumstances attach to the nature of his goal. It is necessary for the objective to be on some kind of definite line, such as a river, a range of mountains or a coastline. It does not need, of course, to be a straight line. The great thing, however, is that if your goal *is* on such a line you need no positive landmark until you reach the line.

This shows the value of the calculated intentional error—a simple method which can bring the traveller to the base line of his desired goal in no doubt whatever (unless he has been guilty of a really gross miscalculation) as to which way to turn. Any normal unconscious deviation is swallowed up in this intentional margin: by purposely aiming for a point either to the right or to the left of his objective, the navigator eliminates this uncertainty and is sure of his homefall.

CHAPTER VI

THE USE OF THE EARS

SOME YEARS ago that famous traveller and explorer, the late F. Spencer Chapman, was kayaking along the east coast of Greenland with an Eskimo hunting party. The coast was free from ice, and in the heavy swell the waves were audibly beating against the shore; so that when a dense fog suddenly came up and reduced visibility to a few yards the party had no difficulty in keeping within sound of the shore. They were some distance from home: and Chapman seriously worried about how they were going to strike the narrow entrance to their home fjord. But, as he writes: " The Eskimos seemed quite unperturbed . . . indeed they beguiled the time by singing verse after verse of their traditional songs and occasionally they threw their harpoons from sheer *joie de vivre*."

It was not until after an hour of steady paddling had passed, that the leading hunter suddenly swung inshore and hit the narrow entrance with complete accuracy. It took some time for Chapman to satisfy himself about the method by which he had navigated with such precision; it was not until he had made some subsequent observations for himself that he could believe the trick. It was a simple one. " All along this coast," he wrote, " there were snow-buntings nesting, and each male bird . . . used to proclaim the ownership of his territory by singing his sweet little song from a· conspicuous boulder. Now each cock snow-bunting had a slightly different song, and the Eskimos had learnt to recognise each individual songster so that as soon as they picked out the notes of the bird who was nesting on the headland of their home fjord, they knew it was time to turn inshore."

It may not occur to many people—and sometimes does not occur to experienced travellers—that they can use their ability to hear and interpret sounds in direction finding. Nearly all the time we hear sounds; but often they scarcely register in our conscious minds—or do not register at all. Only if we distinguish noises and consciously localise them can we use them for orientation on land or at sea. The opportunities for using this auxiliary method of navigation are surprisingly common, once we realise them.

The use of all our senses can be developed with practice, and perhaps none more unexpectedly and usefully than that of hearing. Every familiar noise of everyday life, whether it be a sound of man, or some human activity, or of some domesticated creature, or a sound of nature, can guide the traveller. He can listen to the sound of chopping, sawmills, church bells, whistles, to the rumble of trains and other industrial and highway noises, to the lowing of cattle, the crowing or cackling of poultry, the bleating of sheep, to waterfalls and rapids or the sea's surf. All these sounds can be used as landmarks, can be associated with the places to which they belong in the traveller's mental map, or they can become targets leading the traveller along a forward path indicated by no other sign.

Our human ears, like those of almost every animal, are designed to appreciate the quality and quantity of sound and its *direction*. Most animals which have forward-looking eyes (as opposed to eyes in the sides of their head), and thus " binocular " vision, also have ears formed to collect sounds coming from the front. Man can concentrate both sight and hearing together towards the source of a sound. Most humans have some difference in sensitivity between their two ears: right-handed people are usually more sensitive in the right ear; left-handed people hear better with the left. Provided that it is not overshadowed by true deafness in one ear, this difference in acuteness of hearing between two normal ears is about one-ninth, and is similar to the difference between the power of the right hand over the left in right-handed people. However, any difference in sensitivity between two ears is unlikely to affect the power of direction-finding by sound; for this is almost certainly not usually based on the amount of sound detected by each ear, but on the difference in wave phase. It must be recognised that under the best circumstances it is rarely possible for a human to localise the direction of a sound more accurately than ten degrees in the horizontal plane: in the vertical plane localisation is even less accurate.

No human ear has been found capable of hearing a sound with a frequency much less than 20 or much more than 20,000 vibrations a second. The upper limit is particularly variable in man. If we choose a note with a frequency of 1100 cycles per second, we have a sound which can be heard by every normal man and which has a wavelength of about a foot. If a man turns his head so that the line through his ears makes an angle of 45 degrees with the line joining him to the source of such a sound, the sound will reach one ear about 0.0004 seconds before the other, and the sound waves will be out of phase by about two-fifths of a complete wavelength (cycle).

While sound location by wave phase seems to be the main method among humans and many other animals, it is certain that some other animals, particularly those which can rotate their external ears, can also appreciate and localise sounds by intensity. This may even apply to human sound location when the note to be located is a high one, such as that of the song of many kinds of birds.

The human trying to locate the direction or source of a sound probably unconsciously adopts the correct position for " scanning" the impulses, moving his head so that his ears rotate in the same plane as the source of the sound. Often an observed listener straining to detect a source will stop with his earline at 45 degrees to the soundline. If the sound comes from above ground level the listener tilts his earline; that is, leans his head from one side to the other.

All these things the sensitive listener will do unconsciously, but sound location can often be improved if the listener goes through the scanning movements consciously—deliberately seeks for the angle where the sound waves are most out of place, or for the face-on aspect where the volume of sound received by each ear is approximately equal. The phase detection process is much more an unconscious one than the volume detection process; indeed physiologists and neurologists to this day are not quite sure how it works—how the brain interprets the different stimuli and deduces the direction of the origin of the stimuli from them.

There are further processes in interpreting sounds which can be entrusted only to the conscious mind. Among these are allowance for the velocity and direction of the wind and assessment of the quality of the noise. Moreover, sound travels not only through the air—of course as a disturbance of the air—but through the ground and through water. The American Indian, keen to detect the sounds of galloping horses, puts his ear to the ground. The Fiji Islander, swimming underwater and fearful of sharks, can identify the sound of a shark some distance away—and can even distinguish it from the sounds made by other fish.

More difficult than finding the direction of a sound source is finding its distance. This needs much conscious effort and training, and long experience; but every countryman who is familiar with the intensity of common noises such as the chopping of wood or the crowing of roosters can with experience get a fair estimate of distance by sound volume.

We now know that echo location was invented in the course of evolution independently by at least two orders of animals, the bats and some birds, long before man learned it himself by means of mechanical devices. But man can also use direct and simple echo location, at least when he is at a reasonable distance from the object whose distance he wishes to sound. When fog or darkness obscures vision in hilly country, the echo of a loud call can show the traveller his distance from a mountain side, if he remembers that in air sound takes nearly five seconds to travel a mile. Distance echo sounding is very useful to seamen, for sound often carries a long way over water; and many a vessel, close to a high rock-bound coast in fog or at night, has judged its distance offshore from the reflected sound of a pistol shot, siren blast or shout. Indeed, in the inland waterways of Norway, British

Columbia, Labrador and Alaska, in dirty weather ships' whistles are quite regularly used with stop watches by captains and pilots. Each second between blast and echo means a distance of about 560 feet from the reflecting surface.

So clearly may sound sometimes carry over water that sometimes the seaman can hear the roar of heavy surf long before he can see the shore. But the distances at which he can hear sounds over water are markedly affected by the strength and direction of the wind. When interpreting shore sounds he must always consider this factor and do his best to allow for it. There are innumerable shore sounds. Each roosting or nesting-place of seabirds produces one. It is pretty safe to assume that in most parts of the world the sound of seabirds at night indicates the direction of land. Few seabirds feed at night, and those that do, do so quietly. By day, it is true, seabirds of several kinds may be very noisy when a pack or flock discovers a rewarding feeding ground, but normally all seabirds are quiet except at their shore stations, their colonies. Generally speaking the voice of the seabird—or indeed any bird—is the voice of the land. The land, of course, has many other voices which can be heard at sea. The shore coasting navigator in fog or at night can distinguish the sound of trains, marine fog signals, factory whistles—and other signs of industrial activity. The sea navigator who, in fog, hears a ship's whistle or siren knows he has to make allowance for a moving vessel; he who hears bells at regular intervals, however, knows that the sounds are coming either from a ship at anchor, from a bell-buoy or from some other kind of stationary marker. Always he listens for the sounds of the waves; and he remembers that, if and when he loses such sounds, it may not be because he has moved farther to sea, for the disappearance of breakers may indicate the presence of an inlet or a harbour.

Blind people are in no doubt about the value and possibilities of hearing their way about the world. The more fortunate majority—the seeing ones—usually never consider such things. But they can be most valuable, as helpful as they are unusual.

CHAPTER VII

USING YOUR SENSE OF SMELL

MANY EARLY explorers were led to the land beyond the horizon—by the nose. One wrote of the scent of rosemary off the coast of Spain more than ten leagues out at sea. Louis de Bougainville, when he was off the east coast of Australia in 1768, recounted that " a long time before sunrise a delicious odour announced the vicinity of the land which formed a great gulf open to the south-east."

There were several explorers before de Bougainville who were led on their way by the perfumes of nature, by the breezes carrying the scent of sweet spring flowers, of new-mown hay, of freshly turned earth. A journal of Sir Francis Drake's expedition in the Pacific in 1577 records that: " From hence wee directed our course towards the south-south-west . . . at which time wee had a very sweet smell from the land . . . and wee had sight of the land about 3 of the clocke in the afternoone of the same day."

Nature's smells may not only please but can guide, for various parts of the world have their own particular odours. Many miles to sea from the Falkland Islands the smell of burning peat may be picked up: off the Cape Verde Islands the scent of the orange groves may greet the voyager: to many voyagers in the tropical seas the sweetish rancid odour of the drying coconut may be recognised out of sight of the land from which it comes. Seabird colonies on small islands produce the penetrating guano-smell, with much ammonia—a smell which has before now reached the traveller's nose before the island has reached his eye. Bush fires, forest fires, factories and oil refineries, all kinds of smelly industries indicate land not far off. Beaches and tidal lands have their own characteristic smells; and the sweet smell of new-turned farmland —especially after heavy rain—can float on the breezes many miles to sea.

Often odours are at their strongest when visibility is low, as in fog, mist or rain, or at night. The Polynesians on their long voyages frequently carried pigs with them; pigs have a highly developed sense of smell. On smelling land far out of sight the pigs would become excited; the Polynesians watched them closely. Sea breeze odours tell not only of the nearness of land, but of its direction. New smells are quickly detectable to the sensitive seaman. He becomes accustomed to the ordinary spectrum of smells which belong to his own ship. This spectrum does not shift as does the smell pattern of a town or a village. Any new smell is much more readily distinguished at sea than on land.

Back in 1924, when I was third officer of an oil tanker twenty days at sea from a Californian port, I was on watch. I well remember how the monotonous smells of the ship were suddenly relieved by the fragrance of new-mown hay coming from land eighty miles away. Just at that moment, and at that great distance, I needed no other indication of the fact that we were nearing New Zealand—a fact which of course our modern navigational devices had already announced.

This also brings to mind an incident which happened earlier on the same trip. Our Captain, who rather prided himself on his astuteness, announced that he could smell the distinct odour of tropical flowers from an island. There was a hurried examination of the charts; but nobody could find an island that could possibly have given rise to the smell. I regret to say that a fellow officer and I kept quiet about the fact that we had been blowing incense up the speaking-tube from the engine-room: we did not dare disillusion him.

On or over land the scents are much more numerous and confused, generally speaking, than they are at sea. Nevertheless, there are many—both natural and pertaining to human civilisation—which are diagnostic, readily detectable and useful to the traveller. In desert regions smells are relatively simple. Normally the only odours met with are near oases and human habitations.

Travellers have often been able to follow the direction to a water-hole or oasis for several miles by smell alone, especially when the wind is in the right direction. In a recent paper read to the Institute of Navigation, Brigadier R. A. Bagnold referred to the use of smell in desert areas:

" In desert regions where the weather conditions in the evening and the early morning are generally very favourable and where the wind direction is fairly predictable it is sometimes possible to home on an occupied rendezvous by smell alone. In a lifeless country smells are so rare that one's nose gets almost dog-like. For instance it is possible to home to a doubtfully located water-hole hidden in broken country the size of a small English county after a D.R.[1] approach run of several miles. The author once found such a water-hole entirely by the smell of one camel, which was picked up eight miles away."

In the polar regions, which are in a true sense deserts, explorers have found much the same. Indeed, their own smells and the smells of their own animals in depots are their principal olfactory guides. Good guides, too, they can sometimes be, for almost as a rule dog team sledgers in the polar regions have tried to locate their food depots by steering a little downwind so as to allow their sledge dogs (with their very acute sense of smell) to take the final line and find and close the depot.

Of course not only do dogs have a prodigiously better sense of smell than humans, but they live with their heads much nearer the ground; and scent is nearly always strongest near the ground, based (as it of course is) on tiny particles emitted by objects and floating in the air. Primitive man knew well how to track his quarry by scent, and he was never too proud to put his nose to the ground now and then like a dog.

But for modern man to hunt his game by scent, the game would probably have to be dead—and very well hung. It is not that modern man, compared with the primitive, lacks the capacity to track by scent. He is probably blessed with an equal inherent capacity to do so, and an equally good sense of smell.

[1] D.R., which means Dead Reckoning, is a navigation term for a track or position arrived at by estimation.

But primitive man was aware of his olfactory powers and cultivated them: modern man has lost interest in them.

Yet there are plenty of smells that even the least practised of us modern men can overlook. Only a fool could fail to work upwind in his search for the source of a fire's smoke. More subtle is the traveller who can tell the difference between the different fire smokes, who can distinguish, for instance, between a pine-wood fire and an aspenwood fire. Such a distinction can be a valuable one in the Rocky Mountains of the western United States. As often as not, the smell of burning pine means a forest fire, but as indicated in Chapter I (p. 26) the smell of burning aspen means a homestead, for aspen is the particular favourite of the domestic hearth of the Rocky Mountain cabins.

It is indeed often that a region, large or small, has its signature of smell. Cities have many such signatures. The fish market smells differently from the flower market, and the cattle market from the fish market. Sometimes cities (or parts of them) can smell, if not to high heaven, at least a long way in that direction. I well recall that, many years ago, while flying from Washington to New York with very bad visibility *en route* (and before the days of radio aids) we were able to get a most accurate fix of our position—directly above the glue works outside Philadelphia.

CHAPTER VIII

REFLECTIONS IN THE SKY

With some Notes on Standing Clouds

THE TRAVELLER by land or sea, in nearly every part of the world, will pursue long stretches of his journey under a cloudy sky. The extent and nature of the clouds themselves may indicate the presence of mountain ranges or mountainous islands—I shall have more to say about such " standing clouds " presently—but a general cloud cover and overcast sky such as can be encountered almost anywhere (though it is very rare over certain deserts) is not by any means neutral to the traveller choosing his route or defining his position. There are many kinds of cloud sign that he can make use of; for clouds can, literally, reflect certain elements in the earth's surface below them. Cloud mirrors can, to the experienced natural navigator, indicate all sorts of things that are out of range of his line of sight.

On land off an ice-covered sea the traveller can, for example, detect the presence of open water, simply because it reflects less light than land or ice. The open sea's tell-tale is thus a darkness on the underside of the clouds. Usually it tells the traveller little more than the presence of water: it is an unreliable indicator of the water's extent; even a small lead or pool in an otherwise complete expanse of sea ice can show a broad effect in the sky. Moreover, vapour often rises from open water in an ice-field, especially when the temperature of the air is at or not far below freezing point. This vapour affects the light in such a way as generally to produce a dark-cloud reflection. If the wind is blowing a comparatively small amount of open water can spread its tell-tale over a wide area, and thus inform a navigator a

considerable distance away. It produces what is known as a
" water sky."

During an unsuccessful search in the Arctic for the ill-fated
expedition of Sir John Franklin, Lieutenant de Haven looked for
an open sea to the northward and westward; he saw in that
direction a water sky. Captain Penny later acted on this information, and confirmed the existence of open water in this area.

The Australian Antarctic explorer, Sir Douglas Mawson, also
gives an instance of the value of spotting this particular phenomenon in the absence of other means of navigation. " Soon after
leaving the hills," he wrote, " a direct course to the hut was made.
There was no mark by which to steer, except a ' water sky ' to
the north, the hinterland being clouded over."

The converse of the water sky is ice-blink. An " ice-blink "
is a noticeable patch of brightness in an otherwise grey sky; and
is a sign of an area of floe or shore ice surrounded by water, and
big enough to produce a detectable reflection. Quite a small area
of ice can produce a blink in the sky detectable from a long
distance; and Arctic explorers have always paid considerable
attention to ice-blink. From many examples, I can quote one
written by Henryk Arctowski. " On January 19 [1898]," he
wrote, " Commandant de Gerlache pointed out the ice-blink in
the south. The sky was uniformly covered with a thick layer of
stratus [cloud] and just at the horizon a white line appeared like
a longitudinal slit, detaching itself by its brightness from the grey
of the sky. It was discontinuous, a little undulated, not rising
more than 10 to 25 feet above the horizon. At 8 p.m. Lecointe
reported the first iceberg, which appeared like a dome rising
sharply out of the sea at a distance of about 10 miles."

On land an overcast sky can signal many different things to
the traveller. One of the simplest and most important of these
things is the well-lit human city, town, airfield beacon, or even
powerful lighthouse. The loom of these lights in the sky can
often be seen when their source is actually below the observer's
horizon.

In Arctic or snow mountain country much of the anatomy of
the land surface can be reflected in a high overcast sky—some-

times so distinctly that the sky can be said to provide a sky map. Great sheets of white, such as snow or icefields, may contain a body of open water or exposed and naked rocks; the absence of reflection from these relatively non-reflecting expanses projects, upon the cloud screen if not their image, at least a dark indicator of their presence. Even new ice (blue or green) will show as greyish patches on the lower surface of the cloud layer, if it lies in quantity within a snowfield. Patches of vegetation, or even those extraordinary plants which grow on snowbanks and are known as " pink snow," may be revealed in an overcast sky and sometimes even have a pinkish effect.

Conversely, the presence of ice patches and small snowfields in an otherwise vegetation-covered or bare rocky area will make a tell-tale steel-blue reflection on the under-surface of a cloud. At the edge of a snowfield, where there is a great difference between the heat reflection of the snow and the bare rock, a shimmering of the air can be produced which is detectable in strong sunlight above a ridge.

In deserts the shimmering which is caused by differences in heat reflection can produce a " desert blink " which is detectable, in the clear cloudless sky which is practically permanent over some deserts. An area of white sand can produce a very marked desert blink because of its extra reflecting power. An oasis can produce a desert blink because of its lesser reflecting power.

In the desert the camel-rider's eye is about ten feet from the ground. Oases often lie in hollows, and in some parts of the Sahara may be surrounded by ridges of hills up to a thousand feet in height; so they are often impossible to see from a distance. But the contrast in the radiation of the sun's heat between that of the green-palmed oasis and the surrounding desert sand produces a special kind of haze in the air above the oasis. Such a haze is known to the experienced travellers in the Sahara as " shabur." Shabur can appear over hollows and basins bottomed by pure sand and lacking in water and vegetation. The heat radiation from the surface all around the hollow is visible, while that from the bottom of the depression is in dead ground. At the level which the eye can see there is then a ring of air at a different temperature from the air in the middle. The consequent difference in the refraction of the atmosphere is immediately detectable.

In many parts of the world where the atmosphere is humid, clouds tend to form continuously on mountain tops; and many highlands, coastal ranges and high islands thus tend to have standing clouds or cloud crests around their summits. Often these clouds extend far above the peaks. As the clouds are continually forming at a particular point, they appear fixed in relation to the ordinary moving clouds passing by or above them. They can indicate, for long distances, the presence of peaks which are themselves below the horizon.

The standing cloud tell-tale of high land has been used not only by all primitive peoples but by the early European navigators. De Bougainville and Dampier attached very great importance to it, as their log books testify. La Perouse, one of the early French explorers in the Pacific, lacked many of the modern navigational devices; but as his records show closely watched for the fixed clouds on the horizon that suggested an island or land mass.

Standing clouds often have a much woollier appearance than that of the normal trade-wind clouds, and readily betray the presence of an island by their shape as well as their immobility in the open ocean. Moreover, in the tropics, islands tend to produce not only standing clouds but distinctive reflections upon those clouds. Some islands—and particularly the coral islands— are far from high and mountainous. Flat and low though they are, they can still produce standing clouds simply because the white sands of a coral atoll reflect more heat than the surface of the surrounding water; the sharp kick in the temperature gradient above these islands may be enough to create the conditions in which a cloud can condense. Usually such a cloud is not directly overhead, but a little to the lee side of the island, because of the effect of the prevailing wind; and on the underside of this hovering cloud the lagoon of the atoll—nearly always bright turquoise in contrast to the deeper blue of the surrounding sea—is reflected; such coloured reflections can sometimes be observed miles before low-lying atolls appear above the horizon. Indeed, lagoons or other shallow waters can sometimes cause a reflection in a completely cloudless sky which is surprisingly conspicuous.

In the *Sailing Directions* of Matthew Fontaine Maury, the renowned American oceanographer writes of clouds hovering not only over coral islands, but over shoals:

" They are often seen to overhang the lowest islet of the tropics and even to stand above the coral patches and hidden reefs, a ' cloud by day ' to serve as a beacon to the lonely mariner out there at sea and to warn him of shoals and dangers which no lead nor seaman's eye has ever seen or sounded out."

Lightning from one particular direction in the early hours of the morning before sunrise is usually a sign of land to the tropical sea traveller—particularly when a large land mass or mountainous island carries a standing cloud.

So far I have generalised about standing cloud and cloud reflections. Let me now take a special example; for the study of clouds can help the natural navigator even further if he has a knowledge of local conditions.

When winter comes to the valley of the St. Lawrence River in eastern Canada, the waters of the river and its tributaries are warmer than the air; and a strip of mist-columns is often formed, which is intensified by the spray of the waterfalls. Near Quebec, for instance, stationary clouds are sometimes seen hovering over the cataracts—over the Chaudière and the Montmorency Falls. Later in the winter small, well-defined cumulus clouds can often be seen standing above the falls, at an elevation of three or four hundred feet. Higher up over the surrounding mountains, clouds form on the mountain-tops and may descend some distance down their sides, or remain suspended and " standing " at some height above their summits. Clouds of the first kind are often seen before or after heavy rain, of the last kind usually in fine weather.

When fine warm weather succeeds heavy rains, and the surface of the earth has been exposed for several hours to the heat of the sun, clouds often form over the islands in the estuary of the St. Lawrence River. In good stable weather they appear towards noon. They hover over the small islands which are surrounded by a large area of colder sea. Not far away we can see the opposite of this—clear spaces in the heavens over lakes where a small region of cold sea is encircled by land. This pattern of cloud of course derives from the fact that the sun heats the land more quickly than the sea. Often the clouds of the St. Lawrence valley may be seen resting over the highlands all day, while the sky over the water is clear; and at nightfall the sky over the land becomes clear as it cools, and the clouds shift to lie over the river.

The average traveller does not need specialised knowledge to understand these phenomena. He certainly does not need to be a trained meteorologist to detect the meaning of a stationary isolated cloud, if he studies the local conditions. But many pathfinders who tend to limit their observations to the things on the ground miss their opportunities.

CHAPTER IX

DIRECTIONS FROM THE WIND

THE WINDS of the world differ (of course) from each other in direction, velocity, temperature and humidity. But the differences are far from being haphazard or disorderly. Each district (practically without exception) has its own pattern of winds, usually with a particular wind from a particular direction that dominates at some seasons, and often at all seasons. I could not, of course, attempt to give details of the local prevailing or dominating winds in all parts of the world. It is not important to do so, for all that is necessary for the natural navigator is to find out what they are, learn how to recognise them and navigate with them as guide. Every human resident, almost without exception, of a country district knows his dominant wind or winds and can tell the traveller whether it is hot, cold, violent or gentle and the length of the day or the season for which it can be expected to blow. The dominant wind of any area is nearly always the same as the prevailing wind (*i.e.* that wind which blows longest from a given direction) and is the wind which leaves the biggest impression and directional effect on trees, snow, sand or other objects on the surface of the earth, either by blowing longer than the other winds (in which case it is also the prevailing wind) or by blowing more violently.

Writing entirely generally, it is true to say that at medium latitudes (that is, in most regions of temperate climate) the prevailing wind generally blows from the west in both the northern and southern hemisphere. In lower, more tropical latitudes, the prevailing winds—at least during the greater part of the year—lie between north-east and south-east and at the equator are often from the east. These easterlies are called the Trade Winds; and it is not usually realised that these trade winds blow over the continents as well as over the oceans.

To give an example, the prevailing and dominant wind in the northern South Pacific is from the south-east. It is of medium force and usually blows only during the winter months. It is the most constant wind in velocity, and also blows for the longest period of the year; throughout the year the other winds are more variable in direction and force, and have no marked or lasting effect on the surface of the land.

The compass-less natural navigator can use certain simple and pretty obvious principles in identifying the direction from which winds come—even if he lacks local knowledge. Thus in the northern hemisphere a northerly wind will be generally colder than a southerly wind, and in the southern hemisphere a southerly wind colder than a northerly wind. In the southern hemisphere, moreover, a southerly wind is often accompanied by an extreme clarity of atmosphere which very sharply outlines distant objects. Winds blowing from deserts are unmistakable because they are dry. Those blowing from oceans are moisture-laden—some are rain-bearing. Those blowing from snow-capped mountains often bring a marked drop in temperature. Some winds carry the signature of their origin in the particles of dust, sand or smoke that they bear. Wind can carry fine dust more than half-way across the world: some great volcanic eruptions have tinted the sunsets thousands of miles away for months after. I once myself witnessed an example of the ability of the wind to carry smoke for long distances. I was in Fiji at a time when there were extensive bush fires in Australia. Their smoke was carried 1500 miles to the islands. Any resident in Fiji at the time of the smoke winds could tell the direction of the west simply enough.

Dust in the wind can be carried not only for vast distances, but to great heights. Once I was in an aircraft flying across the United States at a time of strong winds over the dust-bowl region of Kansas and Oklahoma. In broad daylight and at a height of over 10,000 feet we were forced to fly entirely by instruments: the dust obscured all vision.

In nearly all regions the prevailing wind has its own personality of velocity and temperature and humidity, which enables the wind navigator to identify it. He can also identify other winds which may prevail at different times and seasons in the same way. Nearly every coastal region, for instance, suffers both land and sea breezes, simply because the surface of the sea takes longer to heat up than does the land—but retains its heat much longer. After sunset in a coastal region the surface of the earth becomes colder, while the air above the sea remains warm. This warm air rises; and the cold air from the shore flows out to take its place and produces what is known as a land (*i.e.* off-land) breeze. The sea breeze—in the opposite direction—usually blows during the afternoon, while the warmed air over the land is rising and the air from the sea (at that time colder) streams in over the land.

In the open ocean the winds are by no means constant, but the prevailing wind often has not only its characteristic temperature, humidity and force, but its characteristic accompaniment of clouds. While the wind continues to keep its personality, the navigator can be pretty sure that it is not changing seriously in direction and can guide himself by it. All he has to watch for is a change. Below the Equator, for instance, a vessel ploughing along under the stable and easily recognisable conditions of the south-east trades may sometimes experience a sudden decrease in temperature and humidity. Even without a compass its navigator would probably be correct in assuming that the wind had gone around towards the south.

The typical trade-wind clouds of the tropics are small isolated woolly tufts. They generally appear in a uniform layer below 8000 feet, characteristically outlined against the blue sky. If these trade clouds disappear, and the sky becomes overcast with heavy billowing clouds, the navigator can conclude that in all probability the wind has gone around through the south to the south-west or even to the west.

In the tropics and in temperate climates in the summer,

changes of wind after sunset or during the night often mean the presence of nearby land. Often, too, these breezes bring land scent during the night or early morning.

In the polar regions the wind temperature gives the most reliable indication of open water, for this temperature is higher —naturally enough—when it comes from water than from ice or snow. A sudden drop in air temperature without a change in wind direction can conversely give conclusive evidence of the presence of a big iceberg in an up-wind direction.

On land the traveller can use a constant wind both for orientation and for keeping a straight line. He keeps the wind directed to the same part of his body and all the time watches its strength, temperature and moisture content so as to note any changes immediately. Many travellers wet and raise their finger to detect the direction of a very light breeze; they would be better advised to wet a cheek, a much more sensitive region of the body. Of course a slight breeze can be a rather unreliable guide, since it is more likely to vary than a strong one, but it may be of great value in cases where it carries a recognisable odour.

In dense bush it is not often possible to feel the wind, but it is easy to see the sky and to note the direction of movement of the clouds. High clouds are likely to be more constant in movement than low ones and to belong more certainly to the prevailing wind. Further, when the tops of the tall trees are visible, it is useful to observe which way the highest branches bend with the wind. If snow is falling the direction of its drift will also show the wind's direction.

All over the world local winds have such marked personalities that they have been named by the resident humans. The famous Mistral blows from the north-west across the eastern part of the south of France and the delta of the Rhône. It is a chilling wind that comes down from the mountains to take the place of the hot air that rises from the flat lands around the Camargue, so constantly bathed by the Mediterranean sun. The Mistral is accompanied by a bright sky and horizon. Violent, cold and dry, it blows often for periods of from five to nine days; and it is especially strong during the autumn and winter months. Another wind, the Autan, is also very strong, hot and dry; and blows from the south and south-west.

These two typical winds are encountered in a large part of France, but other winds of constant characteristics have become well known to the inhabitants. According to Manciot the Pontias is a north-easter which blows from the Col de Devez to the plains of the Rhône valley, and stops when the snow has disappeared from the mountains. The Pontias is a morning wind; and in the afternoon may be replaced by another coming from the south-west, the Vesine, which blows up the river Aigues, a tributary of the Rhône.

Incidentally, it has always seemed strange to me that winds are named after the direction from which they blow; for nearly all other natural movement, including the movements of the sea, is identified by the direction *to* which it is proceeding. The direction-from system of naming is a very ancient custom and was used before the introduction of the magnet, when the mariners in the Mediterranean divided the horizon into divisions according to the various wind directions. If we trace this Mediterranean dummy compass through the years, we can find all sorts of variations in the names given to the winds and in the number of divisions of the horizon—depending on the historical period and the nationality of the seamen. But throughout the years it is clear that the seamen and travellers were conscious of the character of the wind and of the locality *from* which it blew. One wind coming from the northern snow-capped mountains was named Tramontane. The dominant north-westerly wind of some parts of the Mediterranean was called Magister, or Maestro. Sirocco was, and indeed still is, the name of the hot dust-laden wind blowing off the North African deserts. Greco was the north-west wind which came from Greece.

Even when the prevailing wind is not blowing at the time, the traveller versed in the use of natural signs can identify its direction by observing animals and plants. Spiders cannot lay their webs against the wind (although they may take advantage of eddies or gusts to lay them across it), but the general orientation of the webs can contribute to the picture. A warning is necessary: a web which has been broken and very recently re-made may show the direction of a recent wind which may not be the prevailing wind.

Most animals, especially birds and insects, naturally build their nests in protected positions. Most creatures who live by and with nature are very sensitive to the prevailing wind and use it to their advantage; you can use them to yours.

In the tropics the western side of rock or tree is that which is sheltered from the trade winds, and that where the shelters of the animals are most likely to be found. In higher northern and southern latitudes the eastern side is generally the most sheltered; and it is on the east, south-east or south (where it is usually drier and warmer than on the north or west) that the mice will burrow under dead trunks, the woodpeckers excavate their nests and the open-nesting birds will build. Out in the open, too, birds will tend to frequent and meet each other at places sheltered from the prevailing wind—even repairing to such places by habit when the wind is blowing from another direction. During the breeding season, for instance, many wildfowl will choose the edge of a lake or stream and congregate under the bank sheltered from the prevailing wind.

In South Africa protection from the wind is best found on the south-east of trees and rocks. Dr. S. H. Skaife of Hout Bay, Cape Province, has written very detailed accounts of the common carpenter bee of that region; and he informs me that this insect always has its burrow in that part of a dead trunk or branch which faces south-east. The rain-bearing winds of South Africa come from the north-west; this carpenter bee cannot tolerate dampness as it brings a fungus disease which is very harmful to it.

We see, then, that the wind can be your guide; and indeed it has guided many explorers of uncharted areas in the world— who have used winds at times when they had no other means of telling their direction. From the experiences of his most famous Antarctic expedition, Sir Douglas Mawson found that " In dense drift it was not a simple matter to steer a correct course for the Hut and it was essential not to deviate, as the rocky foreshores near which it stood extended only for a mile east and west; on either side abutting on vertical ice-cliffs. With a compelling force like a hurricane at our backs, it was not a nice thing to contemplate finding ourselves on the brink of a precipice. The wind, however, was steady, and we knew at what angle to steer to keep a rough course."

CHAPTER X

SOME SPECIAL EFFECTS OF
SUN AND WIND

THE PREVAILING slant of the sun's rays and the prevailing direction of the wind may leave their signatures on the country in special ways. The experienced traveller can readily spot these signatures in certain kinds of country, even when the sky is completely overcast and the wind may be blowing in a direction quite different from its prevailing direction—or not blowing at all.

Let us take an example, from mountain country in the northern hemisphere. In such country the southern slopes of the hills receive the most direct rays of, and therefore the greatest amount of radiation from, the sun. On the south slopes, therefore, are found greater extremes of temperature than on the northern slopes. In particular, the effect of alternate cooling at night and heating by day is much greater on the southerly slopes. Erosion by frost is therefore more rapid.

From this springs a general rule of mountain anatomy, namely, that in the northern hemisphere the northern inclines are smoother, less eroded and offer fewer obstacles to the climber than the southern slopes. In the southern hemisphere of course the situation is reversed.

The sun leaves its signature very readily on fields of snow or ice. If such fields slope, the slopes which face the arc of the sun's daytime track will naturally melt more quickly than those tilted away from the sun. Rocks or trees in snowfields will leave " melt-shadows " where they have protected parts of the snowfield from the rays of the sun. Such shadows give a rapid and positive indication of direction in all parts of the world.

In assessing direction by relative melting and by melt-shadows, it is necessary to take into account the direction of the prevailing wind as well as that of the prevailing sun. The modifying effect of the wind can be very substantial. Winds can melt snow quickly and, if of a high temperature, can sometimes have an even greater effect on the melt-rate than the direct rays of the radiating sun. Thus, while in general the snow-line on mountains will be lower on the side protected from the sun, quite substantial exceptions to this rule may be expected. In the southern hemisphere, for instance, the general tendency is for the snow-line to be lower on the south side of a mountain range than on the north; but in the Otago district of New Zealand, as I have myself noticed, the region of low snow-line has been swung through a large arc by the prevailing westerly wind; and in fact the snow-line is lower on the south-east and northern sides of the hills than on the western sides.

The directional melting effect of wind and sun can be observed on the glaciers of the temperate latitudes in a most interesting way. When small dark stones, leaves or other debris lie upon the snow, they absorb more heat than the surrounding white surface. Consequently, melting-holes begin and small basins are formed in which water may lie. The depths of these basins are limited to that which the slanting sun's rays can reach. Usually they are less than one foot in depth, though in some places they have been recorded up to three feet deep. They are useful in direction-finding because the swing of the sun's arc through the day traces a consistent semi-circular edge on one side. In the northern hemisphere the southern edge of the melt hole is straight or almost straight and is aligned east-west; while the northern edge is the true semi-circle with its arc open to the true south. In the Swiss Alps these melt holes in the snow are known as " noon " holes (mittagslöcher) or " meridian holes " (Meridian löcher).

The semi-circular shape of noon holes is naturally best marked in low latitudes. In high latitudes during the summer they are of less value. North of the Arctic Circle the summer sun may never set in summer, and the melting occurs almost equally on all sides; and so the melt holes become practically round and have no directional value. But in the temperate and high tropical parts of the world they provide a constant and useful travellers' guide. It is not even always necessary for small black bodies to be present to start them. In snow already pitted by wind, the shadow effect of the edge of the original wind pit may be enough to start differential melting and bring the pit to its tell-tale semi-circular shape. In many snow areas of the world " pitted snow " or very small holes caused in the process of the melting of snow will show this same semi-circular effect, the rounded edge being on the side farthest from the sun and the flat side nearer to the sun.

Just as small pieces of rock produce tell-tale directional noon holes, so do large pieces of rock on snow produce tell-tales: but these tell-tales are of rather a different kind. Few glaciers which flow through steep-sided valleys are free from rocks and earth eroded from the valleys' sides. Cliffs break in the ordinary process of erosion, and through the course of the years and months shed an intermittent cascade of rock on to the glacier below. Such rocks on a glacier form the beginnings of a lateral moraine; and when two glaciers meet their lateral moraines run together to form a central moraine on the joined glacier. Thus rocks may be carried along by moving glaciers in their middles or at their edges. When heated by the sun, large rocks protect the ice under them from melting, thus affecting it in exactly the opposite way from small dark stones.

The sun's action slowly melts the ice around and underneath the stone slab. Gradually it comes to stand on a pedestal of ice. A big plate-like flat slab becomes a one-legged table; and the bigger it is, the greater is its protective action by shadowing the central core of the ice below it, and the higher does the pedestal become. In most temperate latitudes pedestals seldom become more than two or three feet in height whatever the size of the slab which they support; but in the high snow areas of the tropics where the sun's rays are steeper, the pedestal may be thicker and its height may reach seven, ten or, quite exceptionally, thirteen feet.

These glacier tables or ice tables (Gletschertische) as they are called in the Swiss Alps, are directional because of their tilt. In the northern hemisphere they normally tilt down towards the south simply because the greatest amount of melting takes place on the southern side. Normally the tilt increases as the melting goes on: the slab tilts more and more towards the south until, when the glacier table reaches a certain size, the slab slips off its

Glacier table (*after Manciot*)

pedestal back on to the glacier face. The old pedestal then melts away (though often its remains can be seen) while a new one begins to be melted underneath the slab in its new position. Indeed, when melting is intensive, a new table can be formed under it during the same summer; and north of it the remains of its predecessor—and even occasionally its predecessor's predecessor—can be observed in line. These lines and the fundamental tilt of the slabs show a very reliable north-south direction to the mountaineer in the Swiss Alps. Large tables can be found on the glacier ice (not the winter snow) of the Unteraar, the Lower Grindelwald and Aletsch Glaciers.

In the Arctic, glacier tables are rare and almost valueless for direction because of the low circular path of the summer sun. The sun's rays, falling seldom far from the horizontal, generally melt the ice all around a stone and quite far under it; and simply cause it to sink.

The signature of the prevailing wind may be detected in some kinds of country as readily as those of the prevailing sun. The wind carries erosive agents—water, snow, sand—which set their marks in unmistakable ways on the face of the traveller's terrain. The famous Antarctic explorer, Douglas Mawson, knew well how often the prevailing wind and snowdrift set its mark upon the rocks and upon hard blue ice. Such ice may become channelled and pelted by the action of drift snow; and both snow and ice may become so polished by the prevailing wind that they grow very slippery. In one particular instance in the Antarctic, Mawson noted a differential rock—weathering very similar to that which would have been caused by the sun in a more temperate latitude. The rocks facing the north appeared to be quite different from those facing the south: the southern faces were smooth and rounded by the wind; but their surface was somewhat broken by the chipping and splitting action of frost: the sheltered northern faces were rougher and more broken up.

I must stress that in most latitudes the effects of sun, wind and rain must be interpreted in conjunction with each other. Exposure to the sun may have an effect opposite to or modifying that of the prevailing wind or rain: results are much more pronounced when sun and wind work together. To show how sun and wind can place and write a joint signature across a natural landscape, I have chosen a particular area, the details of which can be appreciated by any interested observer.

In the Palouse region of the south-eastern part of the state of Washington and northern Idaho in the United States, erosion and drift through the centuries have brought about a dune-like topography by working the soil into a succession of hills. In the winter, the wind blows almost continuously from the south-west, and tends to lay bare the windward slopes of the hill-tops, and to pile deep snowdrifts on their leeward slopes immediately below

Plate I. An analysis of this picture can indicate the general region, the time of the year, the time of the day, and the direction in which the house is facing. (*After a photograph from* Coming Events in Britain *by Courtesy of the British Travel & Holidays Association*)

Plate II. The departure of the six canoes from Rarotonga for New Zealand, A.D.1350 (*after Watkins*)

their crests. Over the long years this has made the inclines facing south-west more gradual than those to the leeward, which are inclined to be steep.

In this region then, the location of the thickest snow cover is due principally to the great force of the south-west wind. The difference in the steepness of the slopes is very considerable. Those facing the south-west are gradual—averaging less than eighteen degrees from the horizontal—whereas the north-east slopes incline about fifty degrees from the horizontal. This state of affairs persists throughout nearly the whole of the Palouse region so constantly that in the summer-time any traveller can easily determine his direction anywhere in the area simply by watching the sides of the hills.

CHAPTER XI

DIRECTION FROM TREES
AND OTHER PLANTS

W E SELDOM pause to observe the shape of a tree, and therefore we do not often realise that the different forms of trees can teach us much about the directional influences of the sun and the wind in various localities. To understand how these two elemental forces affect trees, it is necessary to become " shape conscious " and familiarise ourselves with the basic outlines of the various trees. Each kind of tree has its own characteristic form, and it is therefore much easier to differentiate among the species if you think of them in terms of their silhouettes. Start with the shape, and with this impressed on your mind, it will be easier to study the details of leaves and flowers.

It is important for the pathfinder to learn to identify the common species of trees in his locality. In most parts of the world one can obtain popular books describing the trees of the region; a walk with someone who is familiar with the local trees will also be helpful. Moreover, once you have learned which trees are native to your area, you will be able to recognise any introduced species, particularly the ornamentals, which often indicate the proximity of towns and farms.

Nature designed the basic shapes of trees principally in order to satisfy their differing light requirements. The reason for the differences in the forms of various species, comparing the fir tree with the elm, for example, is that each has a greater or lesser need for sunlight, under the various climatic conditions to which they are adapted.

In the cold northern latitudes, many trees are dependent on

NORWAY   WHITE   LOMBARDY   SYCAMORE
SPRUCE   OAK   POPLAR   MAPLE

lateral, diffused or indirect light. They adopt the pyramid shape; of these the most common example is the fir. This tree cannot get overhead light, and there is therefore no advantage in its having a rounded crown such as the elm tree has in lower latitudes. Trees in the high latitudes are more openly branched and leaved than those of low latitudes, so that the light can penetrate even to the branches on the north. The leaves are generally rounded so that they are able to get direct light through the branches and diffused light from all sides.

Some trees of temperate climates, such as the cypresses, also have a pyramid form. They adopt this shape to avoid the excessive heat of the high sun at midday and to obtain the full benefit of front light in the morning and the afternoon.

A spectacular example of a large-leaved, tropical, palm-like tree which has a narrow, vertical form in order to avoid the midday heat and light, is the Traveller's Tree (*Ravenala madagascariensis*). This tree is thought by some people to have been so named because it is aligned in a north-south direction. This is not so; there would be no advantage in such an alignment in the equatorial region, where the sun is practically overhead at midday. Its name was suggested by the abundant store of fresh water found in the trunk at the base of the leaves.

Often, however, valuable indications of direction are given by the modifications of the basic shapes of trees through the effects of wind, sun, or these two elements combined. Even the most casual observer has seen windswept trees growing in exposed places of strong winds and has realised that they clearly show the dominant wind direction. But this knowledge is of little practical value unless it is interpreted in terms of north, south, east and west.

Windblown tree (*totara*) at Auckland, New Zealand

The dominant wind in an area is the one which has the most effect on vegetation, either because of its strength or because of the length of time it blows during the course of the year. It is quite simple for the pathfinder to learn the direction of the dominant wind which causes the leaning of the trees in his own locality and to apply this knowledge in finding his way.

Trees do not necessarily have to lean away from the dominant wind to show its direction. There are other, less obvious and little realised effects. Wind can retard development, for example by damaging or desiccating the young shoots on the windward

Elm trees near Zandvoort, Holland. The right hand side
faces south-east and shows the enhanced growth on the side
sheltered from the wind

side, while the sheltered side of the tree will flourish and produce
more branches and more abundant foliage.

The coconut palm normally leans towards the wind even in
areas exposed to strong winds. During the many years I have
spent in the South Pacific, I have observed hundreds of these
trees, all leaning into the prevailing trade wind, which in this
area is the south-east, not only on my own coconut plantation
island but also on all the others I have visited. In common with

other trees, the coconut palm has a much greater leaf growth on the sheltered side and its head presents a flattened appearance to windward.

When observing trees for directional purposes, it is essential to choose a tree growing in an exposed position and which is not interfered with or sheltered by other trees or buildings. Do not base your conclusion on only one tree, but examine several in similar situations. Be specially careful that the trees you observe have not been pruned by man or damaged by natural causes.

While the direction of the wind has the effect of retarding growth on that side of a tree, the effect of sunlight, on the other hand, is usually to enhance the development of branches and leaves, and its beneficial effects can be seen plainly. In places where the winds are variable, the full effect of greatest sunlight can be very striking in the distinct difference it causes between the northern and southern sides of the tree. In most parts of the Northern Hemisphere the arc of the sun from rising to setting is entirely on the south side of the tree, and the mid-point of this arc is true south. This is the direction of the most abundant foliage in certain species.

Among the trees which develop more foliage on the side which receives most sunlight are the common black and white poplars, the oak, plane tree, beech, Corsican pine, horse chestnut, Norway maple, British maple, ailanthus, box elder and North American black locust tree. Because of their greater branch and foliage development on the side where the light is strongest, in areas where the wind does not modify the effect, these trees often show a slight inclination of the trunk in that direction. Although elms are less affected by the direction of greatest sunlight than other trees of temperate climates, they sometimes show this same inclination of the trunk.

In Surrey, where strong winds are not particularly usual, I have observed that the oak and beech trees in exposed positions were more heavily branched and had greater foliage on the south side. In Virginia, the oaks and long-leaf pines show a decidedly heavier growth on the south side. The illustrations were drawn from photographs of trees which I examined.

Longleaf pine tree. Virginia Beach, U.S.A. The right
side of the tree faces south and shows the greater branch and
foliage growth on that side which received the full daily arch
of the sun. This is in an area where the winds have practically
no effect on direction of the growth

These trees are typical of most of the other species when growing
in positions exposed to full sunlight in the temperate regions of
the Northern Hemisphere.

In these regions the southern branches of many trees are more
horizontal, while the northern ones reach up more vertically in
their endeavour to obtain more light. This provides an excellent
means of determining north and south.

This upward struggle of the northern branches to receive the greatest amount of top light is very pronounced in the horse chestnuts of the eastern United States and of Europe, and also in the European lindens. In the elms, however, it is hardly notice-able. In Connecticut I have found it easy to get my direction from the horse chestnuts merely by glancing out of a train window. In winter, when the trees are leafless, the side of greatest branch growth is more easily seen. In summer a closer inspection of the foliage from either side is sometimes necessary.

Unlike the trees mentioned above, there are some, such as the common spruce, the firs and the pyramid poplars, which usually remain straight and are uniformly branched on all sides in spite of uneven illumination. The cedars also remain straight unless they are very tall, when they have a tendency to bend towards the strongest light.

So far we have considered only the separate effects of the wind and the direction of greatest sunlight on the growth and shape of trees. It is also necessary for the pathfinder to observe the combined effects of wind and light. In some cases these two influences will combine to intensify the effect; in other cases, one reduces the other. The sun has the stronger influence on some kinds of trees, the wind on others.

Early in 1955 my wife and I made a leisurely trip by car from the south of France through Belgium and Holland for the express purpose of observing and photographing the directional charac-teristics of trees. Similar observations were made in England and in the eastern United States. Following winding roads from the Mediterranean coast to Holland, we had no difficulty at any time in determining north, south, east and west by observing the trees through the car windows.

Through Provence in the south of France that chilling wind, the Mistral, blows from the north-west. The farmers in this region call the wind the " mud-eater " (" mange fange ") because its dry, cold gusts have the effect of drying up the ground. The farm-houses of Provence (locally known as " mas ") are built with their backs to the north-west, the direction of the Mistral, and have a minimum of windows on that side. The houses are usually sheltered from the wind by a row of cypresses which also shield the gardens. The position of these windbreaks would make it very easy for anyone to tell his directions, for they are naturally aligned north-east south-west. The Mistral has a striking effect on the growth of individual trees, although it blows only for four or five days at a time, intermittently, during the winter. Every cypress in an exposed or unprotected position shows its bulge of greater growth on that part of the tree which is sheltered from the wind. Although trees in Central Europe actually receive the full benefit of the sun from morning to evening on the southern side, the wind's effects on their growth is much more pronounced than that of the sun. However, the decidedly greater growth of branches and leaves on the south-east is to some extent caused by the southern sun, though not enough to make it a true southerly growth.

Proceeding on our journey, north of Avignon we left the cypresses behind but observed the same marked effect on the common poplar. Although we were out of the area of the violent Mistral, the trees throughout central and northern France, Belgium and Holland clearly showed that the direction of the dominant wind was still north-west. In this region almost all isolated trees, of various species, even if not leaning away from the wind, show evidence of retarded growth on the side where the wind blows strongly. The silhouettes of clumps of trees present a smoothly rounded edge pointing into the prevailing north-west wind. The sheltered sides of these groups of trees have a more ragged configuration. This striking evidence of direction can be seen many miles away.

Summing up, we have to give full consideration to the separate effects of wind and sun on trees, and at times to their combined influence. The information gained in this manner can be applied in finding our way.

In any place where the wind blows predominantly from one direction, the flower plumes of reeds will be found to form a thin wedge only on that side of the stem away from the wind. I have seen this not only throughout Europe but also in many other places in the world, including the vicinity of my home in the Fiji Islands, where the south-east trade is the dominant wind.

It is often stated in boys' books that moss will be found on the north side of trees in the northern hemisphere. This is a rather dangerous generalisation if other factors are not taken into account. Moss and lichens do not necessarily thrive where they receive the most shade but—and this is more important—where the moisture is retained the longest. Humidity is an even greater

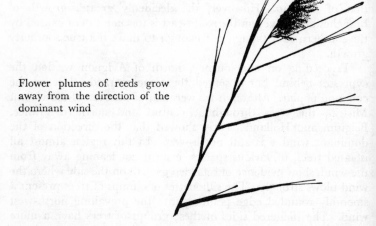

Flower plumes of reeds grow away from the direction of the dominant wind

factor than shade. It is a question of knowing from where the rain-bearing winds in your locality blow, and the direction of the greatest shade. Combining these two factors, you should be able to determine where moisture will be retained longest and where moss will grow. In North America, as a general rule, there is less evaporation on the north and north-east sides of trees and rocks. On the other hand, in the Seine and Burgundy regions in France, mosses and lichens are usually found on the north-west side of trees and rocks and in the Jura, in Switzerland, on the south-west side. Each locality has its differences in climate, and you should determine for yourself which side retains moisture the longest in your particular area. Only in this way can mosses and lichens be a valuable guide to direction.

This information will be all the more worthwhile when evidence is obtained from growths on trees or rocks exposed to all weathers. It may also be of interest to know that some mosses take on a darker brown hue when growing in greater sunlight and are more green or greyish-green when found in more shaded spots.

Other plants growing on trunks or branches of trees can be useful to you in determining direction if you continually observe

NORTH

Section of tree trunk

SOUTH

the habits of each individual species under local conditions. These plants are known as epiphytes. Each species has its particular preference for light, shade or moisture.

The Indians of North America used all possible indications in order to orient themselves in the forests. Père Joseph François Lafitau, speaking of the Iroquois tribe, with whom he spent five years, wrote in 1724: " The savages pay great heed to their ' star ' compass [the Pole Star] in the woods and in the vast prairies of the continent of America, as well as on the rivers whose courses are well known to them. But when the sun or the stars are not visible they have a natural compass in the trees of the forest from which they know the north by almost infallible signs.

" The first is that of their tips, which always lean towards the South, to which they are attracted by the sun. The second is that of their bark, which is more dull and dark on the north side. If they wish to be sure they only have to give the tree a few cuts with an axe; the various tree rings which are formed in the trunk of the tree are thicker on the side which faces north and thin on the south side."

Lafitau's statement that the tips of trees point south is not wholly accurate; in fact the tips of certain trees in North America, such as pines and hemlocks, lean to the south-east.

The tree-ring method known to the Indians was also described by Leonardo da Vinci in Italy more than four hundred years ago. Throughout North America and Europe more recent observations have confirmed da Vinci's statement that as shown by annual tree-rings, the heart of a tree is nearer the bark on the north side, and that the bark of old trees is usually thicker on the north and north-east sides.

In a test made many years ago by the New York State Forest Commission on 700 black spruce trees in the Adirondack Mountains, 94 per cent showed a greater growth of the trunk section towards the north and east, while only six per cent had thicker growth on the south and west.

Plants and trees can give us much help in finding our direction because of their liking for certain environments. Some species flourish in full sunlight, others in shade; some prefer moist conditions while others need arid zones. Many types, such as those with small leaves which spin with the wind, have a tolerance for wind, while other plants, including many with large leaves, need sheltered positions.

Thus we find that in many cold and temperate parts of the Northern Hemisphere the leaf-shedding trees grow on the warmer, south-facing slopes, while the evergreen pines and conifers are found on the northern slopes.

In the Rocky Mountains, limber pines will nearly always be

Plate IIIa (*opposite*) Cypress and farm building in Provence in France. Note the large cypress tree with its bulge of greater growth on the south-east side, sheltered from the mistral. Also of interest is the symmetrical shape of the small cypress sheltered by the large tree. The leafless trees in the foreground on each side of the building show the retarding effect of the dominant wind on the north-west side. The door of the farm building in the sheltered south-east side is typical of the Provence region. All of these features combine to give very positive evidence of direction to the traveller.

Plate IIIa (caption on opposite page)

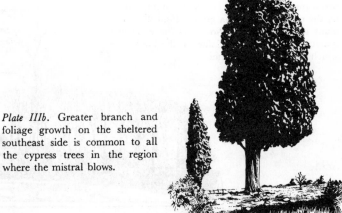

Plate IIIb. Greater branch and foliage growth on the sheltered southeast side is common to all the cypress trees in the region where the mistral blows.

Plate IVa. Poplar tree at Heemstede, Holland. The growth on the right hand side of the tree, which is the northwest side, has been retarded by the dominant northwest wind.

Plate IVb. Beeches and a birch near Heemstede, Holland. The rounded edge of this clump of beech trees points to the Northwest and is caused by the retarding effect on growth from the dominant northwest wind. Note also the enhanced growth on the southeast side of the birch tree which overtops the beeches.

found on the south-facing slopes, while Engelmann spruce trees are on the inclines facing north. Seeing either of these species, you can be very certain which slope you are on.

In the eastern Grass Veld of South Africa the north-facing slopes are exposed to intense sun and hot winds. This results in a vegetation which can stand the dryness, such as thorn trees, milky sap plants, and aloes. On the protected south-facing slopes, however, there are grasslands. These inclines also get the benefit of the rain-bearing winds blowing from between south-west and south-east. In the higher ridges of the Drakenburg and Stormberg Mountains in South Africa this causes patches of forest, usually on the sides facing these winds.

For another example, on the Banks Peninsula in New Zealand, and in the Southern Alps there, the trees and shrubs are invariably found on the southern slopes of the spurs, which face the rain-bearing winds and are also the side protected from the sun. The northern inclines are generally bare.

In the hilly parts of central and southern Europe vineyards are usually situated on the southern slopes because the vines require the greatest possible amount of light and warmth. In European farms and gardens, peaches, nectarines, mulberries, grapes and other sun-loving plants are grown against the southern side of garden walls.

Many plants throughout the world indicate direction because of their need for light or their permanent alignment to avoid the excessive midday light and heat.

For example, there are many species of wild lettuce which are common throughout Europe, Africa and temperate Asia. They have violet or yellow flowers. All of them have vertical leaves and align their edges north and south so that they can get the benefit of the morning and afternoon sun and avoid the full midday heat. The leaves of these species are similar on both sides. Those of most other plants, however, differ on the upper and lower sides, with many more breathing spores or stomata on the lower side, which is protected from the sun.

The yellow-flowered prickly wild lettuce (*Lactuca serriola*) was introduced into the United States in about 1863 and

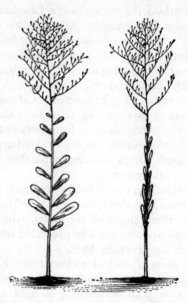

Two views of this plant show its compass-like habit of adjusting the leaves in a north-south direction. The one on the left is seen from the east and the other from the south

is now found very generally throughout the country. It has similar directional characteristics. Some of the narrow-leafed domestic lettuces also align their leaves in a north-south direction when allowed to seed. The Cos and Deertongue varieties are particularly noted for this.

In the United States, too, the pilot weed or resin weed (*Silphium lacinatum*) directs its leaves in a constant north-south direction when it is not growing in the shade. It grows to a height of from three to six feet and is commonly distributed from Ohio to the Rocky Mountains and from Minnesota to Texas. Its directional qualities were well known to the old pioneers to whom it was " the compass plant of the prairies." Longfellow wrote of it in *Evangeline*:

" Look at this vigorous plant that lifts its head from the meadow,
See how its leaves are turned to the north, as true as the magnet;
This is the compass flower, that the finger of God has planted
Here in the houseless wild, to direct the traveller's journey
Over the sea-like, pathless, limitless waste of the desert."

This weed has been introduced into Europe and is often found there as a cultivated plant.

A closely related weed often called Prairie burr-dock (*Silphium terebinthinaceum*), shows the same peculiarity. Only the younger plants of this species, however, manifest this north-south orientation. This weed is widely distributed throughout the southern United States and is often found growing with the Prickly Pear (*Opuntia*) in the South-Western deserts.

In South Africa, a plant which gives direction to the lost traveller by its curious, uncanny growth is the so-called " North Pole " (" Noord Pool ") or " half mens " (*Pachypodium nama-quanum*). It is an amazing sight to see hundreds of these plants with their heads all turned towards the north. A traveller should have no trouble in finding his way in such a locality. The name " half mens," meaning " half a person " in Afrikaans, is given to these plants because from a distance they resemble silhouettes of slender people buried up to their hips in the ground. The crown of this plant, particularly of the taller specimens, always points to the north, and the rosette of leaves on the crown forms an angle of 30 degrees with the horizontal. The " North Pole " plant is found in the mountains on both sides of the lower Orange River in Namaqualand. Plants of these species, which are eighteen inches high, may be as much as twenty-five years old. Their curiously shaped stems are leafless for ten or eleven months of the year, and sometimes in periods of drought they may have no leaves for several years, and look like petrified sentinels on the rocky slopes. When the rains begin, a rosette of greyish-green, felt-like leaves covers the head of each plant. The flowers, which appear in July or August, are large and showy, pale yellow in the lower part of the tube and deep maroon at the mouth.

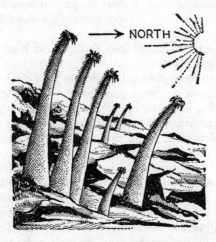

The tops are all leaned permanently to the north to obtain the
full advantage of the midday sun

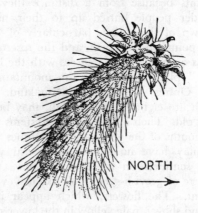

The North Pole plant of South Africa, *Pachypodium namaquanam*
(*after Marloth*)

This plant is not to be confused with a different South African species, *Euphorbia fasciculata*, which shares the name " Noord Pool " and is reputed to bend the apex of its stem towards the north.

In North and Central America the giant barrel cactus, *Ferocactus*, is similarly influenced by the direction of the midday sun and has a permanent lean to the south. In desert areas this plant is a most valuable guide, besides providing a source of water.

In northern temperate climates there is a marked tendency for the flowers of plants to face south or east. This can be important not only to anyone trying to orient himself, but also to the person planning his garden for the most effective display.

In middle northern latitudes such plants include the viola, pansy, daffodil, some lilies and the Shasta daisy. This orientation of the flowers is more pronounced when they are not crowded or shaded but are able to get the full influence of the sun.

Many other plants, especially when shaded, turn their flowers towards the greatest source of illumination. Among these are tulips, phlox, sweet William, coral bells and Canterbury bells.

Some flowers are true sun followers from sunrise to sunset, while others are influenced only by the early sun, after a night of darkness, and give up their chase of the sun by midday. The daisy-like leopard's bane (*Doronicum*) which flowers in the spring throughout Europe and North America, is a true sun-follower. From sunrise to sunset the flowers turn towards the sun, but they are about 40 minutes late (roughly 10 degrees).

Contrary to popular opinion, the common garden sunflower (*Helianthus annus*), does not always point to the sun. It appears to do so in fairly high latitudes, where the sun is always at a low angle, and the light is not so intense as in lower latitudes. In the vicinity of New York, however, one close observer found that 95 per cent of the flower heads of this plant always face east.

Study of the ecology of plants shows that there are many factors which determine why particular plants and trees grow in certain places and not in others. Among these factors are the chemical content of the soil, the temperature, the amount of moisture and drainage, the duration of daylight, the amount of light or shade, and exposure to or protection from winds.

A little known and remarkable fact is that the chemical content of some plants indicates the ore content of the soil in which they are growing. This knowledge can be very useful to those searching for minerals. The Finnish scientist Kalervo Rankama terms this " geobotanical prospecting." The usual procedure is to burn the plant and analyse the ashes. Finnish geochemists actually found a rich copper-nickel deposit by examining the ashes of birch leaves.

In the United States, Mrs. Heleń Cannon, a scientist employed by the U.S. Geological Survey, located several important uranium ore deposits by analysing the ashes of deep-rooted trees in desert areas. Previously these deposits had been missed by prospecting with Geiger counters and spot drilling.

Prospecting for zinc ore has been very successfully carried out this way. There is, for instance, the classical zinc pansy, *Viola calaminaria et zinci*, which shows a decided affinity for zinc and accordingly is found on waste ore dumps of zinc mines in many places in Central Europe. This zinc pansy may contain up to several per cent of zinc oxide. Another zinc indicator of the *Thlaspi* genus, commonly called pennycress, which grows in Germany and Sweden on ground rich in this element, is said to have up to sixteen per cent zinc in the ashes.

The lead plant (*Amorpha canescens*), a shrub two to four feet high, with blue flowers, is found in Missouri in ground containing silver and lead.

Although this method of prospecting has received special attention in recent years because of the present increased interest in rare minerals, it has been known in principle for many years. In 1897, in Northern Australia, it was reported that a small plant, about six inches in height, with large flowers (*Polycarpaea spirostylis*), contained a large percentage of copper and was an actual indicator of copper deposits.

In Norway is found the attractive alpine plant *Lychnis alpina*, less than a foot in height, with pink flowers, which grows in soils rich in copper. In the copper ore deposits of the Roros area of Norway, hardly any other plants than these can survive.

There are even plants which indicate gold. Two of these, commonly called " horsetails " or scouring rushes (*Equisetum arvense* and *Equisetum palustre*), may contain up to $4\frac{1}{2}$ ounces of gold per ton of plant material.

Four species of milk vetches (genus *Astragalus*) are considered the best plants for indicating uranium. They are *Astragalus thompsonae*, *Astragalus confertiflorus*, *Astragalus Preussi* var. *arctus* and *Astragalus Pattersoni*.

Two other good indicators of uranium are the prince's plume (*Stanleya pinnata*) and woody aster (*Aster venustus*).

CHAPTER XII

ANTHILL SIGNPOSTS

ALL INSECTS, being cold-blooded, are sensitive to changes in temperature; and few insects are more so than those highly specialised social creatures, the ants and the (quite unrelated) termites or white ants. Both of these orders of insects build hills to house their communities; and many of these hills are to a greater or less extent oriented to the sun. The ants of cold regions, or regions which are cold in winter, build their nests to get the greatest warmth. Other tropical ants build their nests in the coolest places. Sometimes this results in buildings which have a shape and alignment consistently oriented in a compass direction. What they build, in fact, are signposts for the natural navigator.

In the parts of the Northern Hemisphere which have cold winters, in both the new and old worlds, several kinds of ants build their mounds on hill slopes facing south-east, the direction in which the winter sun rises. So cold are the nights that the ants are almost paralysed by the low temperature: they need the earliest rays of the morning sun to get the longest possible working day. That is why they build their mounds aligned in a south-easterly direction and show a general preference for living on southern or eastern slopes (depending on which kind of slope gets the most heat). When they build their hills close to trees or tree stumps the hills are generally found on the warmer side, which is (in the Northern Hemisphere) the south or south-east side.

Perhaps the most striking example of a signpost ant is the yellow ant of Central Europe. *Lasius flavus* is particularly common in the pasture lands of the Swiss Alps and in the Jura Mountains and it is on their south-eastern slopes that the ants of this species generally build their nests. When their mounds are built in open ground, they are oriented most accurately to the south-east, so much so that the country people of the area often use them to pick up bearings when they are lost in a fog or away from home. The Swiss even have a local name for these directional anthills— " teumons."

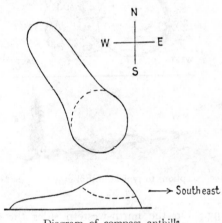

Diagram of compass anthills

These compass anthills are steep on their south-eastern edge to get the greatest amount of warmth; and it is in this part that the ants live, and here that the ants continue to build as they add new earth to their anthill. The result is that the hill slopes gradually to its north-western end; the north-western part, indeed, is often quite abandoned, and represents the home of previous generations.

Established yellow ant mounds usually develop distinct characteristics other than their compass alignment. On their south-eastern side the ground is often loose and sandy with scattered vegetation, with thyme and a fine grey-green grass

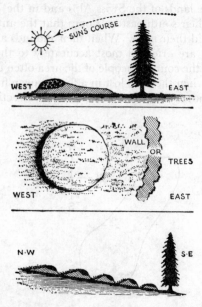

Three exceptions to typical anthill growth (*after Linder*)

predominating. On the north-western sides the soil becomes compacted into a consistent humus—which tends to become covered with low-growing but dense vegetation of bulb type plants, which eventually carpet this part of the mound completely. A big hill of the yellow ant is six to seven feet long, two and a half feet wide and about fifteen inches high. It is in open ground that it is of its most typical oval shape: when the mounds are surrounded by, or built against, a rock wall, or encircled with trees, they are often round; for in such circumstances the ants get their greatest warmth from sun rays striking from above, and there is no longer much advantage in extending the mound towards the direction of the rising sun. Nevertheless, under these conditions the mounds can still be used for direction finding; for the ants still tend to inhabit the south-eastern side of the nests.

Exceptionally though, the ants may inhabit the north-west end of their nests—when the mound is close up to a tree or rock which shields it completely from the south-east.

Another European ant, the black ant, *Lasius niger*, builds nests of pine needles. These nests do not have the oval shape of those of the yellow ants, but their inhabitants consistently tend to live on the eastern side of the hills, which show the greatest activity to the watchful traveller.

In the western part of the United States we can find two further examples of the consistent orientation of anthills. The western harvester ant, *Pogonomyrmex occidentalis*, which is also known as the mound-building prairie ant, builds the only entrance to its mound at the bottom of its south-eastern side. The nests of the silver ant, *Formica argentata*, are similarly oriented in the fields of the lower mountain areas of the State of Colorado.

In desert areas where ants seek cool as opposed to warm conditions, certain ants, like *Messor arenarius* of the Sahara, build the walls of their hills in a crater-like form, with the high side facing the local strong winds—and give safe signposts to the natural navigator—at least if he already knows the direction of the prevailing wind as (we hope this book will have persuaded him by now) he should.

Termites or White Ants

Termites are social insects which belong to an order of insects quite different from the ants. The order has a more exclusively tropical distribution than that of the ants, so it is not surprising that most of the " compass " termites construct and orient their nests to avoid the excessive heat of the midday sun.

Some of the most interesting termite mounds can be found over the vast hot desert areas of northern Australia. They all belong to the well-known termite *Lamitermes meridionalis*. They are most conspicuous structures which have been christened " magnetic anthills." Some of them reach a height of twelve feet; few established hills are less than three feet high. All of them are oriented almost exactly true north and south. On their eastern

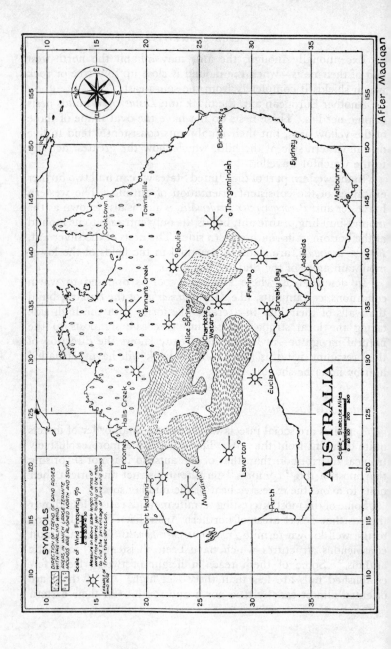

After Madigan

SYMBOLS

DIRECTION OF TREND OF SAND RIDGES

AREAS IN WHICH LARGE TERMITE MOUNDS ARE ALIGNED NORTH AND SOUTH

Scale of Wind Frequency %

Measure on above scale length of arms of wind rose nearest your locality on the map to find percentage of time wind blows from that direction.

AUSTRALIA

Scale - Statute Miles
0 50 100 200 300

Cooktown
Townsville
Tennant Creek
Boulia
Thargomindah
Brisbane
Sydney
Melbourne
Adelaide
Streaky Bay
Farina
Charlotte Waters
Alice Springs
Euclea
Halls Creek
Broome
Port Hedland
Mundiwindi
Laverton
Perth

and western sides they are steeply flattened and their average length is about four or five times their height. They rise to a sharp and serrated top ridge.

Magnetic anthills (if we may forget that termites are not ants and use the popular expression) owe their straight north-south shape to a technical necessity. These hills are built of mud and the termites can only build them under very wet conditions: yet in order to become secure they must dry most rapidly. If they are built north-south the morning sun can dry the eastern side, the afternoon sun the western side, and no part is left in shadow for very long during the day.

A further advantage in the directional shape of this kind of mound is that the termites can move quite quickly from one side of the hill to the other. This they need to do in order to obtain the most comfortable temperature during the day; for they can withstand neither the heat of midday nor the direct heat of the morning or the afternoon sun. In the winter they move in the opposite way, to the east galleries for the morning warmth, to the west side in the afternoon. (See drawing facing page 126.)

These magnetic anthills are one of the most important travellers' guides through the thousands of square miles of northern Australia in which they are found. They have certainly made it difficult for anybody to lose his way in this area. During the last war I was Director of Air Transport for the Allied Air Forces in Australia and New Guinea, and several times I flew over Queensland and over Australia's northern territories. I often saw the military ranks of the magnetic anthills. From the air their number is most spectacular and the consistency of their orientation almost uncanny. Close to the airport townships of Darwin and Katherine I inspected these termite hills on the ground. In this flat monotonous country with no mountains on

Directional characteristics in Australia. This map shows that over a vast area of the Australian continent it is a simple matter to find one's direction from the natural features such as the direction of the sand dunes with the prevailing winds and the area in the north covered with the striking north-south termite mounds.

the horizon, they made living signposts that no traveller could forget and few could fail to use.

Just as in northern Australia, farmers and travellers on the edge of the Kalahari desert in South-West Africa have a termite signpost to guide them. The common termite here, as Dr. S. H. Skaife of Cape Province informs me, builds its mound some ten to fifteen feet high and orients it with the tip bent towards the north.

Plate V. North-South termite mounds of Northern Australia.

CHAPTER XIII

FINDING YOUR WAY IN THE DESERT

THOSE WHO must find their way in deserts know that in all the deserts of the world there are indigenous nomadic people to whom the desert is a familiar home, and for whom the solution of the many difficult problems of travel is second nature. The desert explorer must, through his powers of observation, attain the proficiency of the true desert people. For them navigation is a necessity for survival. From an early age they know it is a matter of life and death.

Naturally enough, the desert nomads have a very well-developed visual memory for topography. In their minds every journey's landmark is engraved and is recalled in succession as they go their way. Their conversation together is of many things, but most particularly of landmarks and travel conditions. Every meeting of nomads in the desert produces talk of the state of going, the condition of water-holes, the amount of feed available at pastures. They are particularly observant of traces of each other's caravans, and can tell with incredible accuracy just how many camels and horses have passed one way and how long ago they passed. In the vast sand-free pebbled surface of most areas of the Sahara even the caravan tracks and the camel tracks (called medjbed) become obliterated. But generations of nomads have marked the way from water-hole to water-hole with rock cairns—with pyramids of stone called amer, or redjem, usually perched on some skyline point so that they can be seen from afar.

I confine this chapter to those methods of navigation which

are peculiar to desert areas or any places in the world containing sand. The desert traveller must remember that these are the special techniques to be used in conjunction with many of the other general techniques described in this book, which of course apply just as much to desert areas as they do to other regions.

Even if we ignore the cold deserts of the Arctic and Antarctic, we find that about a sixth of the land area of the world is desert. No great continent is without a desert or semi-desert arid area. In North Africa lies the Sahara, the largest and best-known desert in the world—three million square miles of level plains, jagged mountains, rock plateaus and sand dunes. Only ten per cent of it is sand; by far the greater part is gravel from which the sand has long ago been blown, to pile up in the depressions where most of the dunes are found. A track in the Sahara's desert gravel lasts for many years. South Africa's Kalahari is another great desert; and from the deserts of Arabia arid zones stretch almost continuously into Syria and through Persia into India's Baluchistan and up into Russia's Turkestan. In central and eastern Asia lie the Ordos desert and the great Gobi, a saucer-like plateau north of China which includes large parts of Inner and Outer Mongolia. Ringed by mountains, its basin stretches as an almost endless, almost level, plain with scattered rocks and buttes. South America has its great desert; Australia its vast central desert; and North America its great basin: the desert area of the south-western United States has flat plains with scanty cactus vegetation and abruptly rising mountain islands which are reminders of parts of the Gobi and the Sahara.

The two special keys to desert navigation are given by the behaviour of sand and the behaviour of animals.

In the desert regions of the earth man has established only the tiniest of communities. Except in the oases, the earth has never been subjected to cultivation; and across the desert's broad sweep the winds have left their marks for man to read. Each desert has its prevailing wind, just as has each ocean; and these winds can make permanent impressions on the landscape which dominate the scenery when it is calm or when the winds are temporarily varying. A temporary wind blowing across a desert in a direction other than that of the dominant wind may leave its marks, but usually these are but ripple marks, and insignificant in comparison with the effects of the dominant wind.

The dominant winds of the desert are really very constant in direction; and since the greatest part of most deserts is plateau land, these winds are not interfered with by local topography as they are in mountainous land. The first thing the desert traveller has to learn is the direction of the prevailing wind and the principal ways in which it arranges the shifting sand.

Desert sand mostly consists of hard mineral grains small enough to be moved by the wind but not small enough to be carried up into the air for long periods and distances and dispersed as dust. Sand is blown, but not at random, for by its very nature it piles up into definite features. Sand dunes have a history and an anatomy: they are not just disorderly masses of sand. They can be classified into three main types, which we shall examine presently.

Sand, when driven by wind, settles in sheltered places, gradually filling in depressions and protected spots. When a rock or some other obstruction rises in the desert, the blown sand accumulates on the leeward side of it, where it ultimately consolidates into a streamlined shape. The crest and the long axis of this sand drift will lie in the direction of the prevailing wind. On the windward side of an obstacle like a rock or shrub, a steep sandbank will heap up. On the sheltered side the bank will slope away more gently as a streamlined dune, or perhaps I should say a near-dune.

The three main kinds of dunes in the desert are the longitudinal dune, the seif dune and the barchan. Of these the commonest is the longitudinal dune. Typically it is a continuous bank of sand of even height which lies parallel with the dominant wind. In the sandy parts of hot deserts longitudinal dunes are very extensive. In the Atlas regions of the Sahara the Great Western and the Great Eastern Erg are composed of a vast system of these longitudinal sandhills running north-west to south-east or north-north-west to south-south-east. In the central Sahara the alignment of the dune system turns southward, and in the Sudanese (eastern) Sahara, towards the south-west and even towards west-south-west. In the Libyan desert—the north-eastern part of the Sahara—the dune axis is north-north-west. Here, as everywhere, it is in the general direction of the prevailing wind.

Such is also the case in Inner Mongolia, where the dunes in the Ordos desert are oriented north-west to south-east parallel with the wind. Some of the dunes are bare, for this desert has an exceptional quantity of loose sand, but others have been consolidated with vegetation and appear as small hills covered with tufts of grass or low brush.

In Australia the inland desert dunes run generally north-west, with a more westerly trend at both the north and south margins of the western desert, and once more this reflects the direction of the winds which blow almost permanently in that region. The dunes are low (on the average about forty feet high, with a maximum of about a hundred feet), straight and naturally parallel, with a rather regular distance of a quarter of a mile between ridges that may be truly hundreds of miles long.

Unlike the longitudinal dune, whose one side is almost a mirror image of the other, the individual seif dune has a form very like that of a sand drift behind a rock. Its length (or axis) lies in the direction of the prevailing wind, but its long crest, unlike that of the longitudinal dune, is sharply ridged, much more steeply on one side than on the other. Indeed, one end often appears as a rounded convex slope while the other falls as a concave slope or even a precipice, so abruptly that it may give the appearance of a collapsed front. This front is at right angles to the dominant wind. And it may change temporarily when a strong wind veers out of its prevailing direction. Seif dunes are seldom found alone; but much more often as a range forming a continuous ridge connecting a succession of summits from sixty to six hundred feet apart. Usually several seif dune lines run parallel with each other at intervals varying (depending on the area, but rather uniform within the area) from anything from four hundred yards to five miles.

A barchan is a crescent dune shaped like a horseshoe. The slopes down to the hollow are steeper than the outside slopes and the hollow faces downwind. In the sandy desert of Peru the barchan dune is known there as medaños; and there it is the sand dune's most typical form. Where other deserts might have longitudinal dunes, this desert has a ragged interrupted line of these rather small crescentic mounds. In the horseshoe's hollow the steep

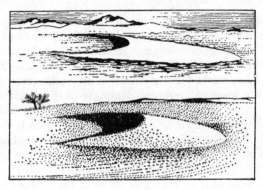

Barchan or crescent dunes in snow (*above*)
and sand (*below*)

slopes are sheltered from the wind; and there the sand lies at the steepest angle of rest, about thirty-three degrees from the horizontal. At any greater angle the sand would slide, for gravity would overcome surface friction. The end of the barchan dune which faces the wind slopes least, only about five or six degrees from the horizontal. The angle of the sides is usually from ten to thirteen degrees.

This desert dune topography is not entirely confined to the world's present deserts, for many great areas in temperate zones date from an arid past, though subsequently conquered by vegetation and cultivation. What we could almost call the " fossil shapes " of their desert dune topography remain, as does even the alignment of the dunes with the prevailing wind—showing, incidentally, that the type of country has changed more than the wind. Old dune formations in Germany, Poland, Hungary and on the moors of Gascony lie east-west, for instance; and the dunes of Sweden are aligned with a föhn wind which comes down the Scandinavian Alps, a dominant westerly, deflected south.

Animals as Desert Guides

The question of survival in deserts might, by a purist, be thought not strictly relevant to a discussion of desert navigation. However, a common-sense view recognises that the two subjects are mixed closely together. The armed forces of many countries, of course, have made detailed studies of desert survival; and there is already a mass of literature dealing with the solution of the problems of exposure and living off the land. One of the most important survival drills which involves navigation is that which enables the traveller to find water. Water-holes may not necessarily be on the intended route of the desert traveller; but a knowledge of their direction can always help him to find his position. Among the best indicators of desert water are animals. Anybody who can spare enough of a desert day to sit quietly and out of sight near a water-hole, will learn a great deal about the behaviour of water-seeking birds and other animals.

There are two hundred and eighty-nine species of pigeons and doves in the world; and there is no desert (apart from the ice deserts of the north and south) which does not have one or more species native to it. Birds of this order are easily recognisable by their shape and style; and nearly every species has a habit of perching in trees or shrubs near desert water-holes, especially towards the evening. Usually the desert pigeons drink once or twice a day. Occasionally they drink at daybreak: always do they drink in the early evening: never do they drink during the heat of the day. It is, then, in the evening that it is important to watch the direction of their flight. An experienced watcher of desert pigeons can even tell whether his birds are on their way to or on their way from their evening drink, for their flight from water is characteristically heavy, and is accompanied by a louder flapping of their wings.

A remarkable story of desert pigeons is told by H. A. Lindsay in his " Bushman's Handbook."

In the desert of the Australian Northern Territory a whole party of surveyors were " bushed " without water. David Lindsay took the strongest camel and went off to look for water. He failed to find it. But on his way back to camp that evening he saw a solitary rock-pigeon flutter across a gorge ahead of him. He followed its flight line up a hill; and, in a spot where nobody would normally think of finding water, came across a rock-hole containing thousands of gallons.

If it had not been for one little bird the entire party might have perished.

Each of the world's deserts has its own particular, sometimes even peculiar, birds—besides pigeons and doves. The Australian desert has its speckled finches, locally known as diamond sparrows, which congregate in thick flocks never far from a water-hole. Among the best indicators of water in the Gobi deserts are wagtails, and larks and other small sand-coloured birds. The Australian desert has cockatoos and other deserts have parrots. Nearly all deserts have quails. When geese migrate through desert country (as they often do) their presence may be considered as an indication of water—particularly when they are flying low, for then they follow rivers or chains of ponds or isolated lakes.

King Solomon is said to have discovered the retreat of Balkis, Queen of Sheba, among the mountains between the Hejaz and the Yemen, by means of a plover which he dispatched in search of water during his progress through Arabia.

Birds are not the only indicators of water, by any means. Gazelles and other desert antelopes herd towards the water-holes, particularly in the evening. Bees and hornets go on watering flights and are excellent guides to water. The tracks of mammals and humans on the desert sand do not of course by themselves invariably lead to water; but when different animal tracks converge they will probably do so.

Not all animals, of course, invariably show the presence or direction of water at evening drinking time. A number of species can go without water for several days. If you see an emu or the large red kangaroo or the grey kangaroo in the Australian desert, for instance, you—and the animals—may easily be from twenty to fifty miles from a drinking place.

CHAPTER XIV

FINDING YOUR WAY IN THE
POLAR REGIONS

THE WORLD'S areas of permanent, or near-permanent, snow and ice are by no means confined to the polar regions. The suggestions in this chapter apply, especially in winter, also to Alaska and Greenland, to the whole northern part of Canada and the Soviet Union, to northern Scandinavia and Finland.

The North Pole area itself is only a large floating mass of ice without any actual land, while the South Pole region is really a very large continent. In the last years the Antarctic has attracted a great deal of attention not only on account of the disputes about sovereignties of that country but also because of the possibilities of the presence of rare minerals. This large unknown land-mass is in my opinion the adventurous area of the next fifty years. It is also the last of the earth's unknown, except for the oceans.

Already I have discussed many methods of pathfinding which apply to snow-covered lands. Among them is the study of reflections in the sky (page 79), the construction of back tracking landmarks (page 62), the direction of the prevailing wind (page 92), the observation of wind-polished rocks, of the movements of high clouds, the directions of sun and shadows, and steering by sighting on companions, whether they be fellow-humans or dogs.

Special to the problems of pathfinding in snow regions is the study of wind-made snow forms. All the accounts of the great polar explorers—Scott, Amundsen, Nansen, Shackleton, Mawson and Byrd—show that they paid very great attention to snow forms in finding their way on their famous journeys. Many of us read and re-read their epic stories full of suspense and self-sacrifice. Just now polar travel is reviving. Explorers are using techniques out of reach of those great pioneers, though no doubt they dreamed of them. I expect the explorers of the present generation will find just as much thrill and drama under extreme conditions as the men of a generation past, and will be poised (as they were) just as excitingly between success and failure.

I am certain they will still be watching and using the sastrugi, the snow mounds, the wind ripples on the snow and the distribution of sea ice to help them in their navigation in the same way as their predecessors did.

The polar regions have much in common with the hot sand deserts. They are themselves cold deserts, for one thing; and for another very cold snow behaves physically in many ways which are similar to the behaviour of sand. Snow crystals are smaller than most of the usual sand particles. But the wind can arrange them in much the same way. In the snow deserts, then, the wind forms snow dunes or snow drifts, just as in the hot deserts it forms sand dunes and sand drifts. What is more, these snow dunes have very much the same shape and properties as sand dunes, though generally speaking they are smaller and less stable. Like the sand dunes, snow dunes reflect the direction of the dominant or prevailing wind, and thus are a very considerable aid to the navigator who is travelling on an Antarctic or an Arctic day when the sun is clouded over, or in the long Antarctic or Arctic night when he cannot see the stars.

One of the commonest snow dunes is the counterpart of the longitudinal sand dune. Over extensive snow-covered areas the prevailing wind drives the drifting snow and packs it hard into ridges, from a few inches to three or four feet in height, which run parallel with the wind's direction. These are known as " sastrugi ": the word is derived from the Russian word " Zastrugi " meaning snow waves. Smaller than the longitudinal sand dunes, sastrugi are almost always placed much closer together; but they are built in the same way.

So many polar explorers have found sastrugi valuable in navigating when other means of orientation were obscured by weather, that accounts of sastrugi have become almost commonplace in the logs of their expeditions. I can quote, for instance (as I often do in this book), from the famous book, *The Home of the Blizzard*, by the eminent Australian Antarctic explorer, Sir Douglas Mawson.

" Close to the Magnetic Pole as we were, the compass was of little use, and to steer a straight course was a difficult task. The only check upon the correctness of the bearing was the direction in which trended the old hard winter sastrugi, channelled out along a line running almost north and south. The newly fallen snow obliterated these, and frequent halts had to be called in order to investigate the buried surface."

Admiral Richard E. Byrd also added his tribute to the directional value of sastrugi in his book *Little America*. This tells of his explorations in and around a famous United States base on the Antarctic Continent, re-colonised (as I write) for the International Geophysical Year.

This is what Admiral Byrd refers to:

" Rough sastrugi which we had to cross diagonally and which made the compass bound about badly, and steering, therefore, difficult. As is always the case (in this region) these sastrugi trend in an ESE to WNW direction. . . . It has been a stimulating afternoon after the almost unchanging travel for the past three weeks over the sastrugi surface of the Barrier."

In just the same way Sir Ernest Shackleton recorded the frequent use of sastrugi in his great book *The Heart of the Antarctic*. In his famous polar dash he was often denied a sun sight for days at a time; but all the time, when low clouds obscured the sun and even prominent surrounding landmarks, he was able to steer by aiming his sledges at a constant angle to the prevailing direction of the sastrugi.

Just as sastrugi are the counterparts of the longitudinal dunes of the sand desert, so does snow occasionally form, or rather drift, into mounds which have a crescentic shape similar to the barchans of the sand deserts. Snow barchans are not only smaller than sand barchans, but their sides are much less steep. In just the same way as those of sand barchans, the hollow part of a snow barchan or snow mound points downwind.

Winds make ripple marks upon the snow in much the same way as they do upon sand. These ripples are very small and never more than a few inches high. They are not valuable as an indication of the prevailing winds, because they can be formed very quickly by any substantial local wind. These temporary snow ripples are set at right angles to the wind, just as are water waves; they are quite different from and much less useful than the sastrugi and the snow barchans, which take the direction of the dominant wind and are much more permanent.

I make no apology for quoting Sir Douglas Mawson once more, as his observations and accounts are always full of the most clever combination of natural navigational methods. Throughout his book we can read of many occasions upon which he used one indication to check another. Here is an example:

" At 11 a.m. on Sunday, November 24, we moved off to the south-east in a wind of fifty miles an hour. The light was bad, and steering had to be done by sastrugi and wind. However, momentary glimpses of the sun served to check the course. The lunch camp was five miles from the depôt, and a good mound with a top of black bunting was left there. At almost every halt, thus far on our journey, the snow cut for pitching the tent had been gathered up into a mound which, in addition to forming a landmark, could often be used as a back-mark for checking the course. Our depot thus had a mound four miles on the southern and five miles on the northern side of it. It was not marked as well as I had hoped, but under the circumstances we could not do better. Moreover, at intervals during the day, some very distinctive snow ramps had appeared in the valley, some five miles to the north-east, and their position was fixed relative to the course."

Sea Ice in Navigation

On the seas of the polar regions true pack-ice, or pancake-ice is continually formed when the temperature of the surface water is somewhat below zero. Such open sea ice rarely if ever appears in any but rounded flat pieces made up of small fragments and occasional large floes.

Icebergs are formed in quite a different method: they are pieces which have broken off glaciers which flow into the sea. Rough and irregular in appearance, they show varying wave erosion marks at different angles—different because as their ice melts or breaks off, their centre of gravity periodically shifts and the whole berg assumes a new position. An iceberg which shows no wave erosion lines cannot have drifted far; but neither icebergs nor large true floes are of much use in navigation, since their position is due to current drift and is relatively unaffected by opposing winds. Considerable local knowledge of dominant currents and dominant winds is necessary before such ice formations can be used to establish position. But from one particular kind of ice formation—" bay ice," more useful conclusions can often be drawn.

Low smooth flat pieces of ice, which look as though they might be part of a jig-saw puzzle, will (if they are fairly close together) not be far from the frozen cove from which the pieces have been broken off by tidal and other effects. Bay ice with fresh edges is seldom far from home: bay ice which is largely dispersed and whose pieces are rounded or edged with a raised rim of crushed fragments, have probably been carried for a long distance by wind or current. Fresh bay ice is the tell-tale of the nearness of a bay; old bay ice, of the general direction of a prevailing wind or current.

While not strictly navigational, one note on sea ice is worth the attention of the polar navigator. Even though true ice floes are formed by the freezing of sea water and contain the sea percentage of salt at the moment of formation, this salt leaches out quite quickly; so that the traveller seeking fresh water has to do no more than cut ice from the upper part of the older, larger floes. When he melts the ice he will find the water quite fresh.

CHAPTER XV

DIRECTIONS FROM HILLS
AND RIVERS

THE TRAVELLER in mountain and valley country has only to study the map to realise that most mountain ranges are arranged in an orderly way and that the rivers which rise in them and flow from them show orderly trends. Not only are the mountain chains themselves prominent landmarks, but the streams which flow down them usually have a directional trend. Only in flat plains do streams and rivers meander to a very great extent; and it is a traveller's drill (as old as travel) that the lost wayfarer has only to follow a river to pick up his bearings or reach some form of civilisation.

Take, for example, the Coastal Range in the North of New South Wales in Australia, which continues almost throughout the length of Queensland. This chain of hills creates a vast watershed on each side of the range. The rain on the coastal side forms into rivers running eastwards to the sea, while on the western slopes the rivers run inland in a westerly direction. As this Coastal Range is followed farther into northern Queensland, the rivers on the west side empty into the Gulf of Carpentaria, while those on the eastern slopes flow into the Coral Sea.

All over the world, mountain ridges and valleys tend to be grouped in more or less parallel series. For instance, from New Hampshire into Maine and the Maritime Provinces of Canada, is found a consistent group of low ridges, locally called " horse-backs." They run in a north-easterly south-easterly direction, nearly parallel with the Appalachian Chain.

These horsebacks occur with reasonable regularity, like ripples on a water-surface. Few of them rise for more than fifty feet above the surrounding country and most of them average between fifteen and thirty feet. On their southerly side the slopes are gradual, on their northerly side steeper.

Such trends in land forms are common features of the surface of the earth and can easily be detected on a small-scale contour map. Every traveller is advised to consult such a map to get a general idea of the trends in the surface anatomy of his region, for this affects not only mountains and rivers, but lakes and ponds. In the horseback area of eastern North America, for instance, many lakes and ponds are embraced by the horsebacks, where natural drainage has somehow become plugged with accumulations of silt. These ponds have a bank several feet above the water, behind which the ground slopes away into a swampy area—swampy probably from seepage through the banks; and the dry land bank bordering many of these ponds is hardly wider than the averaged-sized roadway and may often extend several miles. When it does so it is in a consistent direction—in this case north-easterly.

The river follower should make a point of observing all the other features I have described from which he may naturally navigate, for the ancient drill of pursuing a river may occasionally lead to a serious mistake. There is a famous story from Iceland of a farmer in the north of the island, who travelled up one of the rivers flowing north from the central desert, to round up his sheep. Late in the year great mists often descend upon the barrens of central Iceland; this farmer, becoming lost, actually crossed the water-parting without knowing that he had done so. Obeying the ordinary rules of river following, he made for the nearest stream and pursued it on its way to the sea. Many days later, nearly dead from exposure and exhaustion, he staggered to the door of a farm in the *south* of Iceland. He had followed the wrong river, and only his physical condition and tenacity had brought him to the end of the journey over a hundred miles longer than the path to his own home.

The traveller, then, had best be pretty sure that his river drill will work, when he embarks upon it without auxiliary navigational aids. But in nine cases out of ten rivers will lead, if not home, at least to somebody else's home. It is often extremely difficult to follow a river by walking along its precise bank. Tributaries are frequently most difficult to cross at their mouths. It may be easier for the lost wanderer to follow ridges which are periodically in sight of the river, provided the conditions are not too overcast. In flattish and desert country, where there is little rainfall, or only seasonal rainfall, river beds often dry up; and if the gradient is a gentle one it is often quite difficult to tell which way the river flows when it carries water. But nearly always the river's last flow will have carried shrub-debris or at least a certain amount of floating vegetation. The position in which this is held on the dried bed will indicate very clearly which way the river runs.

To tell direction from rivers is relatively easy over vast areas of the Soviet Union. In the greater part of that country the rivers flow northwards through the great plains to the sea. People without even seeing a river always call the eastern bank the high bank, and the western one the low bank.

The erosion of the eastern banks, causing high bluffs, is undoubtedly due to the piling up of waters by the continuous westerly winds. Another possible contributing factor is the deflecting force (known as Coriolis) caused by the rotation of the earth.

In my opinion, it is quite possible that the reason for the extensive fertile plains in the Soviet Union and Canada is that the northward-flowing rivers have, over hundreds and thousands of years, gradually but continually moved to the east due to the erosion caused by the heaping up of waters by the westerly winds and in small measure by deflection of the moving waters in an easterly direction because of the rotation of the earth.

In mountain country it is sometimes easier to pursue ridges than to pursue rivers. If the country is very steep, this can be dangerous, for ridges may end in sudden precipices, whereas the worst interruption to the path of a river is a waterfall or rapids, whose banks can usually be easily negotiated. Ridge-following pays good dividends in gently rolling country, particularly in densely wooded country. The animals which live in forested hills often pick their routes to feeding grounds along these ridges, and tread natural pathways which can be followed with advantage, especially by the traveller who has studied the general pattern of the local topography beforehand.

CHAPTER XVI

ESTIMATION OF DISTANCE

IT IS very important to be able to judge distances when you are making an overland trip, particularly when the journey involves many detours. Not only should you keep an accurate account, mental or otherwise, of the direction of each detour, but you should also try to remember the distance travelled on each route. Distances can be counted in number of paces, which, for the individual, can be translated into miles depending on the type of country and the average length of the pace. Alternatively, distance can be calculated from the time in relation to the speed of walking in miles per hour.

For the average person walking over fairly flat country, a thirty-inch pace will result in a speed of three miles an hour. If greater accuracy is desired, you can test yourself to find your average length of pace in normal walking.

On occasions when it is necessary to record accurately the distance covered on a particular route, paces may be counted. Instead of counting each pace, try counting only the right-foot paces, and multiply by two when you reach a hundred. To make recording easier, start out with some small pebbles or seeds in one of your pockets, and transfer one pebble from one pocket to the other at each hundred paces. For a thirty-inch pace, one thousand right-foot steps will equal one mile, requiring ten pebbles or seeds to the mile.

Distances very often are found to have been under-estimated when judged before starting out and over-estimated when judged while your trip is in progress and you have become fatigued.

When judging distance ahead of you by eye, certain conditions will cause over-estimation of distances, while others will result in an under-estimation.

Objects look much nearer than they actually are when:

Looking up or down hill.

There is a bright light on the object.

Looking across water, snow or flat sand.

The air is clear.

Objects look much farther away than they actually are when:

The light is poor.

The colour of the object blends with the background.

The object is at the end of a long avenue.

You are looking over undulating ground.

In judging distances, the following table will be found very useful:

At 50 yards	The mouth and eyes of a person can be clearly distinguished.
At 100 yards	The eyes appear as dots.
At 200 yards	The general details of clothing can be distinguished.
At 300 yards	Faces can be seen.
At 500 yards	Colours of clothing can be distinguished.
At 800 yards	A man looks like a post.
At 1 mile (1760 yards)	The trunks of large trees can be seen.
At 2½ miles	Chimneys and windows can be distinguished.
At 6 miles	Windmills, large houses and towers can be recognised.
At 9 miles	An average church steeple can be seen.

A simple means of judging distances which can be used either on land or at sea is the finger method. It is based on the principle that the distance between the eyes is about one-tenth of the distance from the eye to the end of the extended finger. When the width of a distant object is known and you wish to determine how far away it is, proceed as follows:

With the right arm extended in front of you, hold the fore-finger upright and align it with one eye on the end of the distant

object. Without moving the finger, observe with the other eye
and note how many feet along the length of the object it appears
to have moved. The range of the object will be ten times this
distance. When the height of a distant object such as a mountain,
a building or a vessel is known, hold the head sideways and follow
the same procedure.

If you wish to get greater accuracy, measure the distance
between the centre of the eye-pieces of your binoculars when
adjusted to your eyes, and multiply this distance by ten; in this
way the exact distance at which to hold the finger may be
determined readily.

The finger method was used by the British Army during the
First World War and was found to be of very practical value. It
has since been used at sea in place of a range-finder, for keeping
ships in station.

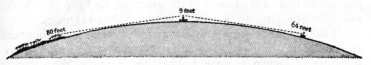

It is useful to know how to judge distance at sea, whether it
be the distance of a ship or of land. Because of the curvature of
the earth, the greater the height of the observer's eye, the greater
his range of vision; that is, the farther away will be his visible
horizon.

For an accurate determination of the distance of the horizon
at sea, take the square root of the height in feet of the observer's
eye, and multiply it by 1.15. The result will be the distance in
miles from the observer to the horizon. For instance, if the height
of the eye is 9 feet above sea-level, by multiplying 3 (the square
root of 9) by 1.15, we find that the horizon is about $3\frac{1}{2}$ miles away.
Hence any low floating object just on the horizon will also be
about $3\frac{1}{2}$ miles away.

When the object whose distance is to be judged is between
you and the horizon, you can estimate the proportionate distance
between yourself and the object and the horizon, and thus get a

close estimate of the object's distance, calling on your familiarity with perspective.

When a ship is partly below the horizon and partly visible above the horizon, if you can form an idea of what type of vessel it is, you can estimate the height above the water-line of the part of the ship just level with the horizon. You then add the square root of its height above the water-line, to the square root of your height above the water-line and multiply by 1.15, which will give you the distance to the ship, even though you cannot see its full outline.

For example, suppose you see the cross-trees on the foremast of what appears to be a large steamship. Although the hull is out of sight, you assume that in a ship of this particular size the cross-trees will be at a height of about 64 feet from the water-line. The square root of the height of the object equals 8. Adding 3, the square root of the height of the observer, we have 11, which, multiplied by 1.15, gives us the answer: about $12\frac{2}{3}$ miles.

If the height of some prominent object, such as a mountain or headland, is known, the same method may be used. Many trees are of known average height; for example, the coconut palms of low islands, the tops of which may be taken with little error as being about eighty feet above the water-line. Thus, if the tops of the palms appear in line with the horizon and the height of the observer's eye is still nine feet, the palms are about $13\frac{3}{4}$ miles from the observer.

If you don't want to bother with multiplying by 1.15, as in the preceding examples, it won't make very much difference for your purposes if you omit this step. Your result will still be out by 13 per cent, at most.

CHAPTER XVII

FINDING YOUR WAY IN TOWNS

As you approach the outskirts of a town there are many indications which announce to you its close proximity. Converging roads, railway lines, telegraph wires and heavy power lines all point the way to a city. As the greater number of people are coming into a town in the morning and are leaving in the afternoon the direction of heavy traffic in or out at these times will show the way to the heart of the city. A number of aircraft climbing or losing altitude is an indication of an airport and, usually, therefore, a town. At night another guide is the red obstruction lights on high buildings in the vicinity of an airport.

Most people will naturally point their television aerials facing a station for better reception. The direction in which the aerials are pointing will be worth noting; most stations abroad, for instance, are located in the centre of a city. This can be useful to aviators. In a town where there is only one television station, it is quite simple to see the general orientation of the aerials. Elsewhere of course where there is more than one station, the value of this indication will depend on your knowledge of where they are situated.

To a newcomer, a strange town presents many of the same problems in direction-finding as those set by pathfinding in dense bush. They are both unknown areas and there is the same need for accurate orientation. Although the consequences of being lost in a city are not likely to be as serious as those of losing your way in the bush, they can sometimes be equally as exasperating especially as it is the habit of most people, when asked, to give confusing directions to a visitor in a town. The average person takes so much for granted because of his familiarity with the place that he will give an absolute jumble of vague directions and follow them up with that most annoying phrase " you can't miss it." Even with the aid of systematically numbered and named houses and streets you can still get lost if you do not quickly orient yourself at the start. The first impression is the most important one.

Begin your visit by learning the general layout of the streets in terms of north, south, east and west. Establish these directions from a known point which may be your hotel or house. Draw a simple map marking in this " home base " and all prominent landmarks. As you travel, keep an imaginary thread connecting you with your home base so that you know exactly at all times the direction of the place from which you started. Mentally record each turn you make; for example, " left home base and walked two streets down, turned to the left for one street then right. . . ." This constant relation of your present position to your starting point will prevent you from being incorrectly oriented. This method was used by primitive peoples who were able to point to the place from which they came at any given time along their route. Combine this method of relating everything to a central point with the more modern one of establishing north, south, east and west and so have the advantage of both.

If there is some high point, a building or a hill which is visible from all parts of the city, you can relate your directions to this as long as it is not too far from your focal point.

There may be circumstances under which you find it difficult to record your turns mentally, in such a case use the street on which your house is situated as a base line and relate all your directions to this. Even if you are not able to go directly to your house you can locate this line and proceed along it to your base.

Everything depends on your early experiences in a new place when associations which become basic are being established. If at the outset you wrongly orient yourself then it is practically impossible to adjust. Most of us have experienced that confused, bewildered and unpleasant feeling of uncertainty which accompanies an illusion of orientation in a strange city. Everything seems reversed and you begin to lose all confidence in your ability to find your way.

In 1929 I accompanied Roscoe Turner on his attempt to break the air record between Los Angeles and New York. It was my first flight to Long Island; and after a long and trying nineteen hours' flying, we landed at Roosevelt Field in very bad weather. It was in the middle of the night. I was overtired, and when I oriented myself on leaving the airfield I established the wrong directions. I kept feeling that I knew my directions perfectly and kept finding that I was absolutely wrong. What is more, on subsequent visits I carried my capacity for illusion with me. Everything seemed reversed. I made mistakes so consistently that I began to lose all confidence in my ability to find my way. For years after that, when I was in the region of Roosevelt Field, I always felt that north should be south and that west should be east; and even though I knew perfectly well that these directions were wrong, I somehow could not rid myself of them and had to translate them correctly in my mind with an act of conscious will each time I visited the area.

I have since found that my experience is not unique. Indeed, it has been shared by most people with whom I have discussed the phenomenon. A first mistake in orientation at the beginning of a visit to a strange town seems to be curiously ineradicable. It can only be prevented if the natural navigator makes sure that he has the right directions when he first establishes his base in a city.

At first glance it may appear that some cities have spread out without any particular pattern, but closer study may reveal some form of alignment. As a newcomer to a city you should endeavour to find out whether this pattern is regular or irregular. In the newer towns which have been planned, and not just evolved from small villages, the tendency is to lay them out symmetrically; and as long as the terrain permits the streets will be at right angles. A true north-south alignment is the easiest pattern to follow. Salt Lake City in the United States is a good example because in this city the main streets run north, south, east and west. The compass point orientation exists even though a river flows through its centre. Once you have established which direction lies north and make it a habit to record your turns, you should travel with confidence in a place like this. Other cities in the United States such as Chicago, Denver and Kansas City are also aligned to the compass points. It is also easy to find your way in Melbourne, Australia, which has been laid out in regular blocks with the streets at right angles to each other.

A river, lake or hill may have an important influence on the way a city is planned. When a river flows through a town, it is probable that the streets conform to the configurations of the shore. A town which is fronted by a lake may be aligned to it. Similarly, when a community is situated between hills the streets will be patterned accordingly.

There are many examples in the United States of this alignment to a physical condition. Cleveland, Ohio, is oriented parallel with Lake Erie and at right angles to the lake shore. If you realise in such a case that the general orientation follows and runs directly parallel with the lake front, it should not be too hard to keep track of your direction. Manhattan, in the city of New York, is aligned running parallel and at right angles with the Hudson River and the East River. Fifth Avenue is practically parallel with these rivers and is nineteen degrees east of north.

The city of Wellington, New Zealand, is built on hills and under these circumstances, the alignment will be irregular because the roads are planned with consideration to the slopes so that they are not too steep for vehicles.

In some cities, streets parallel with each other are distinctively numbered or named. One example is Brisbane in Australia, where the streets running in one direction have women's names while those at right angles have men's. In other cities, the main streets may flow out from a central point such as a square or a circle. In this case memorise the pattern of streets around and from it, and keep your directions related to this point. This method of orientation is particularly necessary in the older cities such as London or Paris which have expanded without a clear plan or pattern.

After you have firmly established in your mind the general

pattern of the streets of a town, consider then the other means of telling direction. The orientation of buildings to sunlight can be very significant. When an architect designs a building, he takes into consideration which area will benefit most from sunlight and faces the house in that direction accordingly. In the temperate and cold climates of the Northern Hemisphere you will find that buildings are generally oriented facing south, which is the direction of the greatest sunlight. In the temperate and cold climates of the Southern Hemisphere the orientation will be opposite, that is facing north.

In cold climates, where possible, the living-rooms face south to get the greatest warmth and light, and kitchens will usually be found on the north side. The long and narrow Friesian farm-houses in Schleswig-Holstein in Germany, face the south to get the greatest warmth from the sun, with the longer sides running east and west. A careful inspection of this district has shown that seventy-seven per cent of the houses are aligned in this way. This orientation has the advantage not only of the greatest warmth from the southern sun but the narrow ends of the houses face the strong cold westerly winds. In other areas in which cold violent winds are prevalent, windows and doors are situated on the side away from the chilling wind. Such an orientation is found in Provence in France.

In the hotter parts of the world the orientation rules of houses may be quite different. Often it is desirable to avoid the sun rather than court it, and to court the wind rather than avoid it. As you descend to the Mediterranean from the hills of the Massif Central of France, you can notice a pretty rapid transition from sun-facing houses to patio-style houses on the coast—houses in which the main living-rooms look on to a central court which can be com-pletely shaded from the hot summer sun. Houses of this style are the norm in nearly the whole of Spain; and were an early invention of the first great western civilisation for the Sumerians built in this way more than five thousand years ago in sunny hot Mesopotamia.

In other parts of the world with hot climates, houses are generally oriented to get the greatest cooling from the prevailing wind. In the islands of the South Pacific, wherever possible, the long axis of the houses is aligned at right angles to the south-east trade wind to get the cooling air through all the rooms.

An additional means of telling north from south is found in Holland by the absence of window shutters on the north side of houses. The thrifty Dutch generally place their shutters only on the south side of their houses because the sun shines only on that side. These shutters, which are hinged back when not in use, are very often gaily decorated and can be a useful sign of direction in this country.

In Christian countries churches have nearly always an east to west orientation. This dates from ancient days, when they were designed with the altar to the rising sun. The tradition has been followed as consistently as possible throughout the evolution of the magnificent church architecture of western Europe. In Spain, Germany, England, France and Italy, and in many parts of Holland and Scandinavia the churches and cathedrals, both medieval and modern, show this east-west alignment. The chancel, which contains the altar and forms the most easterly portion of the church, is nearly always the oldest part of the church and is often lower than its greatest part—the nave. Around the eastern end of the chancel there is often an apse, which is in turn lower than the chancel and forms (usually) a projecting semi-circular part at the church's easternmost end. Between chancel and nave are often found great wings, one north, one south, which give the church or cathedral the shape of a cross, and the towers or spires may be built over this central transept or (more often) over the western end of the nave.

In the populated centres there are still effects of nature which can tell you your direction. These natural signposts, apart from their value to a stranger, also can be informative and interesting to a resident of a town. It will help him practise his observation, increase his awareness and prepare him for the time when he visits a strange city. Both the newcomer to a town and the one who lives there can apply the knowledge gained from this book to interpret some of nature's causes and effects which are peculiar to built-up areas. One of these is the fungus, moss or lichen growth on any building which can be a consistent feature for direction. First of all, find out where the rain-bearing winds come from in your locality, combine this information with a knowledge of the arc of the sun and you will then know the direction which retains the moisture the longest. Once you have established this for a particular town, you will have a perpetual aid for direction finding by noting which sides of buildings have this growth.

The direction of the greatest sunlight will have a bleaching effect on paintwork, particularly on darker colours. By studying which side of structures show this effect provides you with another clear sign of direction. Further to this, interpret the effects of a combination of sun, wind and rain which causes peeling of paint or other deterioration on houses, buildings or fences. This effect also can be seen in the corrosion of ironwork in buildings and bridges. Even though you may be unable to determine which of these forces has the biggest influence you will be able to see a consistency in the direction of the greatest weathering. For example, you may have established that this weathered appearance is on the south-east side of one building; as you travel through the locality you will notice that the same side on most of the buildings is similarly affected. You have, therefore, a constant and automatic directional aid just by observing which side shows this effect.

I have stressed repeatedly throughout this book that to be guided by nature, you must add up all the natural signs. It is the same in the case of finding your way in towns where many of the individual aids and methods to which I have devoted chapters can be used in conjunction with each other. The use of the sun and shadows for telling direction when you are travelling in built-up areas is, as ever, a most reliable guide. The moon and the stars can be used at night in the way I have outlined in these two chapters. The movement of high clouds, the direction of the seasonal and dominant winds for the districts are all aids which can be used also in finding your way in towns.

CHAPTER XVIII

ORIENTING AS A SPORT

NAVIGATION is an art, so it is not in the least surprising that it has been developed into a sport. The sport of orienting[1] is a new one. It originated in Sweden not many years ago and it is now estimated that about 350,000 people (a very high percentage of the Swedish population) now engage in this form of pathfinding. Even more significant is the fact that every year in Sweden about forty thousand boys and girls qualify for orienting proficiency pins. The pastime has certainly become a very popular one.

Essentially, orienting consists of cross-country races on a course that is arranged from point to point. Each point must be reached entirely by map and compass. Many forms of competition have been devised, so that people of all ages and of varying physical condition can take part. In a simple cross-country orienting contest—the most popular form of competition—all the competitors start out with map and compass from one common point at time intervals of about a minute. Upon their maps is marked the compass direction and location of the first control point or " control station." Each participant takes what he estimates to be the shortest possible route to get there. The control point—which may be a hill, a dead tree or some other unmistakable landmark—carries a sign which gives the compass direction and the

[1] I think it is a pity that the Scandinavian enthusiasts have introduced this sport in English-speaking countries under the name " orienteering." I believe that the adoption of this name has hurt their cause. An exact translation of the Swedish word is not " orienteering," but " orienting." This word is already an English word and is widely understood. The coined word does not sound natural.

distance to the next. Competitions are nearly always scored on time; so that each is a race to the finish; but it is a race that tests skill as much as speed.

A less rigorous form of orienting is point orienting, in which the competitors follow on foot a course clearly marked on the terrain, and locate on their maps the exact position of the control points that they come across on their journey. Their log is subsequently judged and awarded appropriate marks. Some orienting competitions are devised in summer by bicycle or by car, in winter on skis or skates. It is even possible to conduct an orienting competition indoors with maps and photographs of the terrain and its landmarks; the contestants have to indicate the compass direction to a number of points on the map. In all these forms of competition skill in the use of map and compass is at a premium.

Another of the less exacting forms of orienting is miniature orienting. This is a game devised to teach children to walk by compass and is an excellent training. In a school yard or park the pupils have to find, by compass direction alone, a succession of control points. Each point is marked by a card which is concealed from the direction in which it is likely to be approached —for instance, by being attached to the back of a tree.

Orienting, pioneered in Sweden, has now become popular in the other Scandinavian countries as well as in Belgium, Holland, Switzerland and France. Lately it has been introduced with some success into the United States, Great Britain, and Australia and New Zealand.

There is no doubt that the spread of orienting through the world owes much to the fact that it can be easily adapted to boy scout programmes. It is a sport wonderfully suited to the temperament of youth. A boy or girl who takes up this keen, active and competitive game will develop in later years into a skilful country rambler. Many a hunter, fisherman, fell walker, rock climber, explorer of the future, will go far afield on guideless trips with perfect efficiency and safety because of his experience in orienting.

There is no doubt that orienting owes much of its success to the fact that it can evoke the pioneering spirit over country that is well explored and well mapped. The Swedish exponents,

Bjorn Kjellstrom and Stig Hedenstrom, who have introduced the sport into many other countries, say that through orienting they can experience the thrill of discovery—that a vista of new adventure is opened up to them.

My only criticism of this excellent sport as at present conducted, concerns its obsession with the use of map and compass. As a professional navigator, I would be the last to condemn any sport designed to improve familiarity and efficiency with these two fundamental instruments; but in my opinion, orienting enthusiasts would derive far more pleasure from their pastime if they were also guided by natural signs. If natural navigation were introduced into orienting competitions—as it could be without any great difficulty—it would not only increase the interest and sheer fun of the sport, but would give the competitors even more accuracy and speed in finding their way, and would also prepare them for the time when they may find themselves without a map and compass.

To take an example, the natural signposts provided by the sun and shadows could be easily used on orienting courses. Nobody can read a compass when he is running; but he can easily look for shadows. In a competition in which time counts, the experienced sun-watcher should easily outstrip the compass-needle-watcher. He needs, of course, to know the rate of movement of the sun at his latitude and season. The tables at the back of this book can be read as easily as a compass and the relevant information memorised without difficulty at the start of an orienting race.

How much more meaningful and adventurous would orienting be if each contestant were to set out to find his way from start to finish using natural navigation, primarily—checked only secondarily by compass and map. The whole sport of orienting arouses the senses of wonder and discovery. How much more dramatically would these senses be aroused if the explorers put a premium on their ability to derive conclusions from nature.

Like many other professional navigators, I must have been playing the game of orienting all my life without knowing it, for it is just that precision which is cultivated in the sport which has appealed to me in my professional job. I know no greater feeling of satisfaction than that which comes with a landfall over a long distance of sea (by ship or by air—it does not matter which), when the point of destination shows up at the exact spot to which the course has been set. An accurate homing at the end of a land journey is perhaps a little less dramatic, but the fascination of the problem is just the same and the satisfaction just as profound.

In the Armed Services, at the present time, the use of map and compass is taught only to specialised groups. I am certain that the simple use of these instruments should form a part of everybody's military training, and should be conducted on lines similar to those followed in the Scandinavian sport of orienting. But I would go farther. I cannot imagine any branch of the armed services in which the usefulness of a man could not be sharpened and his efficiency improved by simple training in the elementary principles of *natural*—as opposed to instrumental—navigation.

CHAPTER XIX

DIRECTIONS FROM WAVES AND SWELLS

M OST NAVIGATORS of to-day would be lost at sea if they were deprived of the use of compass, sextant, chronometer or radio. So accustomed are we to navigating with these instruments that we watch the waves rising and falling with their monotonous regularity, without appreciating that they have a definite order and pattern. The natural navigator can study the anatomy of sea-swells and use them to find his way.

In nearly every part of the world's oceans, some sort of swell is chronic. In mid-ocean even a glassy sea has a detectable up and down movement. Only under quite exceptional conditions is this movement so small as to be invisible. This chronic sea swell is the lasting tell-tale of the direction of the prevailing wind for the prevailing wind arouses it and maintains it. It takes a prolonged and exceptional wind from a direction which is not the prevailing one to divert and re-orient a swell. Normally, the momentum imparted to the swells by the prevailing winds persists throughout all the vagaries of weather. Winds may suddenly change, but the directions of the swells will not. It is important of course to distinguish between swells and waves. When the wind changes, the motion and direction of the surface waves will soon follow these changes; but the fundamental chronic swell will persist for far longer. Soon after the wind has established itself in a direction other than the prevailing direction, we can begin to detect the peculiar effect of wave motion working at an angle to the long fundamental chronic swell.

The natural navigator can in many circumstances (though not all), get useful information from wave motion, and in practi cally all circumstances from swell motion. For instance, waves can sometimes be indicators of the direction of unseen land. When there is fairly high ground near the shore of this unseen land, and a wind is blowing off the land, the benefit of the protection of the land barrier will be felt by mariners even if they are well out of sight of it. For in the wind shadow on the lee side of the land, there is a reduction in the size of the waves and (if the wind blows off the land in its prevailing direction) also of the swells. The voyager, sailing or drifting, who discovers that the sea has subsided although the wind is still blowing with the same strength, can be fairly sure of the direction of the land from which this protection comes.

Of all early pioneers, the Polynesians squeezed most meaning from the ever-changing appearance of the sea. Living as they did, and still do, in the island-dotted Pacific Ocean, they developed a most particular and critical interest in the effects of islands upon the shape, direction and motion of the waves and swells. It was much better for them to watch these things than to try to take soundings; for most of the coral islands of the Pacific Ocean are isolated in waters of very great depth. To Polynesian eyes, wave formations became as useful as landmarks to the landsman.

The Polynesians were not the only native navigators of the Pacific who understood wave marks and swell marks. Even more skilful were the Micronesians—a mixed Polynesian and Mongoloid race which lives in the Caroline and Marshall Island groups. These archipelagos are in the western Pacific, north of the Equator, and consist of hundreds of small, low-lying coral atolls, isolated in large expanses of water, often visible only for short distances, and seldom visible from each other.

Throughout these archipelagos the Micronesians navigated in the same way as did the Polynesians. But they also had something that the Polynesians proper never seem to have invented—charts of the anatomy and topography of local surface waters. These unique charts were, in a sense, models, for they were made out of the ribs of coconut palms tied together with coconut fibre. Within a framework were meticulously arranged bent ribs tied into a sort of net that most accurately represented the curvature

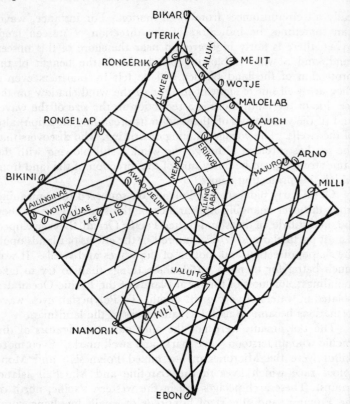

Example of Marshall Island stick chart made from ribs of coconut
palms with shells representing islands

and meeting points of the dominant swells around the islands
The islands themselves were represented on the framework b
small shells. The charts were not made to distance scale, so mucl
as to time scale, for the Micronesians and Polynesians thought c
their journeys only in canoe- or catamaran-days from one plac
to another. On some of these Micronesian charts small island

were shown disproportionately large, because of their sheer importance to the maker and users of the chart. Indeed, the Micronesian charts were ready aids to memory. There were three chief kinds: simple instruction charts used for training; general charts of large areas; charts of local areas.

The Micronesian charts were (as far as we can judge) very personal and individualistic, for each navigator made his own and incorporated in it those ideas which were of particular interest and help to him. It is for this reason that charts of the same areas differ considerably, as we can see by examining the handful in the museums of the world. Unfortunately, there are, as far as I know, only forty-three surviving examples. In a Micronesian chart of a particular archipelago, the directional characteristics of all the swells throughout the group are carefully marked. Further, sticks on the charts indicate the distance from land at which coconut palms can be seen. Other lines showed the position and distance from the island of the meeting of the waters of the oncoming swell and the tide ebbing from the island's lagoon. In many cases, this meeting place is actually out of sight of the land.

As a dominant swell approaches an island, its pattern of parallel ridges begins to be modified. This modification may start at a point out of sight of the island and consists of what is at first a gentle curving of the swell front, as if to embrace the island. As the swell system nears the island, this curvature becomes more and more pronounced until it almost fits the obstruction. At this point that part of the swell directly in front of the island starts to break up into smaller waves which gradually build up and finally collapse as breakers on the reefs. This wave motion from the direction of the prevailing swell is easy to see.

This is not all the story; for we can find on the opposite side of the island a counter-swell. Certainly this is much less noticeable than the prevailing swell on the prevailing-windward side of the island. But anybody who knows enough to look for it, can find it. I have seen this counter-swell particularly well from the air, and have easily recognised its curves, which also embrace the island, though never so closely as the curves of the main swell. The counter-swell and the main swell meet, of course, on a line which runs through a point a little on the lee side of the island, and lies at right angles to the direction of the prevailing swell. The slight eddies and disturbances can be often traced along this line for a considerable distance; and it was this line of meeting of two opposing swells that the Micronesians looked for. When they were steering for an island and by some chance had missed it, they would reach the swell-line and simply sail down it to the island. Moreover, they could even find and use this swell-line at night, for in the tropical seas eddies and turbulence bring up luminescent organisms to the surface and make the swell-line into a subtle, but none the less authentic kind of flare-path.

Not only did the Micronesians seek and use these junction lines of swell and counter-swell, but they also used the crossings of the swells of one island with those of another. They were always sailing from island to island, making mental notes in their heads, or physical notes on their model charts of the expected curvature of this swell, or interruptions to that swell, of the eddies and meeting points of those swells: and of course they also watched the sun and the stars, and studied the flight of birds, and navigated in many other ways that I have already mentioned in this book. Seasoned navigators of my acquaintance have invariably expressed amazement—and in some cases disbelief— when I have described to them the early Micronesian methods of navigation, and have shown how these peoples could success- fully make wonderful inter-island journeys. Necessity, of course, is the mother of invention; but it is undoubtedly astonishing that, a thousand years ago or more, native navigators could observe and make charts of such subtle things as the peculiar ground swell on the prevailing windward side of some islands—which is caused by a reflection of the main swell thrown back by the shore which runs over the top of the oncoming swell and against it. The Micronesians and Polynesians could even distinguish this swell a long way out at sea.

CHAPTER XX

COLOUR OF THE SEA

I T IS popularly supposed that the colour of the sea is derived largely from the reflection of the sky above. It is true that the state of the weather may make a slight difference to the apparent colour of the sea, which tends to be brighter in sunlight and duller under overcast; but every experienced sea voyager knows that the fundamental colour of the waters he travels on depends upon its composition. There are two tendencies, each of which is influenced by more than one factor.

The colour of the sea tends to be green when the quantity of particles or organisms in it is high and when the quantity of salt in it is low. The colour tends to be blue when the quantity of particles or organisms is low and the quantity of salt is high. The intensity of the coloration—green or blue—depends slightly upon the amount of sunlight, but more particularly on the depth of the waters—the deeper the darker.

Following these rules, we find that equatorial waters tend to be blue, temperate and arctic waters green. In hot climates—and particularly in enclosed seas in such climates, like the Red Sea and the Mediterranean—so much evaporation takes place that the sea contains a percentage of salt considerably above the average. This makes it blue, as also does the fact that tropical seas generally contain *fewer* organisms than those of more northerly or southerly latitudes.

Conversely, towards the poles the seas suffer less evaporation and are diluted by melting ice. Their salt content is therefore below average; moreover, right up to the ice edge the cooler seas swarm with organisms. They are consequently very green in colour.

All the same, green water is occasionally found in the tropics. There is a special reason for this. When we mix the primary colours yellow and blue we produce the colour green. This happens when blue tropical seas overlie yellow sand. The green water of the tropics, then, is most often an indication of shallow water. It is not always so, however; for when the bottom sand is not its usual yellow but (as is fairly common in some coral areas) white, the shallow water will be very blue—but a characteristic light blue.

Green water can be also found in tropical regions near the mouths of large rivers such as the Amazon and the River Plate in South America. Both these rivers bring down tremendous quantities of silt which they deposit some distance out to sea. The sediment content near their mouths renders the water a muddy green—not blue. But far beyond the region in which these rivers drop their mud their fresh waters dilute the sea and lower its salinity. This also renders the waters green, and the effect of the water of the River Plate can be noticed a thousand miles out to sea.

Anybody who studies a simple current chart of the oceans of the world will see that the waters are not arranged in simple bands of temperature corresponding to latitude. On the contrary, most parts of all oceans are in a constant state of circulation, both at the surface and at great depths. There are a few areas, of course, in which the circulation is not great; but these are rare. One of the most famous of them is the Sargasso Sea in the tropical North Atlantic Ocean. Here the waters are very saline and almost lacking in living organisms and solid particles—so much so that the Sargasso Sea is bluer and clearer than any other water known, salt or fresh, with the possible exception of the famous, blue, deep, fresh-water lake high up in the mountains of Oregon in the U.S.A.—Crater Lake.

Owing to the constant circulation of the oceans cold green Arctic water penetrates in places almost to the tropics, and warm blue tropical water almost to the Arctic regions. In their passage through the oceans these currents are very well defined; and the boundary lines between the ocean streams can be readily detected by the navigator from the sudden change in colour and in temperature. The contrast between the so-called Gulf Stream and the Labrador Current is so well defined that the line between them extends for hundreds of miles, is readily visible from the deck of a ship, and, being relatively constant in its position, offers a ready and valuable means of determining position.

The Gulf Stream was so named from the erroneous idea that it originated in the Gulf of Mexico; but we now know that it passes from the Strait of Yucatan to the Strait of Florida, and that very little of it enters the Gulf of Mexico. Originating in the tropical Atlantic, this great ocean current has a very high salt content and not enough oxygen to stimulate the growth of many living organisms. It is very warm and very blue and can be readily distinguished from the adjacent waters through or alongside which it passes.

The Labrador Current, on the other hand, flows down from the region of Greenland and the Canadian Arctic along the coast of Labrador, carrying with it many icebergs from the great glaciers of the high arctic regions. It flows along the eastern seaboard of North America between the land and the north-eastward flowing Gulf Stream. It is very cold and contains relatively little salt and a vast quantity of marine life. It is therefore very green. At its convergence with the Gulf Stream the contrast in colour is spectacular and the contrast in temperature even more so, for in places the temperature may suddenly rise or drop 30° F. as the voyager crosses the convergence.

From this example—and there are many others perhaps less spectacular that could be drawn from nearly every sea in the world—we can understand how important changing sea colour and sea temperature was to the early " primitive " and European navigators. In the log books of the latter we can find frequent references to such things as " the green hue of soundings." It is an axiom that all ocean travellers, especially those in small craft, should have a knowledge of ocean currents and enough experience to identify them. All such navigators pay close attention to changes of air temperature and quickly confirm whether such changes also apply to the surface of the sea. When a small change of temperature is noticed in the open sea and there is no local weather change to account for it, it may be readily assumed that it is due to some shore effect or to some current from a polar or equatorial direction.

Less than two hundred years ago the determination of longitude by chronometer was far from commonplace and many voyagers and geographers like Benjamin Franklin and John Williams took pains to encourage a system of what they christened " thermometrical navigation." They made charts giving accurate positions of the warm and cold currents in the Atlantic Ocean and encouraged voyagers to take frequent sea temperatures. Surprisingly accurate results were obtained. With the improvement of the chronometer, and its more general use in navigation, thermometrical navigation fell into disuse. But it is still a useful tool for the natural navigator, who can quickly learn to detect even quite a small change in temperature simply by dipping his hand in the water—just as the Polynesians did throughout the Pacific perhaps a thousand years ago.

But I must return to the subject of colour navigation. We have already seen that in the tropics green water may be a good indication of the presence of sandy shores (provided the sand is yellow) or of the mouths of rivers. There are other colour indications of the presence of land, and of the depths of reefs and passages. Anywhere within the tropics, where coral reefs break the water or great coral heads live under its surface, the experienced mariner has only to watch the colour of the sea to know where he can pass safely; for the depth of the underwater coral heads has its tell-tale in the colour change of the water. Water over coral usually looks yellowish when only a few inches to a couple of feet deep. Beyond this, the deeper the darker. Within the Fiji Islands there are vast areas of water as yet uncharted. Following the old Polynesians (who knew all about this colour change with depth, and who sailed their catamarans with great accuracy and boldness in and around the reefs) I have myself navigated my motor cruiser day after day at full speed, knowing

—entirely by the colour of the coral water ahead—just what uncharted reef we could safely pass over.

I would add one rider to this only. I would never care to boast of having done this in bad weather or when the sun was very low. In such conditions the colour guide becomes unreliable and the method of navigation positively unsafe.

Not all colour changes in the sea are indicators of current convergences or the proximity of land. In many parts of the oceans of the world certain kinds of minute organisms may swarm and produce an orange or red appearance. This does not necessarily show nearby land; but a brown or muddy appearance in the water almost certainly does, for it will be caused by silt; and silt comes only from a river or estuary (or, most exceptionally, a volcanic eruption).

Patches of luminescence in the water usually indicate a reef or a shore line, but do not invariably do so; for some organisms may show in patches in the surface waters of the open ocean and shine at night with their own light. Nevertheless, a so-called " phosphorescent " sea should make the natural navigator careful of a reef. The word phosphorescence is not quite right, incidentally, for the luminescence of marine organisms has nothing to do with phosphorus. Gallego, the early Spanish voyager in the Pacific, showed himself a wise man when he wrote in his journal of 1566 " when the night overtook us we were without knowledge of any port, having much thick weather with wind and rain. Guided by the phosphorescence of the sea, we skirted the reefs; and when I saw that the reefs did not make the sea phosphorescent, I weathered the point and entered a good harbour at the fourth hour of the night."

CHAPTER XXI

THE HABITS OF SEA BIRDS

THE GRACEFUL seabirds have been masters of the sea many thousands of times longer than man. According to the latest enumeration, there are about 8600 known species of birds in the world. Only about 200 of these have become fully specialised inhabitants of the seas and open oceans. Ever since man became a mariner these successful and beautiful birds have guided him at sea. Their lines of flight have led him to land, for seabirds are unerring navigators. The presence of one sort or another has told the navigator that he has moved from one zone of the waters to another; for each part of the ocean has its own particular characteristics of temperature, depth, salinity and movement and supports its own special communities of marine life. It is this marine life that supports the seabirds and each zonal community has its own characteristic set of winged navigators, diving, skimming and flying over the waves.

No voyager at sea should travel without a bird book, such as W. B. Alexander's *Birds of the Ocean* which covers the seabirds of all the world. And no seaman could help but understand the sea better if he read such authoritative works as Dr. Robert Cushman Murphy's *Oceanic Birds of South America* or (if he is interested in the North Atlantic) James Fisher and R. M. Lockley's *Sea Birds*; or the former's monograph, *The Fulmar*, or the latter's monographs *Shearwaters* and *Puffins*.

I should like to begin with a quotation from Dr. Murphy's classic work:

". . . if the quality of the water may tell us something about the birds, the birds should also tell us much about the water. The Snow Petrel requires water which is cool; Tropic Birds prefer water which is clear, dense, saline and moderately warm; the Brown Booby clings to water inhabited by flying fish which, in turn, are limited to water of definite temperature and gaseous content."

From the authorities I have mentioned, and from the works of many other learned ornithologists who have been equally fascinated by the wonderful birds of the sea, I have attempted to distil some of their knowledge which, with some of my own, may be of value to the natural navigator.

A reader of Dr. Murphy's *Oceanic Birds of South America* comes to understand very rapidly and clearly that in the tropical zone of the oceans bird life is generally surprisingly scarce. This is in very striking contrast to conditions in the higher latitudes. On the whole, it is the seabird community of the higher latitudes (both north and south) that tends to include species that range far from their breeding-grounds into those parts of the open ocean most remote from land. The majority of tropical seabirds, on the other hand, do not often range far from their nesting places on island groups and continental coastlines. There are some tropical species, of course, about which we know very little, and some extremely abundant birds like sooty terns and noddies seem to disappear to sea where nobody can find them. Certainly, where conditions are suitable the numbers of the tropical seabirds are somewhat astronomical. In many of the more undisturbed archipelagos in the tropical oceans, especially in the Pacific and Indian Oceans, the seabirds breed truly in millions. Of course nowadays, and particularly on the larger islands, the presence of man and certain inimical animals that he has introduced has succeeded materially in reducing the seabird population. But there are still many small islands whose sky is darkened by the nesting birds.

Despite this, it must be reiterated that the voyager may travel for days across tropical oceans and see no birds at all. One experienced observer recorded, on a long cruise in the tropical

Pacific, an average of only one bird for every 125 miles of open sea. The observer many miles from land in tropical seas may expect no aid to finding his position from the seabirds. He must take advantage of all the other aids to location available to him. It is when he is nearing his landfall that the tropical seabirds become useful to him—the more so if he can make a careful note of their number and rely on his own powers of simple identification.

To give an example : on a voyage between San Francisco and Tahiti it was noted that for the first two days North American coastal birds were seen. After this for five or six days only an occasional petrel was observed. When the observer neared the Equator, scattered woolly clouds became thicker and greyer, the swell increased and rainstorms came. Suddenly, numerous birds appeared. Among these were storm-petrels and red-tailed or white-tailed-tropic birds. Then as islands were approached large numbers of terns were seen. As the ship sailed farther along the birds dropped away again as suddenly as they had appeared.

Most frequently is this sudden appearance and disappearance of seabirds notable to the voyager and natural navigator. Birds appear and disappear as one passes out of or into the doldrums or from the part of the sea dominated by one ocean current to that dominated by another. As we have seen in an earlier chapter, neighbouring waters can differ astonishingly in their characteristics, and birds' distributions can have edges just as sharp as the edges of the currents. One current may be rich in its ability to support bird life, while the next is poor. At the convergences of ocean currents not only may bird distribution suddenly change, but there may also be a great concentration of bird life at the actual meeting place, for here water frequently upwells from the depths and brings food to the surface. There is nearly always a big concentration of bird life along the line where the Gulf Stream meets the Labrador current.

The two charts on pages 172-3, based on the observations of many bird watchers, show the relative frequency of birds in the North and South Atlantic. The first chart shows the average number of birds seen per day. It can be seen, for instance, that birds tend to become more plentiful as the voyager penetrates farther north into richer shallower waters. A hundred birds can be seen a day in the waters around the Faeroe Islands in the North Atlantic; whereas in the middle of the Atlantic sometimes only one may be sighted per day. Thirty-four birds a day were noticed around the Cape Verde Islands and (to illustrate the matter further) on a line between Bermuda and the south of Spain one bird per day was seen in the middle of the Atlantic, increasing to four, seventeen and then fifteen approaching Gibraltar. The second diagram for the South Atlantic shows much the same state of affairs: an increasing number of birds with latitude. Generally speaking, the farther the voyager goes south of the Equator, the richer become the waters through which he sails and the greater the number of seabirds.

As a further aid to the natural navigator, I have summarised the habits of a representative number of seabirds in the following pages, concentrating most on those which are of real value in determining the neighbourhood and direction of land. Forty-three species of seabirds are illustrated, with accompanying descriptions, on plates VI-X. The illustrations have been specially drawn by that great naturalist and observer of the *living* bird, Francis Lee Jaques, who has depicted each species with special accent upon the distinctive features by which it may be easily recognised. Further, since the importance of birds as indicators of land varies much according to the season, and particularly the breeding season, I have compiled a tabled summary which embraces seasonable notes. I must stress that these notes are purely for guidance and that it will be a rule that isolated observations or a small number of observations should not be followed. It is absolutely necessary to take into account the law of averages and all I have made are *reasonable* assumptions about the distance from land that a certain observed number of birds may indicate. No evidence from bird numbers at sea should be regarded as conclusive, unless it involves more than a handful of observations of several different species or unless it is coupled with indications from other natural signs. After all, the art of natural navigation often consists in receiving pieces of

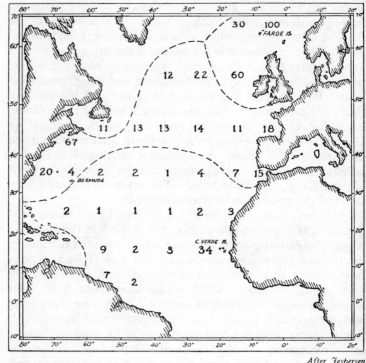

After Jespersen

information from a number of sources, each of which by itself may well be unreliable, but the sum of which when taken together becomes a certain guide.

NOTES ON SPECIALLY USEFUL SEABIRD GUIDES

Penguins

There are fifteen species of penguins in the world, all confined to the Southern Hemisphere and to waters which are at least fairly cool. Half of the species breed on the sub-Antarctic

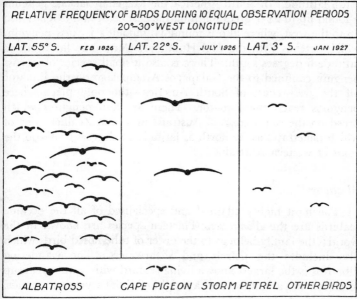

From *Murphy after Spiess*

islands or around the shores of the Antarctic continent itself. Nearly all the penguins breed in large social rookeries where they are very noisy and can be heard for considerable distances. During the breeding season vast numbers will be found swimming towards or from their rookeries close to the shore: however, in the Antarctic and sub-Antarctic large concentrations of swimming penguins are not necessarily an indication of the nearness of a breeding colony, for the birds often congregate where crustacean food is available hundreds of miles from base. Most familiar perhaps to the natural navigator are the more northerly species. Four of these are jackass penguins, characterised by a broad white eye-stripe which widens on the side of the face and neck to join a white breast; the black-footed or common jackass penguin is found along the coast of South Africa as far north as 15 degrees south latitude. In South America the Magellan jackass penguin is found up to 24 degrees south on the east coast and extends also on to the west, where also is found Humboldt's jackass penguin, which extends with the cool Humboldt Current as far north as latitude 6 degrees south. There is also a small species of jackass penguin confined to the Galapagos Archipelago on the Equator off the west coast of South America—the only place where penguins reach the Equator. There are also penguins which breed on the south coast of Australia and New Zealand, one of which penetrates as far north as latitude 22 degrees south on the coast of western Australia.

Albatrosses

The most highly adapted and specialised of all the oceanic seabirds are the *Albatrosses*. Thirteen species are known in the world: the family belongs to the order of tube-nosed birds which also includes the petrels and shearwaters. The wandering albatross is the largest known living seabird with a wing span up to eleven and a half feet and a weight of about seventeen pounds. It has a wide range in the southern oceans between thirty and sixty degrees south. Some individuals come a little north of 30 degrees south in the Humboldt Current on the west coast of South America, penetrating to about 23 degrees south. But four species only regularly live north of this latitude. One of them, the Waved Albatross, nests only in the Galapagos Islands on the Equator and is the only albatross with a tropical breeding distribution. There is no albatross in the North Atlantic Ocean, but three species nest in the North Pacific. Of these, by far the rarest is the white-bodied short-tailed albatross. So scarce was it that recently it was thought to have become entirely extinct. Fortunately this is not so; a colony of ten pairs nested on Torishima an island belonging to Japan, in 1954. The Laysan Albatross has a white head and underparts and dark brown wings and back: it nests in the north-westerly islands of the Hawaiian archipelago. The commonest albatross of the North Pacific is the sooty-brown black-footed albatross, which has a rather wide nesting distribution on the more northerly Pacific Islands from Hawaii to the Marshall Islands, Volcano Islands and Bonin Islands. The North Pacific species of albatross usually breed from April to October. Even at that season small numbers of individuals seen may be a long way from land.

The modern seaman does not seem to believe in the old superstition so solemnly recounted in Coleridge's *Ancient Mariner*. He does not think it unlucky to catch an albatross. I was once an apprentice on a ship running from Australia to New Zealand; and it was quite a common practice for the crew to catch albatrosses to examine them. One method that I used myself was to trail a small open triangle of brass on the end of a line. Attracted by the shining metal, the albatrosses got their curved bills caught in the triangles. It was then quite easy to haul them aboard. Incidentally, an albatross when hauled aboard always becomes violently sick. Many writers have christened this " sea sickness," but I believe myself that it must be a defence mechanism for, on its breeding cliffs, the albatross and its young both vomit at intruders in order to scare them away. Anybody who catches an albatross should study its sharp bill with a good deal of circumspection. It is hooked and very strong and can inflict a nasty wound.

Petrels

Besides the albatrosses, there are three other families in the great order of tube-nosed seabirds. There are nineteen members of the storm-petrel family, many of which are dark with white rumps. The storm-petrels are small and have a flitting moth-like flight, skimming the water closely for surface food. Many but not all of the storm-petrels are ship followers and outside the breeding season can be sighted thousands of miles from base. As far as scientists know, they tend to breed in the season after that in which they are hatched, so that during the breeding seasons there are few or no non-breeding adolescents far to sea. Thus storm-petrel numbers can be a useful indication of the nearness of land where there is an active breeding colony.

One of the most abundant storm-petrels of the world is Wilson's petrel, for from its breeding headquarters on the Antarctic continent and its surrounding islands, it penetrates in the off-season far north into the Pacific Ocean where it certainly crosses the Equator on the west side, and into the Atlantic and Indian Oceans where it regularly crosses the Equator. In the North Atlantic it scarcely ever reaches Britain; but on the west side it is well north of the Sargasso Sea by April and is often seen in numbers off the eastern seaboard of the United States feeding along the convergence of the Gulf Stream and the Labrador Current. Indeed, it is one of the best bird indicators of the Labrador Current. There is some evidence that the return journey to the south of the Wilson's petrels of the North Atlantic is made on the east side of that ocean from the Bay of Biscay along the West African coast. It is occasionally abundant, in June or after, off the coast of Portugal; and birds are still off the West African coast until December and early January. Wilson's petrel can be fairly easily confused with two other storm-petrels, which breed in the North Atlantic—Leach's petrel, whose headquarters are mostly on the western side but of which there are over half a dozen colonies in Britain, The Faeroes and Iceland, and the storm-petrel whose headquarters are in north and west Britain, but which breeds also in Iceland, The Faeroes, north-western France, the Bay of Biscay, Madeira and on islands in the western part of the Mediterranean.

A large family of 50 species embraces the giant petrel or stinker, a great many birds that carry the general name of petrel, and the shearwaters. These birds have a more gliding, albatross-like flight than the little storm-petrels; and while there are always large concentrations of them near their breeding grounds in the proper season, they usually have fairly long periods of adolescence and may be observed sometimes in fair numbers long distances from their breeding grounds at any time of the year. However, a knowledge of the natural history of many of them may be a great aid to the natural navigator.

The commonest petrel of North Atlantic waters, for instance, is the fulmar—a truly oceanic bird which may have a period of adolescence as long as seven years. There is scarcely any part of the northern North Atlantic in which fulmars have not been seen in every month. Nevertheless, a knowledge of this bird has proved often very useful. On one occasion during the Second World War, one of Britain's great " Queens " was making a voyage from Britain to North America. There was, of course, the usual security blackout about the vessel's route, but at least one member of the passenger list who had not been let into the secret was well aware that the great liner was in the Denmark Strait between Iceland and Greenland. The North Atlantic population of fulmars has two main colour phases, one white-headed and white-breasted and the other darkish grey-blue. The dark fulmars nest only in the high Arctic where the temperature of the sea surface in July is around freezing point. Although there are no breeding colonies of dark fulmars very near the Denmark Strait, it is an assembly-place of many of these dark forms from the Arctic; and from January to April the dark birds equal and from May till August, greatly outnumber the light birds in that region—at least in the western part of it fairly close to the Greenland coast.

The fulmar is one of the few birds of the world that is truly bi-polar, for it is either of the same species as, or very closely related to an Antarctic petrel which used to be known as the silver-grey petrel but now is generally called the Antarctic fulmar. This breeds on the Antarctic continent and on some of the sub-Antarctic islands and operates into the Indian, Atlantic and Pacific Oceans, though normally only in the regions of cool water. However, aided by the cool Humboldt Current, it sometimes nearly reaches the Equator on the Pacific Coast of South America and may even occasionally have crossed it. The race of the true fulmar that breeds in the North Pacific is in many ways inter-mediate between the Antarctic fulmar and the Atlantic fulmar; and, ages ago, the North Pacific may have indeed been colonised by fulmars from the Antarctic. Afterwards, they must have spread across the polar basin into the North Atlantic.

The known breeding colonies of the Pacific fulmar at present are in the Kurile Islands, in the Komandorski Islands east of Kamchatka, in certain of the Aleutian Islands, in the Semidi

Islands off the Alaska Peninsula, on the Pribilof, St. Matthew and Hall Islands in the Bering Sea and on certain promontories near the easternmost end of Siberia. The Pacific fulmar is always to be found in the Bering Sea and operates through most of the year a long distance down the Pacific coast of North America; however, there are very few records indeed of fulmars as far south as the state of California between May and August.

The North Atlantic fulmar nests in some eastern islands of the Canadian Arctic archipelago, Greenland, Iceland, The Faeroes, Britain, Jan Mayen, on one island in Norway, on Bear Island, in Spitsbergen, Franz Josef Land and Novaya Zemlya. There is so much ice around the western part of this range that fulmars are almost entirely absent from Davis Strait and Baffin Bay in November and December and withdraw yet farther—even from the Labrador coast and most of that of Newfoundland—in January and February. A steamer travelling eastwards from New York to London in the winter is seldom likely to pick up fulmars until it reaches the eastern part of the Grand Banks of Newfoundland. Generally speaking, the southward limit of fulmars at sea in the North Atlantic Ocean is about 49 degrees or 50 degrees on the east side; on the west the distribution dips down in particular strength to about 41 degrees or 42 degrees north on longitude 50 degrees west, which is south-east of the Newfoundland Banks, a most favoured feeding ground for fulmars. There are useful maps of the fulmar's distribution through the year in James Fisher's monograph, *The Fulmar* (*New Naturalist* series, 1952).

A typical petrel of the southern oceans is the Cape pigeon. Like the fulmar, it is a regular follower of ships and can be often seen far from land. Nevertheless, the observation of large numbers of these birds may generally be taken as an indication of nearby land, for even outside the breeding season they tend to congregate in feeding packs not far from shore, or from the edge of the Antarctic ice. The Cape pigeon breeds on the more southerly of the sub-Antarctic islands—South Georgia, the South Orkneys, the South Shetlands, the islands of Graham Land, and Kerguelen Island, possibly also on Bouvet and the Crozets. Away from its breeding grounds, it has a wide distribution in the southern oceans, extending north with cool currents as far as (for instance) northern Peru in the Humboldt Current, and the Marquesas. On the African Coast it reaches Angola and Mozambique; and it also reaches Australia, but it very rarely crosses the Equator.

A typical petrel of lower latitudes in the southern oceans is the Kermadec petrel, one of the many species of petrels and shear-waters that have white underparts. This petrel nests on the island of Juan Fernandez in the South Pacific, also on the Kermadecs, Lord Howe Island, and the Austral and Tuamotu Islands; formerly it also nested on Norfolk Island. A closely related petrel nests on South Trinidad Island in the South Atlantic. The Kermadec petrel roams some distance across the Equator, often to 15 degrees north, reaching the coast of Mexico; isolated individuals of this species at sea should not be taken as indicators of land. A few have been recorded as far as 210 miles from their breeding grounds on Juan Fernandez, but large numbers do not begin to build up until the breeding land is approached.

One of the most interesting and important of the shearwater group of the petrel family breeds in such large numbers on the islands of Bass Straits, between Tasmania and the south coast of Australia, that smoking and salting the young birds for the local market has become a large industry. An experienced observer saw what he estimated to be 150 million of these short-tailed shearwaters at one time *en route* to their breeding-grounds on these islands. In its off-season from March to November, this bird may be encountered far to sea especially when migrating through the western Pacific north to eastern Siberia, and the Bering Sea, where it can be very numerous within sight of the Alaskan Islands. It appears in the Bering Sea most commonly between April and October. Not many short-tailed shearwaters cross to the eastern Pacific at latitudes lower than the Bering Sea, but small numbers are occasionally seen off the coast of California, which are believed to be individuals that have linked up with the flocks of the sooty shearwater, which normally migrates along an easterly Pacific route from its winter home in the Bering Sea and adjacent waters, to its breeding grounds in and around New Zealand and South America.

Indeed, among the shearwaters, there are several examples of birds which breed in the Southern Hemisphere and migrate to spend their off-season in the northern summer. It must be stressed that while on migration and while in their winter quarters, their presence and direction of flight may give no indication whatever of the proximity of land. An important species which falls into this category is the great shearwater, or Tristan great shearwater of the Atlantic Ocean. Its only known breeding place is in the archipelago of Tristan da Cunha in the South Atlantic, one of the most isolated island groups in the world. This great shearwater appears to spend our summer entirely in the North Atlantic. In May the birds begin to arrive off the east coast of the United States and when their population builds up, groups of a hundred or more may be seen in favourite places, such as at the convergence of the Gulf Stream and the Labrador Current or off the New-foundland Banks. The great shearwaters swing eastwards across the North Atlantic and often arrive off the western shores of Britain in June. They work their way home down the eastern North Atlantic, departing from European waters in November. In effect this species makes a slow roundabout cruise of the North Atlantic during its off-season and at each point in this roundabout there is an appropriate time when a peak abundance can be expected. For instance, on a line from Nantucket Island, Cape Cod and Nova Scotia to the mid-Atlantic in 51 degrees north 30 degrees west, the great shearwater peak is in about the last week of May. In the first week of June the species is abundant on the Grand Banks.

James Fisher has seen great shearwaters at Rockall, about 300 miles west of the mainland of Scotland, as early as May, but the peak visitation in West Britain is in about July and not until later is the species common off the Scilly Isles and to be met with occasionally in large flocks off the Cornish coast.

Another important shearwater is the Manx shearwater. This is a species more resident than some of the great wanderers from the Southern Hemisphere; and within its curiously scattered world range it has several well-marked races. Such races nest in New Zealand, the Hawaiian Islands, the west coast of Mexico and on islands off it, the Mediterranean and the North Atlantic. The Mediterranean and North Atlantic races are sufficiently different to be distinguished in the field. We now know from marking records that the North Atlantic race migrates from the British Isles across the Equator to the eastern coast of South America. But when the Manx shearwater is not migrating, it usually stays within 200 miles of shore or at least over the shallow waters of the 100 fathom continental shelf. During the summer breeding season in the Northern Hemisphere, big " rafts " of Manx shearwaters sitting on the water or big packs in flight mean birds which are operating from some land base. As Manx shearwaters relieve each other on the nest at intervals of up to a week, their operational range from base can be quite considerable. Many of the birds that breed in Wales regularly feed in the Bay of Biscay. At the end of the season, the Mediterranean birds pass out of the Straits of Gibraltar and turn north reaching as far as the entrance to the English Channel. The Manx shearwater is rare on the American side of the North Atlantic; it is not certain that it still nests in Bermuda; and the New England coast is certainly well out of its range. Yet, a bird taken from its burrow in Wales and flown to Boston, returned under its own power across the Atlantic in less than a fortnight.

I should mention the last and smallest family of the tube-nosed birds, the diving-petrels, of which there are four species confined to the cooler waters of the Southern Hemisphere and sub-Antarctic. These extraordinary little birds are shrimp-feeders and can actually swim with their wings under water. At sea they may be sometimes present in quite large numbers a long distance from base in places where sea conditions provide copious food.

The Steganopodes

The Steganopodes is an order of seabirds comprising the tropic-bird family, the frigate-bird family, the cormorant family, the gannet family and the pelican family. Not all the members of these families are marine, though the order certainly must have evolved in the oceans of the world.

Tropic-Birds

The curious tropic-bird family contains three members, all of which are indeed mainly tropical in their distribution. Tropic-birds are useful guides to the natural navigator, for normally they are seldom observed in groups of three or more unless land is close.

During the summer around Bermuda the white-tailed tropic-birds which nest there operate to a distance of sixty or seventy miles, flying out to the feeding grounds early in the morning, returning shortly before sunset. A group of three or more such birds seen flying at these times of day will surely indicate by the direction of their flight the direction of the land. The white-tailed tropic-bird is found in all three tropical oceans: in the Atlantic it breeds not only on Bermuda, but at many islands in the Bahamas and West Indies, possibly in the Guianas, on Fernando Noronha just south of the Equator, on Ascension, and on islands off the West African coast just on the Equator. It has a wide breeding range in the central and western Pacific and in the Indian Ocean. Where tropic-birds breed on inhabited islands they can sometimes be seen flying about without their tail feathers: these slender and beautiful plumes are often removed by the natives who highly prize them.

The white-tailed tropic-bird is one of the few species seen in the area of the Sargasso Sea; though it is not very common there except in its western part. A voyager travelling from this sea area towards the West Indies or Bermuda during the tropic-bird's breeding season (May–August) can observe the increasing numbers build up as he goes.

The red-billed tropic-bird is found in West Mexico, Central America, the south-eastern West Indies, the Cape Verde Islands, St. Helena, Ascension, Fernando Noronha and Rocas Rock. These last four breeding places are on islands in the Atlantic just south of the Equator. The species also breeds on the coast of

Ecuador and in the Galapagos Islands; and at the south-eastern end of the Red Sea and near its entrance to the Indian Ocean.

The red-tailed tropic-bird is not an Atlantic species, but breeds in the Indian and Pacific Oceans over a wide area from Madagascar to the Galapagos Islands and from the oceanic islands off south Japan to the Hawaiian Islands and the Kermadec Islands and northern Australia.

Frigate-Birds

Of all the seabirds the fantastic frigate-birds, with an enormous wing expanse in proportion to their weight, are the most skilful and manœuvrable aviators. Their advanced design serves them well, for they are interceptor fighters in their role as marauders of the skies. Though frigate-birds are true seabirds, they are essentially land based—and hence of value to the natural navigator. If they land on the water for any length of time their plumage actually becomes waterlogged. They eat almost entirely fish, but rarely catch fish themselves. Normally they sit and wait and intercept and rob a returning fish-laden booby or tern. As their victim comes in they take off, gain altitude and power dive at it until it disgorges its belly-load of fish—which the interceptor deftly catches in the air. I have stood on a small Pacific island around sunset and ducked my head from what sounded like a landing aeroplane; it was only a booby trying to land before a frigate-bird could catch up with it.

The frigate-birds are not always easy to distinguish from each other. There are five species in the world, all tropical, which range more or less throughout the coasts and islands that lie in the belt 1800 miles north and south of the Equator. On the west coast of America they range between southern California, and northern Peru and Sala y Gomez Island off the coast of Chile; and in the open Pacific as far north as Hawaii, as far south as New Caledonia, north almost to Japan, south to New Zealand, Tonga, and northern Australia. They are widespread in the tropical parts of the Indian Ocean.

It is altogether exceptional to record a frigate-bird as far as three hundred miles from land; and the presence of any large number of them almost certainly means land within a hundred miles. Since they do not normally settle on the water they shun nights at sea, so that the direction of their flight at dusk will normally be towards land and is well worth observing. Incidentally, frigate-birds have very keen vision; and a bird seen passing at a respectable height above the voyager is extremely likely to be homing directly by sight.

Apropos of frigate-birds, I can cite a good example of the principle I have been trying to establish in this chapter—namely, that there are exceptions to every rule and observations should be as varied as possible before a collection can be made from which conclusions can be drawn. I remember the case of a French doctor who, failing in his attempt to swim the English Channel, sought fame by drifting across the Atlantic on a raft. With him he took my former publication, *The Raft Book*, which was designed to help people adrift at sea during the Second World War. In this book I repeatedly stressed that reliance should not be placed on any *one* sign.

Ignoring these warnings, this doctor put his trust in one single observation of a frigate-bird to estimate his nearness to land. If indeed he correctly identified his bird as a frigate-bird, his observation of it when many miles from land was most exceptional, in view of all the recorded observations of others over many years. Doctor Robert Cushman Murphy expressed the situation well in a recent letter to me:

". . . a storm driven waif once in a thousand years or perhaps in ten thousand years would probably account for the present situation of Frigate Birds of several species distributed widely over the warmer ocean waters. The fact that the distinctness of the present day species is in several distinct oceanic areas is further proof that they are essentially relatively local in their habits."

He added further:

" During the preparation of my book, *Oceanic Birds of*

South America, I ran down many alleged records of Frigate Birds in remote oceanic areas, and I found that an error was involved in nearly all such instances."

Cormorants (or Shags)

There are thirty species of cormorants or shags in the world, not all of which are seabirds, and few, indeed, of which are birds of the open sea. So much is the average cormorant a coastal bird that in olden times it was called the sea-crow or sea-raven and was the shore-sighting bird carried by primitive European navigators. Captain Cook noted that cormorants were never seen more than twenty-five miles from the shore; and all the vast experience of bird watchers in recent times has done no more than confirm this figure. So if the natural navigator sees a cormorant, and better still, cormorants, he is pretty certain to be within twenty-five miles from land.

Cormorants and shags have a very wide range through all parts of the marine world (and some inland waters) except the islands of the central Pacific. On the whole, they are more numerous and have a slightly greater variety of species in the Southern Hemisphere. One particular cormorant is the dominant bird in what is perhaps the greatest community of seabirds in the world; for the guanay or guanay cormorant is the most abundant species all along the bird islands of the guano coast of Chile and Peru.

Cormorants are seldom found on any islands remote from continents, though on the Galapagos islands a peculiar isolated flightless form occurs; and some species have colonised the sub-Antarctic islands in very great numbers.

Gannets and Boobies

Gannets and boobies are always good indicators of land, for they breed in large numbers on many oceanic islands, yet do not normally operate on ration runs far beyond the hundred fathom continental shelf. The family, of which there are nine members, are all great fishermen, and the birds may be seen leaving land on their way to their fishing grounds, especially in the early morning. Normally there is two-way traffic through much of the middle of the day, and in the evening a procession of incomers with their bellies full of the last load of fish for their young.

The visitor to a gannet or booby colony can often walk among the nests, for many species nest on flat ground or even in the branches of bushes. As he walks through, the adults and young often readily disgorge freshly caught or freshly fed fish, no doubt a form of intimidative display.

In these modern days such a habit might seem only in the remotest sense useful to the traveller: at least, this is what I thought myself until one day in the Pacific the whale boat in which I was landing capsized off Baker Island. Our party was unable to return to our schooner for five days, and during this time I used my knowledge of the regurgitating habits of the boobies to provide us with meals of freshly caught and quite edible fish.

The six boobies are of tropical distribution, the three gannets of temperate distribution. Perhaps the most widespread booby is the brown booby, which breeds on the oceanic islands of the tropical Atlantic (not St. Helena), on several islands off the West African coast, on many in the West Indies, and widely in the Pacific from Mexico to Colombia, from Hawaii to the Kermadec Islands, from Formosa to northern Australia. It breeds also on islands on the tropical belt, in the Indian Ocean and in the Red Sea.

Usually the brown booby fishes within a range of about thirty miles from its nesting grounds. The farthest that a single brown booby has been recorded from land is a hundred and twenty miles, in the Caribbean Sea. Normally, it would be pretty safe to assume an outside limit of seventy-five miles from base for several brown boobies seen at sea. At dawn such boobies are likely to be flying from land, at dusk towards it. A dozen or more together are almost certain to be within thirty miles from land.

The red-footed booby breeds on bushes, not on the ground, and is confined to islands which can provide woody vegetation.

Apparently it finds too much difficulty in taking off from the ground. Notwithstanding this limitation, it is rather more widely distributed than the brown booby in the tropical parts of the Indian Ocean and western and central Pacific. It has fewer colonies than the brown booby around the tropical Americas. In the central Atlantic, unlike the brown booby, it may breed on St. Helena.

Red-footed boobies are at their most plentiful within twenty-five miles from base; smaller numbers range to fifty miles and only individuals, and that rarely, beyond seventy-five miles.

The blue-faced or masked booby has a similar distribution to the other species, though the number of colonies known is not quite so great. Like the red-footed booby, it is absent from the islands off the coast of West Africa.

The three boobies that I have just described are the most widespread, and useful maps of the distribution of each of them are published by Fisher and Lockley in their *Sea-Birds* (*New Naturalist*, 1954).

Like the boobies, the gannets seldom wander off the hundred-fathom continental shelf, which means that they are unusual more than a hundred miles to sea and decidedly rare over three hundred miles from the coast. When a gannet is breeding it relieves its mate at the nest at least once a day, and the operational range of adult North Atlantic gannets from their colonies is probably between sixty and ninety miles, a matter of five or six hours' flying and feeding time for this powerful bird: with its six-foot wing-span and seven and a half pounds weight the gannet is the largest seabird of the North Atlantic.

Every colony of the North Atlantic gannet has been found and, indeed, the number of nests of these colonies are now counted every ten years by Fisher, Vevers, Lockley and their colleagues. At the last census in 1949, there was one colony off the coast of Brittany, two in the Channel Islands, one in Wales, three in Ireland, one in England, eight in Scotland, one in Norway, one in The Faroes, five in Iceland; and on the western side of the Atlantic three in the Gulf of St. Lawrence and one on the coast of Newfoundland and two on islands off it. About

100,000 nests were occupied in all in that year. The breeding season of the gannet begins with the arrival of adults as early as January or February in Britain—in March or April in North America. Egg-laying starts in May and the young are away early in September. Young gannets are distinguishable from their white parents, going through various stages of dark plumage in their four years of immaturity. During this period they operate to sea farther than the adults and reach quite a distance down the west coast of Africa. Gannets penetrate the Mediterranean out of season, sometimes even as far as Palestine. Occasionally they reach the Gulf of Mexico on the American side. The winter distribution of the main pack of gannets on the North American eastern seaboard depends somewhat on the state of the Labrador Current. Suffice it to say that the adult gannet is in the nesting season always a good indicator of the direction of land, indeed of a particular rock (for the number of colonies is so limited that we can usually fix a flight line on a particular one). Out of season all gannets, young and old, are certain indicators of the continental shelf.

Very similar to the northern or North Atlantic gannet is the Cape gannet, which breeds on islands off the coast of South Africa from Hollams Bird Island to Algoa Bay, and which in the off-season migrates a considerable distance up the coast of West Africa, sometimes crossing the Equator.

Closely allied also is the Australasian gannet. One race of this breeds on islands in the Bass Strait and around Tasmania, from July to January, and is distributed when young or in the off-season, in the neighbouring seas and as far as Point Cloats in western Australia and Brisbane in Queensland. The other race of the Australasian gannet is confined to New Zealand.

In the season of 1946-47 a census of the dozen or so occupied colonies of the New Zealand gannet (two were off the South Island, all the rest off North Island) showed that the population of this race was between 18,000 and 24,000 pairs. The Australian race nests probably in five colonies only and may total about two thousand pairs.

Pelicans

Of the six pelicans in the world, only one, the brown pelican of America, can seriously be regarded as a seabird. The other great birds, if they do not live inland, are birds of estuaries and lagoons and scarcely ever range out of sight of land. But the brown pelican breeds and roams on the Pacific coast of tropical America from Chile to California and on the Atlantic coast from Florida to the Amazon. Like the gannet, it secures its food by diving from a height, but unlike the gannet it seldom travels to the limit of the continental shelf, except in parts of its range among the guano islands off Chile and Peru. Normally, the brown pelican operates within twenty-five miles from shore and any string of pelicans flying can be regarded as at this distance or less.

In the big gull-wader order of birds six families—the sheath-bills, the phalaropes, the skuas (or jaegers), the gulls, the terns and the auks, are seabirds or mostly so. The sheathbills comprise two curious pigeon-like species confined to the Antarctic and the sub-Antarctic and seldom ranging far from the seabird colonies on which they are modest predators and professional scavengers.

Phalaropes

One of the most extraordinary transitions in nature is found among the waders; for two slight and delicate birds, which breed on the Arctic tundras in the summer (and behave very much like their relations the stints and sandpipers) become—in winter—birds of the open ocean. The grey phalarope, or red phalarope in America, breeds all round the Arctic regions, in a belt somewhat more· northerly than (but much overlapping with) that in which breeds its cousin the red-necked or northern phalarope.

The sea voyager sees the phalaropes in their grey winter plumage, a much more modest dress than that which they wear in the breeding season. The passage south of the grey (or red) phalarope takes place partly over land (at least in the North American continent and western Europe), but also over sea, particularly in the northern half of the North Atlantic. By no means sufficient information has yet come to hand for us to establish the precise wintering places of the bulk of the grey phalarope population. We know that some birds reach South Africa and even New Zealand; but it appears that the bulk of the winterers remain concentrated in three main sea areas. One of these is in the Humboldt Current to the west of the border between Chile and Peru. Another is certainly along the extreme western part of West Africa and around the Cape Verde Islands. A third is in the north-western part of the Indian Ocean and towards the entrance of the Red Sea.

From its rather wider breeding distribution in the Arctic and northern regions of both old and new world, the red-necked phalarope or northern phalarope also migrates south overland and over sea. Probably more individuals of this smaller species than of grey phalaropes take the land route. We can be certain that one of the wintering concentrations of the red-necked phalarope is (like the greys) in the north-western part of the Indian Ocean and the south-east entrance to the Red Sea. Winterers are also seen on the waters of the Persian Gulf and rather widely in the seas of the East Indies, around the Philippines, Borneo, Celebes, the Moluccas and New Guinea. Very few, if any, grey phalaropes winter here.

Only a few red-necked phalaropes appear to migrate to South America and its adjacent seas, or to South and West Africa.

Skuas (or Jaegers)

The skuas are four, all gull-like birds which have become marine birds of prey and which migrate enormous distances, often across the Equator. Only when large numbers of one kind of skua are seen can the navigator infer the presence of nearby land. Small packs may operate hundreds of miles from land when there are other seabirds to parasitise—for the skuas earn much of their living by pursuing other birds and by compelling them to disgorge the contents of their stomachs.

Largest of the skuas is the bonxie or great skua. Like the fulmar it is one of the few bi-polar birds in the world. Its breeding headquarters is in the south. One race actually nests on the Antarctic continent and other forms are found in all the sub-Antarctic islands and as far north as Tristan da Cunha. The species breeds also in the Falkland Islands, in Chile and South Argentina, and in the South Island of New Zealand and its adjoining oceanic islands.

An extraordinary outpost breeds on the other side of the world in the North Atlantic Ocean, where it is confined to the northern part of the British Isles (particularly Shetland), the Faroe Islands and south-east Iceland.

From these bases the great skuas appear to operate widely over the oceans. Individuals of various races have been observed in the Pacific as far as Japan on the west, and British Columbia on the east. Others penetrate into the Indian Ocean nearly as far as the Equator; and great skuas have been seen in the central Atlantic which may have been either from the southern colonies or from the north—nobody has yet been able to find out whether the wandering range of the two widely-separated breeding populations overlaps. Certainly in the North Atlantic the great skua ranges very widely, reaching the eastern seaboard of North America, most of the North Atlantic oceanic islands, Baffin Island, Greenland, Spitsbergen and the north coast of Russia; and individuals have penetrated at least half-way into the Mediterranean and some distance into the Baltic Sea.

The Arctic skua or parasitic jaeger has an entirely northern breeding range, nesting near coasts and also hundreds of miles inland on suitable moors and tundras, widely around the old and new worlds north of latitude 60° N.—and in some cases, as in Kamchatka, south almost to 50° N. From this breeding head-quarters it migrates over land and sea tremendous distances, and has reached islands not far from the Antarctic continent. Undoubtedly a good proportion of the Arctic skuas winter in the tropical seas, but many certainly push on as far as South Africa,

South-East Australia, the South Island of New Zealand and southern South America.

The pomarine or twist-tailed skua or jaeger has a rather more northerly breeding distribution than the Arctic skua and a smaller population. There is no evidence that it penetrates as far south as the Arctic skua, for it has not so far been observed in southern South America or near the Antarctic continent. Certainly a great many winter just north of the Equator in the seas west of the western bulge of Africa. Others also reach South-East Australia and New Zealand.

The smallest of the skuas is the long-tailed skua, which also breeds in the Arctic north. Migrating over land and sea, it does not appear to winter into Asia beyond Japan or to visit Australasia; but it has been recorded in the tropical Atlantic, in West Africa and in South America. There is a considerable mystery, still, about the true wintering headquarters of the long-tailed skua.

Gulls

There are forty-two species of gulls in the world. I might have headed this paragraph " Sea-Gulls," were it not for the fact that about half the gulls in the world (both individuals and species) see relatively little of the sea; and some never see it at all.

Gulls, in fact, are primarily shore birds. Of all the gulls in the world only two species—the kittiwakes—are truly oceanic. Perhaps we should call all the other gulls " shore-gulls."

Most shore-gulls are beach feeders or inland feeders and thrive on seaweed, molluscs, star-fishes, sea-urchins and crustaceans. Inter-tidal feeders, they are also great opportunist scavengers, and to a certain extent predators. They haunt the colonies of other seabirds to pick up anything they can get (and a living egg or young one if possible). Great numbers of gulls of several species have become parasitic on the world's coastal fishing industry, haunting fish-curing wharfs and trawler docks to feed on scraps. Normally, no shore-gull is ever found at a greater distance from the shore than fifty miles, though some members of some species will occasionally work as far as the edge of the continental shelf when this is more than fifty miles from the coast. Most exceptions to this rule occur when gulls follow ships, especially trawlers. Certainly most trawlers of all the nations that work the North Atlantic and Arctic waters carry with them their own wake of expectant gulls (and in some areas also very many fulmars). Most gulls will leave an ordinary vessel before it gets out of sight of land, and return to their scavenging occupation on the shore; but they do not always leave a trawler or drifter, and it seems that quite regularly gulls will accompany the Fleetwood and Milford Haven trawlers right out through the north entrance to the Irish Sea and all the further 250 to 300 miles to the Rockall Bank. James Fisher has even once seen a black-headed gull at Rockall—and the black-headed gull is the most inland of all the British gulls, and must have needed a strong stimulus to go so far out of sight of land.

The commonest gull of the Northern Hemisphere is the herring-gull, though in parts of western Europe its close relation, the lesser black-backed gull, is almost as common. The herring-gull has a very wide distribution on the coasts and to a certain extent also the inland rivers and lakes of the north temperate and sub-Arctic regions of all the lands around the North Pole. It migrates to a certain extent in the autumn, though not as far as the lesser black-backed, ranging mostly coastwise in rather desultory exploration of new territory.

Many of the big light-headed gulls are dark-mantled and dark-winged. The southern black-backed, Dominican or kelp-gull is the only large black-backed and wholly white-tailed gull in the Southern Hemisphere. It is darker on the mantle than any other gull, even the great black-backed of the Northern Hemisphere. It breeds in southern South America, South Africa and New Zealand, on Tristan da Cunha and Gough Island, and on practically all of the chain of sub-Antarctic islands that embraces the Antarctic continent.

About half the gulls of the world are dark-hooded or at least assume chocolate or black heads in the breeding season. A typical example is the handsome laughing gull of North America. This breeds in Central America, the Caribbean, and northwards on the west to Southern California, on the east to New England, and coasts south in the autumn to winter as far as Brazil and northern Peru.

A typical resident coastal gull of the Southern Hemisphere is the silver gull, which is found on the South African coast north to about 30° S. and is also common in New Caledonia, Australia, Tasmania, New Zealand and some of its satellite oceanic islands such as the Chatham and Auckland Islands.

As previously mentioned, the only gulls which are truly oceanic birds are kittiwakes. Of the two species, the red-legged kittiwake is extremely rare and as far as is known breeds only in three small island groups in the Bering Sea. But the common kittiwake has a wide breeding range in the North Pacific and North Atlantic Oceans and adjacent parts of the Arctic. Indeed, the kittiwake's breeding distribution extends to the northernmost high Arctic lands: it is a very successful species. To the south it breeds in the Atlantic as far as the Gulf of St. Lawrence on the west and Brittany on the east. Its breeding range on the Pacific does not extend beyond western Alaska and the Kurile Islands.

Much has yet to be learned about the kittiwake's distribution at sea and its life cycle. It is certainly true that the kittiwake is absent or at least exceptionally rare in mid-Atlantic from mid-June to mid-August. In the winter kittiwakes wander freely in the North Atlantic, reaching latitudes much farther south than do the fulmars. Some even reach 24° N. occasionally. At all times of year kittiwakes are very common off both eastern and western Atlantic seaboards between 40° and 50° N.

Terns and Noddies—with a note on Skimmers

There are thirty-nine kinds of terns in the world and three kinds of the closely-allied but peculiar skimmers. Terns are smaller and more swallow-like than the gulls and are not difficult to identify as a family. They usually breed in large colonies, sometimes—in the tropics—*very* large colonies. Terns of one kind or another are found almost from Pole to Pole; and one species in particular, the Arctic tern, makes what are certainly the longest migratory journeys of any bird.

The most beautiful of all the seabirds, in my opinion, is the white tern, with its streamlined delicate appearance. It was in 1935 that I first saw these tropical terns—on Palmyra, an island eleven hundred miles south of the Hawaiian Islands. The lovely creatures were so tame that when I tried to photograph them they hovered around my head too close for a clear snapshot. The white tern builds no nest, yet nests on shrubs and trees. It just lays its egg on a round branch, fixing it with a sticky mixture of its own making.

The white tern seldom operates farther than forty miles to sea, and is therefore a useful indicator of land, for the voyager who sees several together can be pretty sure of his maximum distance from land.

The white tern breeds on the oceanic islands of the South Atlantic just south of the Equator (Fernando Noronha, South Trinidad, Ascension and St. Helena) in the Seychelles in the Indian Ocean and probably on some other archipelagos, and in many islands in the Pacific Ocean, from Laysan in the north to the Kermadecs in the south.

Perhaps the most typical of the tropical terns—certainly the most abundant—are the noddy and sooty terns. These wander more than the white tern, and their presence over the seas is by no means a sure indication of the nearness of land. The sooty tern is the more venturesome of the two and ranges farther off-shore. A lot remains to be discovered about the distribution at sea of these two species. Both species are almost confined, in and out of the breeding season, to the belt of the world between the Tropics of Cancer and Capricorn, though both breed a short distance north of the Tropic of Cancer in the Dry Tortugas off Florida, the only tropical seabird colony in the United States of America. The breeding season of the sooty tern differs much from one place to another, and on Ascension Island is not annual, but at approximately ten-month intervals.

The Arctic tern is typical of a largish group of black-capped terns. It has been proved by ringing that an Arctic tern hatched in West Greenland can double the Cape of Good Hope and reach Natal on the east coast of South Africa in the autumn of the same year, a distance by sea of over eleven thousand miles. The breeding distribution of the Arctic tern extends to the highest Arctic regions from the north temperate and sub-Arctic regions all round the Pole. From these high latitudes many individuals migrate all the way to the Antarctic continent. The Atlantic element of this migrant population crosses from the American Arctic to the west coast of Africa by flying the North Atlantic diagonally from north-west to south-east. It can be understood that on migration the Arctic tern cannot be relied on as an indicator of the nearness of land.

In general, terns are rarely seen on the water because they are poor swimmers. They prefer to hover over schools of fish and crustacea, making quick swoops to the surface (or just below it) for their prey. Nobody has ever seen an Arctic tern alight on the North Atlantic during its long migration across that ocean; but terns at sea will sometimes rest on any driftwood available, or on ships.

The curious skimmers, of which there are three species in the world, can scarcely be described as seabirds. They are usually denizens of tropical estuaries and enclosed lagoons, as well as rivers and other fresh waters. Occasionally they will feed in the shallows offshore, but never do so, as far as I am aware, out of sight of land. With their curiously elongated lower mandibles, the skimmers fly to and fro ploughing a furrow in the water. It is commonly believed that they feed in this way, but Dr. Robert Cushman Murphy points out that during this manœuvre their bill is usually closed. He considers that the skimmer " ploughs the main " with its bright-red bill in order to lure small fish to the surface, which it catches by doubling on its tracks.

Auks

Our last family of seabirds certainly originated in evolution in the northern part of the Pacific Ocean, possibly the Bering Sea, for in those waters the auks attain to-day their greatest diversity. Essentially auks are seabirds which have specialised in being able to fly both over and under the surface of the water. They manage to swim with their wings with great skill and at a speed which approaches, though does not attain, that of a penguin.

On the whole, all the members of the auk family—puffins, guillemots and auklets—operate from their bases to the edge of the continental shelf, and are seldom found more than about seventy miles from shore unless the continental shelf extends farther. Very rarely are any species seen over deep waters or in mid-ocean.

The largest surviving members of the auk family are the puffins. The tufted puffin of the Pacific has a wide distribution from the Bering Sea to California, and is a familiar bird to most visitors to the western seaboard of the U.S.A. In the Pacific is also found the handsome horned puffin which has a close counterpart in the common puffin of the North Atlantic. Though puffins, like most other auks, seldom operate beyond the continental shelf, individuals quite often appear to cross the long deeps between the Scottish continental shelf and the isolated Rockall Bank; and there have been a few transatlantic recoveries of marked puffins. Thus the observation of a few puffins cannot safely be relied on to indicate the nearness or direction of land.

The Atlantic puffin moves a fair distance south in the winter, and at that time quite a number can reach not only the Canaries but the Azores, which involves them in at least a half-Atlantic crossing, during which they probably swim as great a distance as they fly.

Abundant are the two members of the guillemot or murre genus. Both species are found in the North Pacific, the North Atlantic and parts of the Arctic Ocean in between, though the Arctic guillemot is alone found in the higher latitudes as a breeder.

I use the name " Arctic guillemot " to avoid a good deal of confusion; because in the Atlantic this species is known as Brünnich's
guillemot or Brünnich's murre, and in the Pacific as Pallas's
murre. Similarly the more southern species, the common guillemot or common murre, is known in the Pacific as the California
murre. Neither of these two guillemots often operates farther
than the edge of the continental shelf. Of the two the Arctic
guillemot in the winter is the more likely to penetrate towards
the deep ocean. In places where the continental shelf extends an
unusual distance, such as the south-easterly edge of the Grand
Banks, both guillemots (but particularly the Arctic guillemot)
can be sometimes abundant, and occasionally, in the summer,
rather large numbers of the Arctic guillemot have been seen east
of the southern tip of Greenland nearly a hundred and fifty miles
from land and over rather deep water. But normally both species
coast in the off-season and pursue fish by diving to fair depths in
the coastal waters above the shelf.

There is a fair confusion between the two sides of the Atlantic
over the vernacular names of some of the auks. In America the
word guillemot is used almost exclusively to describe the black
guillemot (or, as it is called in the Pacific, the pigeon-guillemot).
This widespread Arctic and sub-Arctic species is a particularly
resident and coastal bird, staying near its breeding places in the
winter even in the Arctic, where it can find a living in the " leads "
in the floe ice. The natural navigator should learn this bird in
both its distinctive summer and subtle winter plumage, for it is
a very useful indicator of the proximity of land, feeding as it does
in shallows, hardly ever migrating, and living a somewhat self-
sufficient life in pairs and little flocks—never in big packs.

In contrast to the black guillemot, the little auk—the smallest
of the auk family in the North Atlantic—is perhaps the least
coastal of the Atlantic auks. Breeding in the high Arctic, it moves
far south of the edge of the sea ice only in some winters, when it
may suddenly invade more southerly seas in exceptional numbers.
Interested as it is, more in ice-edge than land-edge, it can be seen
(in winter particularly) quite frequently in mid-ocean and in fair
numbers.

In the Pacific the little auk has many counterparts which, like it, are plankton (mainly crustacean) feeders. The crested and paroquet auklets are not often seen in great numbers off the continental shelves, and when moving out of the breeding season tend to coast or island-hop. They are fairly reliable indicators of the proximity of coasts throughout the year.

Smallest of the auk family is the tiny least auklet. Like the crested and paroquet auklets, this breeds in and around the Bering Sea, the home of the auks. In winter it coasts out of the Bering Sea as far as the sea of Okhotsk and the islands north-east of Formosa; on the American side of the North Pacific as far as the State of Washington.

1. WANDERING ALBATROSS. 1a. *Swimming.* Adult albatross, principally white, with black and white markings on upper parts of wings and tail; sides of head usually have pink or orange patch; bill, pink or yellow.

Young albatross, mostly brown and black on top of wings, white underneath.

This, the largest of the albatrosses, has a maximum wing span of a little more than 11 feet. The Wandering Albatross is similar to royal and other predominantly white southern albatrosses.

2. SOOTY ALBATROSS. Adult, sooty grey or brown, darkest on wings and head, black bill and flesh-coloured feet. Younger birds similar except for white markings on neck.

It is representative of the dark southern albatrosses.

3. BLACK-FOOTED ALBATROSS. 3a. *End view.* Adult, sooty-brown, with white around reddish-brown bill. Feet black.

Young similar but with lighter upper parts. ·

From the descriptions of this albatross and ones depicted in figures 1 and 2, any of other ten species may be identified as belonging to albatross family.

4. KERMADEC PETREL. 4a. *End view.* Body, brown above, with either white or dark under surface. Head sometimes white; white patches on under side of wing tips. Bill, black. Feet, black or yellow.

The Kermadec Petrel is similar to the many other petrels and shearwaters that have white underparts.

5. SHORT-TAILED SHEARWATER. Head. tail feathers and upper parts of body, sooty-black; under surface, sooty-brown; bill, blackish-brown; feet purplish-black. General appearance similar to Sooty Shearwater and to other dark petrels and shearwaters.

6. FULMAR. 6a. *On water:* 6b. *End view,* Head, neck and under surface, white, with dark spot in front of eye. Bill, grey, green or yellow. Upper part of tail, pearl grey. Main upper surface wing, slate-grey with whitish patch. Feet, grey or flesh-coloured. High Arctic colour phase in Atlantic much darker, greyish blue replacing white. In Pacific this colour phase has more *southerly* distribution than white phase.

Although somewhat similar in colour to many gulls, the fulmar should not be confused with them. Its flight is quite distinctive, much more stiff-winged and dynamically soaring. It glides much greater distances than gulls, much more swiftly, and in gliding its wings are held stiffly almost straight out: those of gliding gulls are " angled."

Plate VI

7. NORTH ATLANTIC GANNET. 7a. *End view*. Body, mainly white; head and neck, yellow with patch of dark blue skin on throat; quill feathers blackish-brown; bill, white; feet, black.

Young, dark greyish-brown above with white spots, and white underneath.

8. AUSTRALASIAN GANNET. Adult similar in appearance to North Atlantic and Cape Gannets, but with outer tail feathers white and central tail feathers greyish-brown. Head, yellow with slate blue patch of naked skin, on throat. Bill, slate-coloured; feet, greyish-black.

Young, white spotted greyish-brown above, and white underneath, with brown blotches on throat and sides.

9. RED-FOOTED BOOBY (*White phase*). 9a. (*Grey phase*). Adult, generally white with variable yellowish tint on head, neck, back and tail. Outer wing feathers, dark brown with tapering band of brown along rear edge of wing. Tail, longest of any of boobies. Bill, in males, blue with red at base. Legs and feet, both sexes, red. Young, generally brownish.

A variation of this bird, found in great numbers among those with white plumage, is predominantly grey with dark brown wing tips and white tail. This grey phase is shown in 9a.

This same bird may also be seen with brown colouring and white tail. It can be distinguished from the masked or blue-faced booby by its smaller size and bright red feet.

10. MASKED OR BLUE-FACED BOOBY. Adult plumage, white, except for dark brown wing tips, tail and rear half of wing. Skin of face, black; bill, horn colour with bright orange at base in males and pink or light red in females; legs and feet, olive drab in males, and lead colour in females. Young birds have head, neck and upper parts smoky-brown, somewhat mixed with white feathers.

Being larger than any of the other boobies, it may be distinguished from the red-footed booby, and although the feet may vary in colour, they are never red. It may also be recognised by its black tail.

11. BROWN BOOBY. Head, neck and chest, chocolate brown; under parts of body and wing white with paler brown under wing towards tip; top of wing pale brown; base of bill yellow, and bluish-white towards tip; legs and feet yellow.

Young birds, greyish-brown above, slightly lighter on belly and darker on breast. General effect, brownish-grey instead of white. Bills, darker than those of adults.

12. RED-TAILED TROPIC-BIRD. 12a. *Turning in flight*. Adult, silky-white, sometimes with rosy tinge on back; distinct black crescent before and over eye; black bar on wings; wings and tail streaked with black; two long, slender, deep red feathers extending from tail, a length of about 18 inches or more; bill, yellow or red.

12a shows red-tailed tropic-bird in flight using its tail feathers and foot in a characteristic turn.

Young similar but with very short tail feathers.

The white-tailed tropic-bird is mainly white with rosy tinge; black crescent in front and over eyes; black feathers on wings; a long tail up to 21 inches in length; yellow, black or red bill; yellow legs and toes; and black feet.

Young, smaller and without long tail feathers.

The red-billed tropic-bird is white, with black band through eyes; black bars on upper parts and on wings. Tail feathers are white and up to about 20 inches in length; bill, red or orange; legs and toes, yellowish or greyish-white; feet, black.

The young are smaller, but with more black on head and tail and with short tail feathers.

The red-tailed tropic-bird is illustrated as representative of the three species which are found around the warm waters in all oceans. The white-tailed tropic-bird and the red-billed tropic-bird are very similar in appearance to the red-tailed species, the main distinction being that the white-tailed is smaller, and the red-billed has a wavy barred back.

Plate VII

13. FRIGATE-BIRD (white breasted). 13a. *Frigate-Bird (dark)*; 13b. *End view.* Adult, black, with very long wings, long forked tail, and short legs. Some adult frigate-birds have white areas underneath. Bill, long and slender with sharp hook at end.

The young have white heads.

Frigate-birds are most easily recognised of all seabirds, but in normal flight the tail is not spread and its forked nature is not always apparent. When the birds are manœuvring in the air they frequently open and close the tail with a scissor-like effect.

14. CORMORANT. 14a. *Swimming.* Plumage, glossy-green, or bluish-black; face and under part of bill white; bill and naked skin of face yellow; feet, black.

The common cormorant has black plumage in Europe, Asia and Australia, but some species in tropical and southern Africa have white breasts.

Young, brownish-black with usually lighter colour and sometimes white underneath.

The numerous members of the cormorant family vary somewhat in colour but are otherwise similar in appearance.

15. JACKASS PENGUIN. 15a. *Swimming.* Bluish-grey or black above and white below. Narrow band of black, in shape of horseshoe across breast and sides; white spot on tail; bill long and thick, feet black.

Young have upper parts black with white underneath.

The jackass penguin, named for noisy braying sound it makes whether ashore or afloat, is found along the coasts of South Africa as far north as 16° South of Equator. There are sixteen other species of penguins all similar in general appearance to jackass penguin, but differing in size, the arrangement of black and white on face and throat, and colour of bill and feet.

16. BROWN PELICAN. Back of head, white; front and top of head, yellow; neck and back, brown; under parts, greyish-brown; wings, black-brown with grey; skin around eye, blue; bill, greyish; feet, black.

Other species of pelicans are similar in outline and general appearance.

17. GREAT SKUA. Plumage, dark greyish-brown; conspicuous white patches underneath wings; heavy build. Short, square tail, stout curved upper bill.

Young are similar but with slightly different markings.

18. ARCTIC SKUA. Top of head, greyish-brown; rest of head, white; tail and upper parts of wings greyish-brown; neck and under parts, white. At times the arctic skua is completely sooty-brown except for neck which is tinged with yellow. Tail, long and wedge-shaped with long projecting central tail feathers.

The arctic skua is similar to the long-tailed and pomarine skuas.

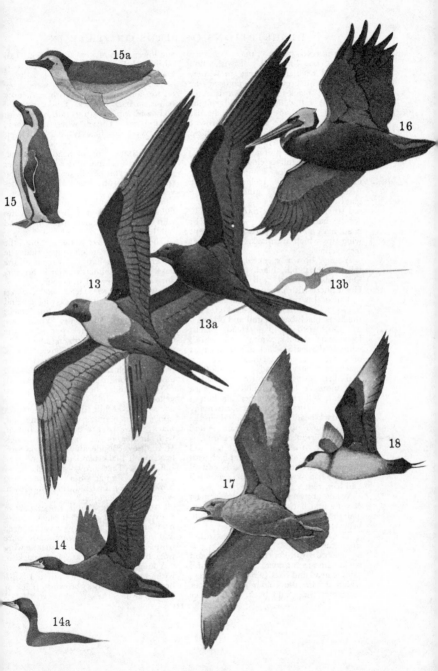

Plate VIII

19. HERRING-GULL. *19a. Swimming* *19b. End view.* Large sea-gulls with white head and neck in summer; in winter, speckled with grey; white underneath; tail white; black feathers towards outer wing tips; bill, yellow feet; flesh colour.

Young have greyish-brown heads; streaked with white and light brown; greyer underneath; tail, brownish-black, spotted with white. Young, distinguished by their very dark plumage.

The herring-gull is closely related to many other species, among them the California gull, the Iceland gull, the lesser black-backed gull and the glaucous-winged gull.

20. SOUTHERN BLACK-BACKED GULL. Adult, back and above wings, black; head, neck and under parts white, except wing tips which are black. Bill, yellow; feet, yellow.

Young, brown, speckled with white; tail blackish; bill, black; feet, brown. Only black-backed gull in Southern Hemisphere with pure white tail.

This gull is similar in appearance and habits to the great black-backed gull, the lesser black-backed gull and others.

21. LAUGHING GULL. Head, black; lower part of neck, white; tail, white; white underneath; back and upper part of wing, dark grey. Top of wing tips, black in winter; head, white mottled with brownish-grey on top and sides; eyes more or less surrounded by dark crescent. Bill, red in summer, blackish in winter; feet, brown. It is similar to many other dark-headed gulls, among them the black-headed gull of western Europe and the Mediterranean black-headed gull.

22. SILVER GULL. Head, dark; tail and under parts, white; wing tips, black with prominent white patch towards end of the tip. Top of wing and back, grey; bill and feet, red.

Young are very similar but upper part of wing and back, speckled with brown. Tail has a narrow brown band; bill, brown; feet, grey.

This gull is similar to several other small gulls.

23, 23a. COMMON KITTIWAKE. Head and neck, white in summer; winter, top and sides of head and back of neck, dark grey, which is also the colour of the upper surface of wings and back. Both upper

and lower parts of wing tips, black. Tail white; bill, greenish-yellow; feet, blackish.

Young have white heads, some grey on top and lower part, with dark grey bands on back of neck. Under parts of body and wings, white; tail, white with black band. Top of wings and back, grey. Wing tips, black; bill, black; feet, brown.

24. SKIMMER. Top of head and neck, black; forehead and under parts, white; tail, mostly white; bill, bright vermilion red with black tip; legs and feet, orange-vermilion.

Young, similar but with upper parts, light brown streaked with greyish-white with black spots; under parts white; and bill, legs, and feet, dull red.

The skimmer has a unique bill, the lower part being much longer than the upper and both flattened except at the base. Other skimmers similar in appearance differ somewhat in colour.

25. WHITE TERN. Head, body, wings and tail, white with black ring around eyes, and long forked tail. Bill, black; feet, black or light blue. Young are similar, but with a black spot behind the eye and black streaks in wing and tail.

26. ARCTIC TERN. *26a. Sitting.* Top of head, black; throat, breast and under parts, pale neutral grey; tail, very long and dark grey; bill, rich red; feet, coral red.

Young similar but with black-tipped yellow bill.

27. NODDY. Adult, dark brown above; upper main feathers of wing and tail, black; lower part of body, dark brown, with lighter brown under the wings. Head, grey, considerably lighter on forehead, with black band in front of eyes. Bill, black. Feet, brownish-black.

Young, similar but lighter and browner. Top of head, greyish-brown, white line above eyes.

28. SOOTY TERN. Adult, upper part of body, wings and tail, dull black. Forehead and side of head, lower part of neck and under parts of wings and body, pure white. Wings, greyish underneath wing tips. Bill, black; legs and feet, blackish.

Young, upper parts, deep sooty-brown, with upper tail surface tipped with brownish white. Bill, brownish-black or dark brown.

Plate IX

29. COMMON DIVING-PETREL. 29a. *Swimming*. Upper surface, black; wings, glossy black, tinged brown; under wing, tinged grey; sides, mouse grey; under neck and breast, dark grey. Bill, black; legs and feet, bluish.

30. 30a. WILSON'S PETREL. Generally blackish-brown, paler on throat, belly and under wings; darkest on wings and tail; square tail conspicuously white above; legs, long and black; feet, yellow.

31. TRISTAN GREAT SHEARWATER. Head above line from bill, dark sooty-brown; rest of body, sooty-brown; neck, white; under part, white, with brown patch on belly; under wings, white with brown streaks; bill, dark; feet, flesh colour.

32. MANX SHEARWATER. Body, including head, wings and tail, sooty-black; cheeks and behind ears, sides of neck and breast, speckled grey or sooty-brown ; under wings and body, white; dark under tail; bill, black; feet, flesh colour.

33. SOOTY STORM-PETREL. Body, sooty; wings, blackish-brown; tail, forked, upper surface greyish, with white shafts; bill and feet, black.

34. GREY PHALAROPE. In winter, head, neck and under parts, white; back of head and around eyes, slate; upper parts, light bluish-grey, darker on wings and tail. In summer, female, tip of head and below bill, dark grey. In male top of head and back of neck streaked black and buff; cheeks, white; neck and under parts, reddish-brown; back, buff striped with black; under wings, white; bill, yellow; feet, yellowish. Short bill and white-barred wing always identifies.

35. RED-NECKED PHALAROPE. In winter: forehead, sides of head, neck, under parts, white; sides of chest, mixed pale grey; top of head, greyish with blackish spot in front of eye; upper parts, grey. In summer: upper part slate; back striped with light brown, white bar on wing; under parts, white; bill, black; feet, bluish-grey.

36. TUFTED PUFFIN. 36a. *Swimming* (*winter plumage*). Upper parts, sooty-black with yellow on side of head; under wings, brownish-grey; under body, greyish-brown. Forehead and around eyes white; bill, very large, salmon red tip, olive green base; skin on side of bill, vermilion; feet, salmon-red.

37. HORNED PUFFIN. 37a. *Swimming* (*winter plumage*). Crown, greyish-brown; neck and upper parts, black; sides of face, white in summer, grey in winter. Underparts, white but brownish-grey towards wing tips. Bill, large and brownish-red; feet vermilion. Similar to Atlantic puffin, it breeds and ranges in about same areas as tufted puffin. The Atlantic puffin differs in its large triangular bright beak, greyish-blue base, vermilion tip, crossed with yellow.

38. 38a. COMMON GUILLEMOT. 38b. *Swimming* (*winter plumage*). Head, neck, upper parts, sooty-brown; breast, underparts, white; bill, long, black and pointed; feet, bluish. Arctic guillemot has a stouter bill.

39. PIGEON-GUILLEMOT. 39a. *Swimming* (*winter plumage*). In summer, sooty-black, with white under wings barred with black. In winter, wings often all black. Bill, black; feet, vermilion. Black guillemot in Atlantic and Arctic.

40. CRESTED AUKLET. Upper parts, slate-black, black crest on greyish forehead, long white feathers behind eye and across face. Under parts, brownish-grey; bill, short, orange-red, whitish tip; feet, pale violet-grey. Young, no crest or feathers on face.

41. PAROQUET AUKLET. Slate above; white plumes behind eyes and across face in summer; throat, front of neck, sides dull grey in summer, white in winter; greyish-brown under wings; white under body; bill, short and orange-red, lower part curved upwards; feet, bluish-grey.

42. LEAST AUKLET. Slate-black above. Shoulders partly white; in summer, white-pointed feathers on forehead, behind eyes and across face. In winter, white and grey; cheeks and under bill, dark slate; mostly white under body; bill, small, dark, with reddish tip; feet, brown.

43. CAPE PIGEON. Black and white petrel with chequered back. General body colour black; head, top of wings and feet, sides of face and neck, black, except for speckled throat; rest of back and upper tail surfaces, white. Feathers have black spots at end, giving speckled appearance.

Plate X

BIRD PLATE NO.	NAME OF BIRD	HABITAT PAGE NO.	TIME OF YEAR	NUMBER SEEN AT ONE TIME	REASONABLE ASSUMPTION
vi	Wandering Albatross, Sooty, and other Southern Albatrosses	178	Any month	Any number	May be far from land
vi	Black-footed and Laysan Albatross	178	April-October November-March	Any number 12 or more	May be far from land Within 100 miles of breeding place
vi	Kermadec Petrel	183	Any month	6 or less Increasing numbers	May be far from land Show proximity to land Direction of flight at dawn and dusk shows direction of land
vi	Short-tailed Shearwater	180	November-March April-October	6 or more Any number	Within 100 miles of breeding places. Direction of flight at dawn and dusk gives direction of land, and increasing numbers show proximity to land. May be far from land
vi	Fulmar	181	During Northern Summer During Northern Winter—all across Atlantic All year	6 or less Any number Increasing numbers	May be far from land May be far from land Show proximity to land
x	Cape Pigeon	182	Any month	Any number Increasing numbers	May be far from land Show proximity to land
vii	North Atlantic Gannet Australasian Gannet Cape Gannet	189-92	Any month	Exceptional cases of single birds 3 or more	Up to 300 miles Up to 100 miles
vii	Red-footed Booby	191	Any month	3 or more 6 or more 12 or more	Within 75 miles Within 50 miles Within 25 miles
vii	Masked (Blue-faced) Booby	191	Any month	3 or more 6 or more 12 or more	Within 75 miles Within 50 miles Within 25 miles

BIRD PLATE NO.	NAME OF BIRD	HABITAT PAGE NO.	TIME OF YEAR	NUMBER SEEN AT ONE TIME	REASONABLE ASSUMPTION
vii	Brown Booby	191	Any month	1 bird (only 1 case recorded—Caribbean Sea)	120 miles
				3 or more	75 miles
				6 or more	Usually within 30 miles
vii	Tropic-Birds Red-tailed ⎫ Red-billed ⎬ White-tailed ⎭	186	Any month	1 or 2	May be far from land
				3 or more	60-80 miles
viii	Frigate-Bird	187	Any month	3 or more	100 miles
				6 or more	Within 75 miles. The direction of flight of *even* 1 bird at dusk generally points to land, as they *never* sleep on the water
viii	Cormorants	189	Any month	Any number	25 mile limit
viii	Penguins	177	Any month	Any number	May be far from land throughout the year—except when breeding
				Increasing numbers	Show approach to breeding places
viii	Brown, or other Pelicans	193	Any month	More than one	25-mile limit; usually much less.
				Increasing numbers	Show approach to land
viii	Great Skua	195	Summer months either hemisphere	Increasing numbers	Show proximity to land
			Winter months either hemisphere	Any number	May be far from land
viii	Other Skuas	195-6	October-May	Any number	Far out
			June-September	Any number	Close to land (north of Arctic Circle)
xi	Herring-Gull and all other Gulls except the Kittiwake	196-8	Any month	3 or more	50 miles (or within the 100-fathom line off coasts)
				Increasing numbers	Show approach to land

BIRD PLATE NO.	NAME OF BIRD	HABITAT PAGE NO.	TIME OF YEAR	NUMBER SEEN AT ONE TIME	REASONABLE ASSUMPTION
ix	Kittiwake	198	April-July	6 or more	Close to shore Within 50 miles
			August-March	Any number	May be far at sea
ix	Black Skimmer	200	Any month	1 or more	Within 25 miles
ix	White Tern	199	Any month	1 or more	Within 40 miles
ix	Arctic Tern	200	May-July	6 or more	(Arctic)—close to shore within 100 miles
			December-February	6 or more	(South and Antarctic) close to shore within 100 miles
			Remainder of year	Any number	May be far at sea
ix	Noddy, Sooty and other Terns, except White Terns	199	Any month	Any number	May be far at sea
x	Diving-Petrels	185	July-November	6 or more	Within 75 miles
			Remainder of year	Any number	May be far at sea
x	Storm-Petrels in Southern Hemisphere	180	December-February	6 or more	Within 75 miles
			Remainder of yr.	Any number	May be far at sea
	Storm-Petrels in Northern Hemisphere		June-August	6 or more	Within 75 miles
			Remainder of yr.	Any number	May be far at sea
x	Tristan Great Shearwater	184	Beginning of October to middle of May	6 or more	100 miles
			Remainder of year	Any number Greater nos. Smaller nos.	May be far at sea Inshore Far out
x	Manx Shearwater	184	April-August	3 or more 12 or more	Within 200 miles Within 100 miles Direction of flight at dawn and dusk gives direction of land
			September-March	Increasing numbers	Show proximity to land

BIRD PLATE NO.	NAME OF BIRD	HABITAT PAGE NO.	TIME OF YEAR	NUMBER SEEN AT ONE TIME	REASONABLE ASSUMPTION
x	Other Shear-waters, Southern Hemisphere, except Short-tailed Shearwater	183	December to February	3 or more 12 or more	Within 200 miles Within 100 miles Direction of flight at dawn and dusk gives direction of land
			Remainder of year	Any number	May be far from land
x	Sooty Storm-Petrel	180	January Remainder of year	6 or more 3 or less	100 miles May be more than 200 miles off shore
x	Grey Phalarope or Red-necked Plalarope	193	June-July August-November February-May December-January	3 or more Any number Any number 3 or more	75 miles May be far from land (migrating) May be far from land (migrating) 75 miles
x	Tufted Puffin, Horned Puffin, Atlantic Puffin, Common Guillemot	201	Any month	3 or more 6 or more	Within 150 miles Direction of flight at dawn and dusk shows direction of land 70 miles. Direction of flight at dawn and dusk shows direction of land
x	Arctic or Brün-nich's Guillemot or Pallas's Murre (similar to Common Guillemot)	202	May and June Any month	Any number Increasing numbers	Limit of 220 miles in Atlantic, and then off Grand Banks Show proximity to land
x	Black Guillemots and Auklets	202	Any month	1 or more 6 or more	50 miles 25 miles

East   *West*

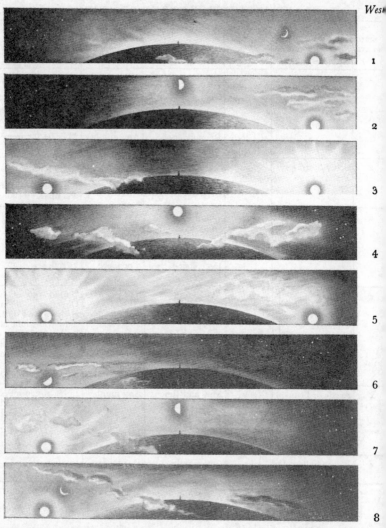

1
2
3
4
5
6
7
8

Plate XI. 1. New crescent moon (waxing) always close behind the sun. 2. First quarter moon at highest point (north or south) as sun is setting. 3. When full moon is rising the sun is always setting. 4. Full moon always at its highest point (north or south) at midnight. 5. When the full moon is setting the sun is always rising. 6. Last quarter moon always rises at midnight. 7. Last quarter moon at highest point (i.e., directly north or south) at sunrise. 8. Old crescent moon (waning) rises at dawn just before the sun.

CHAPTER XXII

WHAT THE MOON CAN TELL YOU

MANY PEOPLE travel at night, from fishermen to foresters, from campers to cross-country walkers. All these sportsmen and natural navigators will find that the moon can be an effective guide. For the moon can give direction, the time of night, and light. On all but a few nights in the month anybody can travel at night in reasonably clear weather with confidence in his ability to find his way by the moon.

The moon produces no light itself; it shines only by the reflection of the light of the sun and (to a very minor extent) other heavenly bodies. The illuminated surface of the moon will thus always point towards the sun and will show the sun's position even when it has set. An imaginary line through the horns of the crescent moon will always lie more or less north and south. A perpendicular erected on the mid-point of this line will point through the illuminated side to the sun's position, whether it is above or below the horizon.

Only in certain places, and at certain times of year, does the sun rise in the precise east and set in the precise west. But quite accurate directions can be obtained from the moon by an observer who knows the true direction and time of sunset or sunrise, or who can work them out from the information in the following chapter.

The full moon is always directly opposite the sun; it rises as the sun sets, reaches its highest point at midnight, sets as the sun rises next morning. A waxing half-moon one week old (called " first quarter ") rises when the sun is at its highest peak, that is at noon. The first quarter moon will in its turn reach its own highest peak in the heavens at sunset. A waning half-moon three weeks old ("last quarter") rises at midnight and reaches its highest point at sunrise. (See Plate XI, facing page 202.)

It is important to keep in mind that the moon rises and sets an average of approximately fifty minutes later every night.

The "age of the moon" corresponds directly to the shape and size of its illuminated or shining area. The moon takes a little over seven days to grow from the slimmest hair-line crescent to a perfect half-moon; a little over seven days more and it is completely full, in yet another seven days and a bit it has waned into an old half-moon; and at the end of the full cycle of about twenty-nine and a half days it has completed the cycle by diminishing into a new moon again. It is worth setting out the moon's ages (correct to the nearest day) in the form of a table:

New Moon is	0	days of age
First Quarter is	7	,, ,, ,,
Full Moon is	15	,, ,, ,,
Last Quarter is	22	,, ,, ,,
New Moon is	30	,, ,, ,,

An observer who has become familiar with the face of the moon above his homeland is often surprised when he travels to a different latitude, for he will instantly note that the surface features are tilted. All heavenly bodies appear upside down in the Southern Hemisphere to people who come from the north; and the moon is no exception to this rule.

The natural navigator planning a night journey is not however, particularly interested in which way up the moon appears to be. But he is often anxious to predict the time at which the moon will rise; how much of a moon there will be; and the period of night in which he can expect to benefit from its light. As we will see, it is quite easy to commit to memory enough information to work the necessary prediction out quite simply.

By way of example, let us suppose that we wish to find the age of the moon for 16th August, 1956. We need but one piece only of given information—the age of the moon on a known previous date. We know, then, that the age of the moon on 1st March, 1955, was seven days; and can base the whole of our reckoning on this fact.

For each full year of twelve months following 1st March, 1955, we add eleven days to this number (seven). If the sum of these two numbers exceeds thirty, we subtract thirty. The age of the moon on 1st March, 1956, is therefore 7 + 11 = 18 days.

For each month following March, including the month in question (in this case August), we add one further day. For each day of our required date in the month we also add one day. If the final sum exceeds thirty once more we subtract thirty.

Thus on 16th August, 1956, the age of the moon would be:

                18 days on 1st March, 1956.
        Plus 5   ,,   April, May, June, July, August
        Plus 16   ,,   for 16th August.
              ──
                39   ,,
        Less 30   ,,
              ──

The moon therefore would be 9 days old.

Now this calculation may appear involved. Anyone who has been through it, however, will see that it is necessary to remember only the age of the moon on a previous first of March and the numbers 11 and 30.

From our discovery, by this method of calculation, that the moon was nine days old on 16th August, 1956, we can predict the amount of light. At nine days the moon is two days past the first quarter. Thus, provided the sky is clear, the light will be considerable. We can also easily work out the period in which the light will be available; for a first quarter moon rises when the sun is overhead and will itself be overhead at sunset. Since the moon rises an average of fifty minutes later each day, at two days past first quarter it will rise approximately at 1.40 p.m. and will be overhead at approximately 7.52 p.m.

Let us suppose then that we wish to find the approximate

time at a point during our journey. On studying the moon we note that it has long passed its highest point—and, indeed, is about half-way between this point and its setting point on the horizon. The time must then be about three hours after the time of the moon's highest point. As the moon was at its highest point at 7.52 p.m., the time must be about 11 p.m.

If you are going on a trip at night and you have a choice of dates on which to set out, you would naturally choose the time of full moon because you would get the greatest amount of moonlight and benefit from this light from sunset to sunrise.

When tables are not available and you wish to find the time of high or low tide in your locality, the following method will be generally correct for most practical purposes. Either from your own observations or by inquiry, determine the time difference between moonrise and the high or low tide for your locality. This will be a constant difference for a particular place. Thus by observing the position of the moon in the sky you will note what time has elapsed since moonrise and therefore what the tide is at any moment.

When I was writing this part of the book, I happened to be on my island Katafanga, in the Fiji Group. In this part of Fiji high tide happens to coincide with moonrise and moonset, and when the moon is at its highest point it is low tide. This is quite a coincidence and I wish to repeat that the opposite will be the case in some other places in the world and there will be constant time differences between the moonrise and high or low tide. Once established, the difference will remain a constant for each locality.

Also at Katafanga at the time was a friend who was very anxious to do some spear-fishing at low tide during the daytime and we all wanted to get out on the reef at night to catch crawfish. This crawfish is called spiny lobster in some places, while the French call it langouste; and to catch it the hunter needs a moonless night and low tide on the reef.

I therefore needed to know how much of a moon there would be and at what time it would be low tide to go crawfishing, also at what time low tide would be in the daytime for spear-fishing.

I should explain here that in most parts of the world there are four tides a day, two high and two low, which are about six hours apart. Actually, they are about six hours and twelve minutes apart because each day the same tide is an average of fifty minutes later than on the previous day which makes each change of tide during the day about twelve minutes later. For our particular locality it will be high tide at the time of moonrise and moonset, and when the moon is at its highest point it will be low tide. In our case the approximate time of high and low water was found as follows:

The date was 21st March, 1955.
By our method the moon was 7 days old on 1st March, 1955.
Add 21 days for the 21st March.
The moon is 28 days old on 21st March, 1955.
This is 2 days before new moon (30 days old).
Because the moon rises an average of 50 minutes later each day = 2 × 50 = 1 hour 40 minutes.
New moon rises at 6 a.m. (high tide for our locality).
Therefore on 21st March the moon rises 1 hour and 40 minutes earlier, that is 4.20 a.m. which equals high tide.
The morning low tide will be 6 hours and 12 minutes later, or 10.32 a.m. (for spear-fishing).
The afternoon high tide will be 4.44 p.m. (remember each change of tide in a day is about 12 minutes later).
The evening low tide (for crawfishing) will be 10.56 p.m.

From these calculations we discovered that we had perfect conditions for our expedition on the reef at night with a low tide at 11 p.m. and no moon. On a dark night, with the aid of petrol lamps to momentarily blind the crawfish and with leather gloves to protect our hands, we caught over two dozen averaging about $1\frac{1}{2}$ pounds each, and very delicious they were.

CHAPTER XXIII

DIRECTIONS FROM THE SUN

I F BIRDS and other animals could talk, they would tell us that the sun provides a more ready means of telling direction than almost anything else. The simplest and most fundamental method for the natural navigator is the sun method: the business of relating the direction of the sun (or shadows) to the desired path or to the compass points around the horizon.

For some time after sunset, of course, the western sky near the horizon will be lighter than the rest of the sky, and during the early morning the eastern sky will be brighter. This, however, will give you only a general idea of east and west, because it is only a few times of the year that the sun will rise due east and set due west.

When you are in a latitude where the midday sun is north of you, the sun's rising point is somewhat north of east, and its setting point equally north of west. When the sun at noon is south of you, the rising point is south of east and the setting point south of west. When the sun reaches its highest point at noon, its direction will be either true south or true north.

In the Arctic and Antarctic regions the sun may be above the horizon all the time, in which case when the sun is at its lowest point or highest point it is in the true north in the Northern Hemisphere and in the true south in the Southern Hemisphere.

Even with an overcast sky, it is often possible to find the direction of the sun by holding a knife blade vertically on your thumb nail or on some light background such as a piece of paper. When the blade is rotated the finest shadow will show the sun's direction.

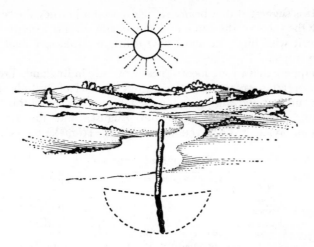

Shadow of stick shortest at noon when it points either north or
south according to your locality and time of the year

In using the sun or shadows as a reference point to enable
you to maintain a straight line while walking, it is useful to know
that in normal latitudes the sun changes in direction an average
of about 15 degrees per hour.

For greater accuracy simple tables of the sun's direction are
given at the back of this book. These tables cover all times of the
year from Latitude 60 degrees North of the Equator to Latitude
50 degrees South of the Equator.

The ordinary tables of directions of the sun, or azimuth tables,
as they are called, are made for navigators and surveyors, and are
bulky and complicated. They are compiled for extreme accuracy
and are not practical for the amateur.

The tables that I have provided will be found accurate within
5 degrees, which is all that is required for cross-country trips on
foot. It is as well to keep in mind that the resultant error of one
degree will be one mile in a 60-mile walk, so that a 5-degree
deviation to one side of your desired track would amount to an
error of 5 miles to one side of your objective in that distance.

It is suggested that before setting out on a journey the reader copy the table of the sun's direction made for his locality, and carry it with him. To show how to use the tables, I shall give an example.

Suppose that we are located near Coventry in England. From a map or atlas we see that the nearest parallel of latitude (such lines run east and west) given in the tables at the end of this book is $52\frac{1}{2}°$ North. It is the 10th August, and the time is 10 a.m. What is the direction of the sun? To make the calcula-

LATITUDE $52\frac{1}{2}°$ NORTH

Hours from Noon	MAR 21 → SEP 23	MAR 31 SEP 13	APR 11 SEP 2	APR 22 AUG 22	MAY 1 AUG 12	MAY 12 AUG 2	MAY 26 JUL 19	JUN 10 JUL 3 ←
0	180	180	180	180	180	180	180	180
1	161	160	159	158	157	155	154	153
2	144	142	140	138	136	134	132	131
3	128	126	124	121	119	117	115	113
4	115	112	110	107	105	103	101	99
5	102	99	97	94	92	90	88	87
6	90	88	85	83	81	79	77	75
7				71	69	67	66	64
8							54	53
Rises & Sets	90°	83°	77°	70°	65°	59°	54°	50°

Hours from Noon	SEP 23 → MAR 21	OCT 4 MAR 11	OCT 14 MAR 1	OCT 25 FEB 18	NOV 3 FEB 9	NOV 14 JAN 29	NOV 27 JAN 16	DEC 11 JAN 2 ←
0	180	180	180	180	180	180	180	180
1	161	162	163	164	164	165	165	166
2	144	146	147	149	150	151	151	152
3	128	130	132	134	136	137	138	139
4	115	117	119	121	123	124	126	
5	102	104	107					
6	90							
Rises & Sets	90°	97°	103°	110°	115°	121°	126°	130°

Before noon read all angles from North to East. *After* noon read all angles from North to West.

tion clearer, I here repeat the table for Latitude $52\frac{1}{2}°$ North from page 259 at the end of the book,

The left-hand column is headed "Hours from Noon" : this applies equally to hours before noon and hours after noon, a device which reduces the bulk of the tables by half. The bearing of the sun from true north is the same number of degrees an hour before noon as an hour after noon, although its direction is different.

10 a.m. is two hours from noon. We follow the table horizontally until we reach the date nearest to 10th August. This is 12th August and quite close enough for our purposes. For this date and time the direction of the sun is 136°. As it is morning, we measure this from north towards east.

The 360° division of the horizon is now generally adopted. To find the angle that the sun lies east of south we thus subtract our 136° from half 360°, i.e. 180°. This gives us 44°. The sun is therefore 44° east of south.

A method of finding the north and south points commonly used and trusted, especially by youthful explorers, but which cannot be recommended, is by means of a pocket watch. Just in case you have not heard of it, you are supposed to hold your watch horizontally, set on local time and with the hour hand turned to the sun. If you are in the Northern Hemisphere, a line midway between the hour hand and 12 is then supposedly taken as pointing south. In the Southern Hemisphere, this line is to be taken as indicating north.

It is a great pity to destroy illusions, but in this case it is necessary to do so, because the apparent simplicity of this method may give a very wrong impression as to its accuracy. There are times and places where such use of the watch will be reasonably correct, but there are others where serious errors will result from it. It is hard to understand how a rule which may be as much as 24 degrees in error has become so universally accepted as reliable. In latitudes between 40 degrees and 60 degrees north or south of the Equator at certain times of the year, the results got by this method will be somewhat close to the truth. But the corrections necessary, even for these latitudes, make the method too complicated to be of any practical use. The only times when no correction is necessary are at sunrise and sunset on 21st March and 23rd September, and at noon on any day, at any place where the sun is directly north or south, but then only if your watch happens to be running on *accurate local time*. The watch method is, of course, entirely impractical anywhere near the North or South Poles, where the change in local time with distance east and west increases steadily the closer one approaches the Pole.

CHAPTER XXIV

DIRECTIONS FROM THE STARS

O N A CLEAR night the stars provide a most useful means of maintaining a desired direction. If we, like the Polynesians, consider the overhead night sky as·the inside of a huge half-shell on which are strewn multitudes of bright points, we see that these points, or stars, are carried around as if they were revolving on a fixed axis. The stars stay in the same relation to one another, pass over the same places on the earth night after night, but rise four minutes earlier each night.

We see the stars rise at the same points each night on the eastern horizon and set at the same points on the western horizon. If we are in the Northern Hemisphere and turn to the south, we notice that the groups of stars which pass above the horizon somewhat to the east of south, attain but a slight elevation when at their highest in the south, and when descending set as far to the west of the south as they had risen to the east of it.

Turning to the north, we see that there are groups of stars which remain visible the whole night, wheeling around a fixed point, the Pole Star, and describing circles of greater or less magnitude according to whether they are at a greater or less distance from that point.

Unlike the sun and the moon, which fluctuate in a north and south direction each day, the star sphere has such a uniform motion as to provide excellent reference points as long as we take into consideration their westward movement in terms of time.

In order to recognise the principal stars visible in the night sky, the ancients divided them into groups, which, with a little imagination, suggested designs of people, animals, birds, fish, etc.

They named these groups or constellations accordingly. It takes quite a stretch of the imagination to see some of the designs as they pictured them. .

So that you will not be lost in a maze of stars, which at first sight look so much alike, it will be helpful to recognise the patterns of the principal constellations—those which include the brightest stars in all parts of the heavens. Thus you will be able to identify any other star by taking its direction and position from stars in nearby constellations.

In the star diagrams shown on Plates XII to XVI, the principal constellations are shown in such a way that if you will follow the dotted lines and form these pictures in your mind, the imaginary connection between certain of the principal stars will enable you to recognise them in the heavens.

In addition to recognising the stars from their patterns, it is useful to know that the colour of certain stars will identify them even if the rest of the sky is clouded over. This is particularly so if the star's position in the sky is also taken into consideration. The distinguishing colours of certain stars are as follows:

> Antares, Aldebaran and Betelgeux—reddish.
> Arcturus, Procyon and Pollux—yellowish.
> Vega and Altair—bluish-white.
> Capella, Canopus and Sirius, and a number of other stars are brilliantly white.

The eight diagrams include constellations covering all part of the sky and two of stars around the Poles. The stars making a complete revolution around either Pole, above the horizon, are called circumpolar stars. Which ones completely revolve above your horizon depends how far you are from the Equator. The diagrams of the stars around the Poles in Plates XII and XIII will be valuable for directional purposes.

In observing the heavens you will see in various parts of the sky very bright star-like bodies which must not be confused with the stars. These are the planets, four of which are bright—Venus, Mars, Jupiter and Saturn. Unless you recognise these a planets you may become confused in trying to find them on the star diagrams. They are not shown on these plates, because their movement is different from that of the stars. It is very difficult to keep track of the position of the planets in the heavens without complicated tables.

To avoid confusing planets with any of the bright stars, the following points may be useful:

At sea level stars usually twinkle, but planets shine with a steady lustre.

Planets are all overhead at points on the earth within 30 degrees north and south of the Equator.

Venus, a brilliant planet, is always near the sun, either ahead of it or behind it, and never more than 47 degrees, or 3 hours from the sun. This means that Venus is always seen before or after sunrise or before or after sunset. Venus may frequently be seen throughout the daylight hours if you know where to look for it.

Mars may be recógnised by its colour, which is ruddy.

These wanderers in the heavens can best be identified by watching their position each night, when they will be seen to have moved in relation to the stars around them.

In the Northern Hemisphere on a clear night, the easiest way of finding your north point is by the Pole Star. The star diagram in Plate XII will assist in locating this star. If the Pole Star is not visible, or you cannot identify it, look for the point in the heavens around which the stars are pivoting in small circles; this will be True North.

The following are four ways of finding the North Pole in the heavens:

Refer to the star diagram of the North Polar area on Plate XII. Look for the two pointers in the Big Dipper. From a point midway between Merak and Dubhe, measure through Dubhe two thumb and middle finger spans of 15 degrees, and this will be the position of the Pole Star. With the arm outstretched as far as possible the average person's span between the thumb and middle finger—the fingers extended comfortably—will measure an angle of about 15 degrees.

On a continuation of a line from Arcturus through Benetnasch (Plate XII) measure three similar spans from Benetnasch, and this will give you the position of the North Pole of the heavens.

The Pole Star can also be found two spans of 15 degrees each from Ruchbah, in the constellation of Cassiopeia (Plate XV) towards Mizar, which is in the handle of the Big Dipper. The constellation of Cassiopeia appears as a " W," the top centre of which points towards, and is two spans of 15 degrees each away from, the Pole Star.

With a clear sky you can roughly distinguish the eastern horizon by watching where the stars suddenly appear above it; and the western horizon by the point where the stars are sinking below it. In these parts of the horizon the movement of the stars is most easily noticed.

If you are in the Northern Hemisphere you can determine true south from the stars, even if you cannot identify any of them, by finding the part of the horizon where the stars low down are moving almost directly horizontally to the right. You will not have to look very long to recognise which way the stars are moving, and you can take the central point of these low stars moving in a short, flat arc, as true south.

Similarly in the Southern Hemisphere, stars low down on the northern horizon move fairly horizontally, and provided it is a clear night you should have no difficulty in finding the north point in this manner.

Near the Southern Cross (Plate XIII), you will note two bright stars known as " the Pointers." Two middle finger to thumb spans, which will be equal to one-half the distance along a line towards Achenar, from the designated point between the Southern Cross and the near Pointer, will give the position of the South Pole of the heavens. The Southern Cross is visible anywhere in the Southern Hemisphere and as far as about 25 degrees north of the Equator.

When you are near the Equator, the best indication of true directions will be from the east and west points of the horizon, where stars rising exactly east of you will ascend vertically, and after passing overhead will set directly on the western horizon.

At all other points of the horizon they appear to the observer to arch away from the vertical.

If the brightest and most beautiful of all constellations, Orion, is visible, you will see from the diagram in Plate XVI, that a continuation from Saiph through Betelgeux will give you an approximate north and south line. It is also important to remember that the northern one of the three stars of Orion's belt is practically over the Equator. Orion rises, on its side, due east, irrespective of the observer's latitude, reaches its highest point in the heavens over the Equator, and sets due west. Seven hours after Orion has passed overhead the Southern Cross will be seen far to the south in its highest position, and can be used as previously described.

Remember that stars rise and set at the same points on the horizon as long as the observer remains in the same latitude, but that they rise and set approximately four minutes earlier each night. A star rising due east of you does not pass directly overhead unless you are at the Equator.

To an observer standing at either Pole, stars will revolve in small circles above him and in gradually widening circles parallel to the horizon. The Pole Star is at no time visible at sea level more than one degree south of the Equator. In the southern sky, unfortunately, there is no Pole Star by which to orient yourself.

In the absence of a compass, or even as a means of checking a compass, a convenient method of determining true south is by observing the Southern Cross. This well-known constellation appears nearly upright when it reaches its highest point, and an observer facing it at that time is looking very nearly directly south, with his right hand to the west, his left hand to the east and his back to the north.

CHAPTER XXV

TELLING THE TIME BY THE STARS

THE STARS which appear to revolve round the North and South Pole of the heavens provide a natural clock to tell the local time. In the Northern Hemisphere the two bright stars in the Big Dipper (or the Great Bear), which are known as the Pointers to the Pole Star, can be used as the hour hand; and the position of the Pole Star can be taken as the imaginary centre around which the hand rotates.

In order to tell the time by the stars it is necessary for us to determine Local Star Time—which is significant only to a navigator or astronomer; and from this, to obtain our Local Sun Time —which is what is shown on our everyday clocks and watches.

The steps to be taken to arrive at the local time can be seen in the following example:

The date is 28th August and the Pointers of the Big Dipper are at 7 o'clock on the imaginary Star Clock (12-hour clock). To find first of all the Local Star Time:

Subtract the time on the Star Clock:
    7 hours from 12 = 5
    Multiply by 2   = 10
    Add 11 (always) = 21 hours = Local Star Time.

Local Star Time is faster than sun time (civil time), which is the time usually kept on our clocks, by one day a year; which equals two hours a month, or four minutes a day.

So in order to find the Local Sun Time we must convert the Local Star Time in the following manner:

Subtract two hours for each full month since March 23 and

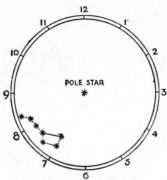

The Big Dipper or Great Bear

four minutes for each day of the remaining part of the month.

Our date is 28th August.

March 23rd to August 23rd = 5 months × 2 hours

                            = 10 hours

August 23rd to August 28th = 5 days × 4 minutes a day

                            = 20 minutes.

Total: 10 hours 20 minutes.

Subtract this from the Local Star Time 21 hours

                           — 10 hour 20 minutes

              = Local Civil Time: 10 hours 40 min. p.m.

If the Big Dipper is below the horizon or not visible because of clouds, we can use another conspicuous group of stars, Cassiopeia, to tell the time. This constellation has the shape of a straggly W, and revolves around the Pole Star.

As Cassiopeia is on the opposite side of the Pole Star from the Big Dipper, there will be many occasions when you can use it if the Big Dipper is below the horizon.

The numbers around the accompanying diagram are not dates or hours of your day but are figures to facilitate the conversion of the position of the stars to your local time.

One particular star of Cassiopeia is used—the right hand star of the group forming the W when it is upright, named Caph (Plate XV).

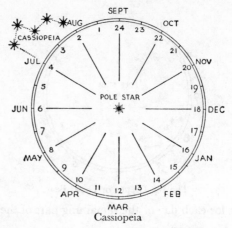

Cassiopeia

To tell the time from this star proceed as follows:

The imaginary clock dial has the Pole Star at the centre, and is divided into 24 parts, starting with 24 on top and numbered counter-clockwise.

Read the number on this circle which corresponds with the imaginary hand connecting the Pole Star with Caph. In this case it is 4.

To this add the number corresponding to your approximate date, which in this example is February 1. The number is 14.

$$4 \text{ plus } 14 = 18 \text{ hours} = 6 \text{ p.m.}$$

If the addition comes to more than 24, subtract 24.

This does not take into account any error resulting from Daylight Saving Time, which we may have in our locality; or a Zone Time used for convenience. Any local difference can be found by inquiry.

It is not always realised that the Big Dipper and Cassiopeia are visible well south of the Equator on their upward revolution around the Pole Star. They can be used, therefore, by most people in southern latitudes for telling the time at night.

Those too far south to observe these constellations, or who find them clouded over, can obtain time from the position of the

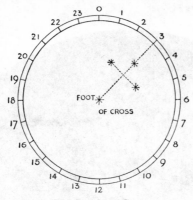

The Southern Cross

Southern Cross. Although there is no star in the position of the South Pole in the heavens, the place in the sky of the focal point of movement can be found by extending the long axis of the cross 4½ times from the bottom of the cross.

Taking the long axis of the cross as the hand of the clock, and the foot of the cross as the centre of the dial, we can make an imaginary division of the dial into 24 hours instead of the conventional twelve.

Reading the " time " from the position of the long axis of the cross, we subtract 2 hours for every month and 4 minutes for each day since the last March 29th. The result will be the time after midnight on the 24-hour clock.

Example:

Date: May 31st.

Time on star clock, 3 hours.

Borrow 24 hours.

3 hours plus 24 hours = 27 hours.

March 29 to May 29 = 2 (months) × 2 hours = 4 hours.

May 29 to May 31 = 2 (days) × 4 minutes = 8 minutes.

Subtract 4 hours, 8 minutes from 27 hours = 22 hours, 52 minutes.

Subtract 12 hours = local time: 10.52 p.m.

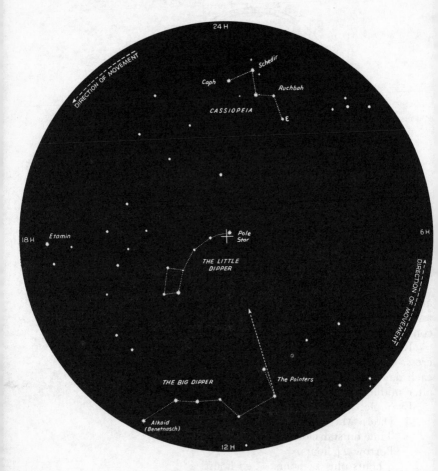

Plate XII. North Polar Area

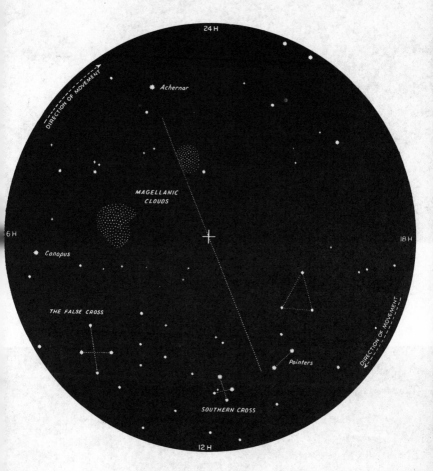

Plate XIII. South Polar Area

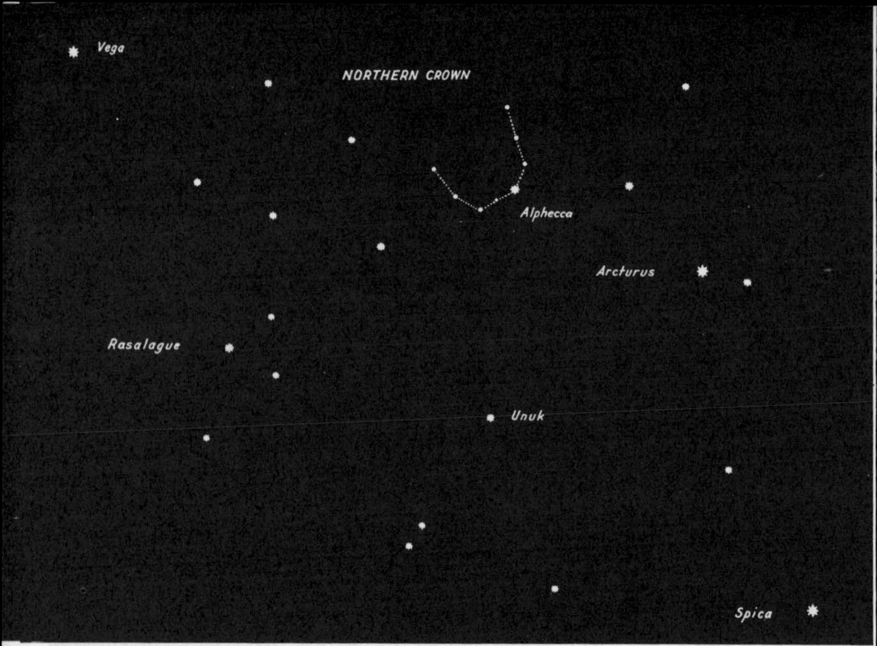

Vega

NORTHERN CROWN

Alphecca

Arcturus

Rasalague

Unuk

Spica

Plate XIV

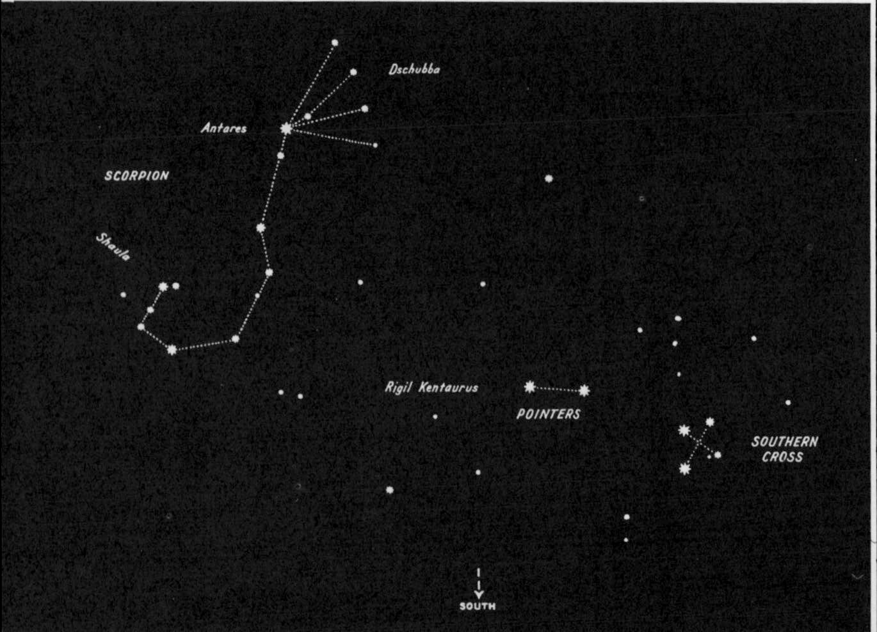

Dschubba

Antares

SCORPION

Shaula

Rigil Kentaurus

POINTERS

SOUTHERN
CROSS

↑
SOUTH

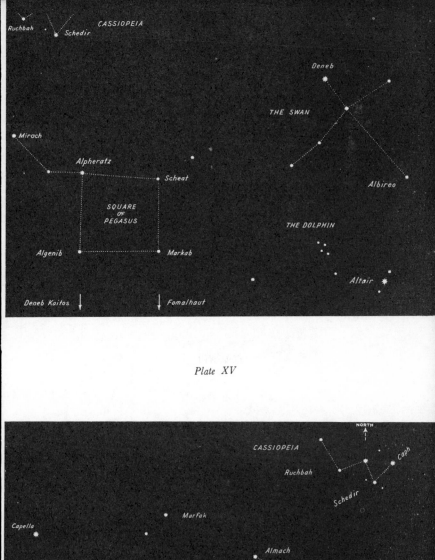

Plate XV

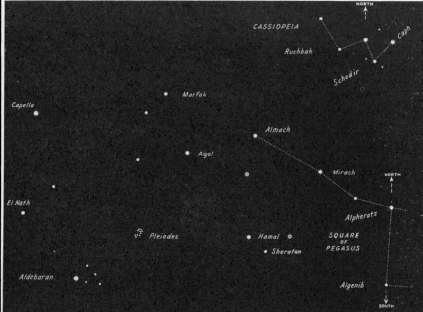

Plate XVI

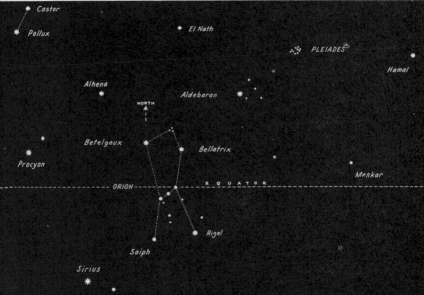

SELECTIVE BIBLIOGRAPHY

ALEXANDER, W. B. (1955). Birds of the Ocean. London, Putnam, 2nd ed.

ARCTOWSKI, Henryk (1901). Exploration of Antarctic Lands. *Geogr. J.* 17: 150-80.

AUFRÈRE, L. (1930, L'orientation des dunes continentales. *Proc. Int. Geogr Congr.* (Cambridge, 1928) 12: 220-31.

BAER, K. E. von (1857). Why are the right banks of our rivers flowing north-wards high, and the left depressed? (in Russian). Moscow.

BAGNOLD, R. A. (1953). Navigation ashore. *Navig.* 6: 184-93.

BIERVLIET, J. J. van (1901). L'homme droit et l'homme gauche. Paris.

BONNIER, Pierre (1910). La question de l'orientation lointaine. *Rev. Sci. Paris* (5) 2: 837-39.

BOUGAINVILLE, Louis Antoine de (1772). A voyage round the world in the years 1766, 1767, 1768 and 1769. London.

BYRD, Richard E. (1930). Little America: aerial exploration in the Antarctic: the flight to the South Pole. New York and London.

CABOT, Thomas D. (1935). Finding the way, pp. 180-82. *Handbook of travel.* Cambridge, Mass.

CAMPBELL, D. (1916). Notes on Scouting. *J. Roy. United Serv. Instn. London* 61: 375-91.

CANNON, Helen L. (1954). Botanical methods of prospecting for uranium. *Mining Eng. (Feb.):* 217-20.

CANNON, Helen L. (1952). The effects of uranium—vanadium deposits on the vegetation of the Colorado Plateau. *Amer. J. Sci,* 250: 735-70.

CHAPMAN, F. Spencer (1955). On not getting lost, pp. 39-48 *of* The boys' country book, ed, John Moore. London, Collins.

CHARLEVOIX, Francois-Xavier de (1744). Journal d'un voyage dans l'Amérique septentrionale. Vol. 3 *of* Histoire et description générales de la Nouvelle—France. Paris, p. 304.

CLIFFE, Edward. The Voyage of Mr. John Winter into the South Sea by the Streight of Magellan, in consort with Francis Drake begun in the yeere 1577. Hakluyt, Vol. 8, p. 91.

CRICHTON, A. (1833). History of Arabia. Edinburgh. 2 vols. (1: 111).

CUILLANDRE, Joseph (1944). La droite et la gauche dans les poemes homeriques en concordance avec la doctrine pythagoricienne et avec la tradition celtique. Paris pp. 460-81.

DARWIN, Charles (1873). A letter. *Nature,* 8: 396.

DIDEROT, D. (1916). Letter on the blind, pp. 68-141 *of* Early philosophical works. Chicago, transl. and ed. M. Jourdain.

DODGE, Richard I. (1890). Our wild Indians. Hartford, Conn.

245

DRESCO, Édouard (1945). L'orientation en randonnée. Paris, p. 66.

DRESSLAR, F. B. (1893). On the pressure sense of the drum of the ear and facial vision. *Amer. J. Psychol.* 5: 344–50.

DUMAS, J. B. (1938). L'homme à la main heureuse. La droite et la gauche. Unpublished MS. in Bibliothèque nationale Paris.

Explorer Scout Manual (1946). New York. p. 382.

FALGER, Dr. F. (1924). Das Orientierungsvermögen Deutscher und Oster-reichischen Alpenverein Mitteilungen. Munich. pp. 201–2.

FARROW, Edward S. (1881). Mountain scouting. New York. pp. 100–06.

FISCHER, M. H. (1931). Die Orientierung im Raume bei Wirbeltieren und beim Menschen. Vol. 15, part 2, of *Hanb. norm. path. Physiol.* Berlin.

FISHER, James (1952). The Fulmar. London, Collins' *New Naturalist*.

FISHER, James and LOCKLEY, R. M. (1954). Sea-birds. London, Collins' *New Naturalist*.

FREE, Montague (1953). Who says plants follow the sun? *Home Garden*, 22: (Nov.) 62–65.

FRERE, H. Bartle E. (1870). Notes on the Runn of Cutch and neighbouring region. *J. Roy. Geogr. Soc.* 40: 181–207.

GATTY, Harold (1943). The Raft Book. New York.

GULDBERG, F. O. (1897). Die Circularbewegung als thierische Grund-bewegung, ihre Ursache, Phänomenalität und Bedeutung. *Z. Biol.* 35: 419–58.

GULDBERG, G. A. (1896). Uber die morphologische und functionelle Asym-metric der Gliedmassen beim Menschen und bei den höheren Vertebraten. *Biol. Centralbl.* 16: 806–13.

HEINE-GELDERN, Robert (1950). Heyerdahl's hypothesis of Polynesian origins: a criticism. *Geogr. J.* 116: 183–92.

HELLER, Th. (1904). Studien zur Blindenpsychologie. Leipzig.

HENSHAW, Henry W. (1918). The book of birds. Washington, Nat. Geogr. Soc. pp. 187–90.

HERTZ, R. (1909). La Pré-eminence de la main droite. *Rev. phil.* 2: 553.

HORNELL, James (1946). The role of birds in early navigation. *Antiquity*, 79: 142–49.

HOUZEAU, J. C. (1872). Études sur les facultés mentales des animaux comparées à celles de l'homme. Leipzig.

HOWITT, A. W. (1873). A letter. *Nature*, 8: 323.

IDRIESS, Ion L. (1943). The scout. Sydney. p. 123.

JACCARD, Pierre (1926). Une enquête sur la désorientation en montagne. *Bull. Soc. vaud. Sci. nat.* 56: 151–59.

JACCARD, Pierre (1932). Le sens de la direction et l'orientation lointaine chez l'homme. Paris, pp. 354.

JARVAL, Emile (1905). The sixth sense pp. 152–69 of On becoming blind.

JESPERSEN, P. (1929). On the frequency of birds over the high Atlantic Ocean. *1st Orn. Congr. Copenhagen* (1926) 6-163-72.

KELLY, William (1845). On the stationary clouds of the St. Lawrence. *Naut. Mag.* 1845: 303–09.

KING, W. J. H. (1931). Pioneer desert exploration. *Geogr. J.* 77: 541–47.

KLEBELSBERG, R. von (1948). Handbuch der Gletscherkunde und Glatial-geologie. Vienna, Vol. 1: 127–31.

LAFITAU, Joseph-François (1724). Les moeurs des sauvages américains comparées aux moeurs des premiers temps. Paris. 2 vols. (2: 240, 241)

LANE, Frank W. (1948). Have animals a time-sense? pp. 93-110 *of* Animal wonderland . . . London.

LEECHMAN, Douglas (1944). The hiker's handbook. New York, p. 220.

LINDER, Ch. (1938). Observations sur les fourmilières-boussoles. *Bull. Soc. vaud. Sci. nat.* 44: 303–10.

LINDSAY, H. A. (1950). The bushman's handbook. Sydney.

LINSCHOTEN, J. H. van (1598). Voyages. London.

LOCKLEY, R. M. (1942). Shearwaters. London, Dent.

LOCKLEY, R. M. (1953). Puffins, London, Dent.

LUND, F. H. Physical asymmetries and disorientation. *Amer. J. Psychol.* 42: 51–62.

MACH, E. (1897). Uber Orientierungsempfindungen. *Schr. Var. Verbr. naturw. Kenntn. Wien*, 37:

MacLEOD, R. B. and ROFF, M. F. (1936). An experiment in temporal disorientation. *Acta psychol. Hague*, 1: 381–423.

MADIGAN, C. T. (1936). The Australian sand-ridge deserts. *Geogr. Rev.* 26: 205–27.

MAGAREY, A. T. (1899). Tracking by the Australian aborigine. *Proc. Roy. Geogr. Soc. Australasia*, 3: 120.

MANCIOT, André (1943). Orientation manuel pratique, *in* Collection de la revue *Camping*. Paris.

MARLOTH, R. (1932). The flora of South Africa. London.

MAWSON, Douglas (1915). The home of the blizzard. London. 2 vols.

MILLS, Enos Abigail (1920). The adventures of a nature guide. New York.

MURPHY, Robert Cushman (1936). Oceanic Birds of South America. New York. 2 vols.

POST, Wiley and GATTY, Harold   Around the World in Eight Days. London. 1931.

PRINSEP, James (1928). Note on the nautical instruments of the Arabs, *in* Gabriel Ferrand's Introduction à l'astronomie nautique arabe. Paris.

RANKAMA, Kalervo (1947). Some recent trends in prospecting: chemical, biogeochemical and geobotanical methods. *Mining and Metallurgy* (June), 1947: 282–84.

RATCLIFFE, F. N., GAY, F. J. and GREAVES, T. (1952). Australian termites. Melbourne.

ROCKIE, W. A. Snowdrift erosion in the Palouse. *Geogr. Rev.* (*July*) 1951: 457–63.

Ryan, T. A. and M. S. (1940). Geographical orientation. *American J. Psychol.* *Ithaca* 53: 204–15.

Salt (Periodical) (1944). Living off the land, a manual of bushcraft. Melbourne.

Sandstrom, Carl Ivar (1951). Orientation in the present space. Stockholm. pp. 128–91.

Saussure, Léopold de (1928). L'origine de la rose des vents et l'invention de la boussole, *in* Gabriel Ferrand's Introduction à l'astronomie nautique arabe. Paris.

Schaeffer, A. A. (1928). Spiral movement in man. *J. Morph. Physio.* 45: 293–98.

Scott, Robert Falcon (1913). The journals of Captain R. F. Scott. Vol. 1 *of* Scott's last expedition. London, 2 vols. ed. Leonard Huxley.

Seton, Ernest Thompson (*c.* 1921). The book of woodcraft. New York.

Shackleton, Ernest H. (1910). The heart of the Antarctic . . . London. 2 vols.

Sommerfelt, Carl Jacob (1946). Orienteringsboka, händbök i tur og kongurranseorientering. Oslo.

Speiss, F. (1928). Die ' Meteor ' Fahrt. Berlin.

Supa, Michael, Cotzin, Milton and Dallenbach, Karl M. (1944). "Facial vision ": the perception of obstacles by the blind. *Amer. J. Psychol.* 57: 133–83.

Szymanski, J. S. (1913). Versuche über den Richtungsinn beim Menschen. *Arch. Physiol. Bonn,* 1913: 158–70.

Trowbridge, C. C. (1913). On fundamental methods of orientation and " imaginary maps." *Science, N.Y.* (*n.s.*) 38: 888–897.

Truschel, L. (1906–07). Der sechste Sinn der Blinden. *Exper. Pädagogik,* 3: 109–42; 4: 129–55; 5: 66–77.

Villey, Pierre (1930). The world of the blind: a psychological study, London. pp. 101–31.

Widmer, Charles (1927). Die Desorientierung in den Bergen. *Die Alpen, Bern,* 3: 218–32.

Wiesner, Julius von (1907). Der Lichtgenuss der Pflanzen, photometrische und physiologische Untersuchungen Leipzig, 322 pp.

Wrangell, F. von (1840). Narrative of an Expedition to the Polar Sea in 1820–23. London.

Wright, John Kirtland (1932). Primitive cartography. *Geogr. Rev.* 22: 491–92.

Yoshioka, Joseph (1942). " A direction-orientation study with visitors at the New York World's Fair." *J. Gen. Psychol.* 27: 3–33.

LATITUDE 0° (EQUATOR)

Hours from Noon	MAR 21 / SEP 23 ↘	MAR 31 / SEP 13	APR 11 / SEP 2	APR 22 / AUG 22	MAY 1 / AUG 12	MAY 12 / AUG 2	MAY 26 / JUL 19	JUN 10 / JUL 3 ↓
0	x	x	x	0	0	0	0	0
1	90	75	61	51	44	39	34	31
2	90	82	74	67	62	57	52	50
3	90	84	79	73	69	65	61	59
4	90	85	81	76	73	69	66	64
5	90	86	82	78	74	71	68	66
6	90	86	82	78	75	72	69	67
Rises & Sets	90°	86°	82°	78°	75°	72°	69°	67°

Hours from Noon	SEP 23 / MAR 21 ↘	OCT 4 / MAR 11	OCT 14 / MAR 1	OCT 25 / FEB 18	NOV 3 / FEB 9	NOV 14 / JAN 29	NOV 27 / JAN 16	DEC 11 / JAN 2 ↓
0	x	x	x	180	180	180	180	180
1	90	105	119	129	136	141	146	149
2	90	98	106	113	118	123	128	130
3	90	96	101	107	111	115	119	121
4	90	95	99	104	107	111	114	116
5	90	94	98	102	106	109	112	114
6	90	94	98	102	105	108	111	113
Rises & Sets	90°	94°	98°	102°	105°	108°	111°	113°

LATITUDE 2½° NORTH

Hours from Noon	MAR 21 / SEP 23 ↘	MAR 31 / SEP 13	APR 11 / SEP 2	APR 22 / AUG 22	MAY 1 / AUG 12	MAY 12 / AUG 2	MAY 26 / JUL 19	JUN 10 / JUL 3 ↓
0	180	x	0	0	0	0	0	0
1	99	84	69	57	49	42	37	34
2	94	86	78	71	65	60	55	52
3	92	87	81	76	71	67	63	61
4	91	87	82	78	74	71	67	65
5	91	87	82	78	75	72	69	67
6	90	86	82	78	75	72	69	67
Rises & Sets	90°	86°	82°	78°	75°	72°	69°	67°

Hours from Noon	SEP 23 / MAR 21 ↘	OCT 4 / MAR 11	OCT 14 / MAR 1	OCT 25 / FEB 18	NOV 3 / FEB 9	NOV 14 / JAN 29	NOV 27 / JAN 16	DEC 11 / JAN 2 ↓
0	180	180	180	180	180	180	180	180
1	99	113	125	134	140	145	149	151
2	94	102	110	116	121	126	130	132
3	92	98	104	109	113	117	120	122
4	91	96	101	105	108	112	115	117
5	91	95	99	103	106	109	112	114
Rises & Sets	90°	94°	98°	102°	105°	108°	111°	113°

Before noon read all angles from North to East. *After* noon read all angles from North to West. Where an X appears the sun's direction is changing too rapidly to be of any practical value.

LATITUDE 5° NORTH

Hours from Noon	MAR → 21 / SEP 23	MAR 31 / SEP 13	APR 11 / SEP 2	APR 22 / AUG 22	MAY 1 / AUG 12	MAY 12 / AUG 2	MAY 26 / JUL 19	JUN 10 / JUL 3 ↓
0	180	180	x	0	0	0	0	0
1	108	93	78	64	55	47	41	37
2	99	91	83	75	69	64	58	55
3	95	89	84	78	74	70	66	63
4	93	88	84	79	76	72	69	66
5	91	87	83	79	76	73	70	67
6	90	86	82	78	75	72	69	67
Rises & Sets	90°	86°	82°	78°	75°	72°	69°	67°

Hours from Noon	SEP → 23 / MAR 21	OCT 4 / MAR 11	OCT 14 / MAR 1	OCT 25 / FEB 18	NOV 3 / FEB 9	NOV 14 / JAN 29	NOV 27 / JAN 16	DEC 11 / JAN 2 ↓
0	180	180	180	180	180	180	180	180
1	108	121	131	139	144	148	151	153
2	99	106	113	120	124	129	132	135
3	95	101	106	111	115	119	122	124
4	93	97	102	106	110	113	116	118
5	91	95	100	104	107	110	113	115
6								
Rises & Sets	90°	94°	98°	102°	105°	108°	111°	113°

LATITUDE 7½° NORTH

Hours from Noon	MAR → 21 / SEP 23	MAR 31 / SEP 13	APR 11 / SEP 2	APR 22 / AUG 22	MAY 1 / AUG 12	MAY 12 / AUG 2	MAY 26 / JUL 19	JUN 10 / JUL 3 ↓
0	180	180	x	x	0	0	0	0
1	116	103	87	72	62	53	44	41
2	103	95	87	79	73	67	62	58
3	97	92	86	80	76	72	68	65
4	94	89	85	80	77	73	70	68
5	92	88	84	80	76	73	70	68
6	90	86	82	78	75	72	69	67
Rises & Sets	90°	86°	82°	78°	75°	72°	69°	67°

Hours from Noon	SEP → 23 / MAR 21	OCT 4 / MAR 11	OCT 14 / MAR 1	OCT 25 / FEB 18	NOV 3 / FEB 9	NOV 14 / JAN 29	NOV 27 / JAN 16	DEC 11 / JAN 2 ↓
0	180	180	180	180	180	180	180	180
1	116	127	136	142	147	150	153	155
2	103	110	116	123	127	131	135	137
3	97	103	108	113	117	120	124	126
4	94	99	103	108	111	114	117	119
5	92	96	100	104	107	110	113	115
6								
Rises & Sets	90°	94°	98°	102°	105°	108°	111°	113°

Before noon read all angles from North to East. *After* noon read all angles from North to West. Where an X appears the sun's direction is changing too rapidly to be of any practical value.

LATITUDE 10° NORTH

Hours from Noon	MAR 21 ← / SEP 23	MAR 31 / SEP 13	APR 11 / SEP 2	APR 22 / AUG 22	MAY 1 / AUG 12	MAY 12 / AUG 2	MAY 26 / JUL 19	JUN 10 / JUL 3 ↓
0	180	180	180	x	x	x	x	x
1	123	111	96	81	70	60	51	46
2	107	99	91	83	77	71	66	62
3	100	94	89	83	79	74	70	67
4	96	91	87	82	78	75	71	69
5	93	89	84	80	77	74	71	69
6	90	86	82	78	75	72	69	67
Rises & Sets	90°	86°	82°	78°	75°	72°	69°	67°

Hours from Noon	SEP 23 ← / MAR 21	OCT 4 / MAR 11	OCT 14 / MAR 1	OCT 25 / FEB 18	NOV 3 / FEB 9	NOV 14 / JAN 29	NOV 27 / JAN 16	DEC 11 / JAN 2 ↓
0	180	180	180	180	180	180	180	180
1	123	132	140	146	149	152	155	156
2	107	114	120	126	130	133	137	139
3	100	105	110	115	119	122	125	127
4	96	100	105	109	112	115	118	120
5	93	97	101	105	108	111	114	116
6	90							
Rises & Sets	90°	94°	98°	102°	105°	108°	111°	113°

LATITUDE 12½° NORTH

Hours from Noon	MAR 21 ← / SEP 23	MAR 31 / SEP 13	APR 11 / SEP 2	APR 22 / AUG 22	MAY 1 / AUG 12	MAY 12 / AUG 2	MAY 26 / JUL 19	JUN 10 / JUL 3 ↓
0	180	180	180	x	x	x	x	x
1	129	119	105	90	79	67	57	52
2	111	103	96	88	82	75	69	66
3	102	97	91	86	81	77	72	70
4	97	93	88	83	80	76	73	71
5	93	89	85	81	78	75	72	70
6	90	86	82	78	75	72	69	67
Rises & Sets	90°	86°	82°	78°	75°	72°	68°	66°

Hours from Noon	SEP 23 ← / MAR 21	OCT 4 / MAR 11	OCT 14 / MAR 1	OCT 25 / FEB 18	NOV 3 / FEB 9	NOV 14 / JAN 29	NOV 27 / JAN 16	DEC 11 / JAN 2 ↓
0	180	180	180	180	180	180	180	180
1	129	137	143	148	151	154	156	157
2	111	117	123	128	131	135	138	140
3	102	107	112	117	120	124	127	128
4	97	102	106	110	113	116	119	121
5	93	97	101	105	108	111	114	116
6	90							
Rises & Sets	90°	94°	98°	102°	105°	108°	111°	114°

Before noon read all angles from North to East. After noon read all angles from North to West. Where an X appears the sun's direction is changing too rapidly to be of any practical value.

LATITUDE 17½° NORTH

Hours from Noon	MAR 21 → / SEP 23	MAR 31 / SEP 13	APR 11 / SEP 2	APR 22 / AUG 22	MAY 1 / AUG 12	MAY 12 / AUG 2	MAY 26 / JUL 19	JUN 10 / JUL 3 ↓
0	180	180	180	180	180	x	x	x
1	138	131	121	109	98	86	74	66
2	117	111	104	97	91	84	78	74
3	107	102	96	91	87	82	78	75
4	100	96	91	87	83	80	76	74
5	95	91	87	83	80	76	73	71
6	90	86	82	79	76	73	70	68
Rises & Sets	90°	86°	82°	77°	74°	71°	68°	66°

Hours from Noon	SEP 23 → / MAR 21	OCT 4 / MAR 11	OCT 14 / MAR 1	OCT 25 / FEB 18	NOV 3 / FEB 9	NOV 14 / JAN 29	NOV 27 / JAN 16	DEC 11 / JAN 2 ↓
0	180	180	180	180	180	180	180	180
1	138	144	149	152	155	157	158	160
2	117	123	128	133	136	139	141	143
3	107	112	116	120	123	126	129	131
4	100	104	108	112	115	118	121	123
5	95	98	102	106	109	112	115	117
Rises & Sets	90°	94°	98°	103°	106°	109°	112°	114°

LATITUDE 15° NORTH

Hours from Noon	MAR 21 → / SEP 23	MAR 31 / SEP 13	APR 11 / SEP 2	APR 22 / AUG 22	MAY 1 / AUG 12	MAY 12 / AUG 2	MAY 26 / JUL 19	JUN 10 / JUL 3 ↓
0	180	180	180	180	180	x	x	x
1	134	125	114	100	88	76	65	58
2	114	107	100	92	86	80	74	70
3	105	99	94	88	84	80	75	72
4	98	94	90	85	81	78	74	72
5	94	90	86	82	79	76	73	70
6	90	86	82	78	75	73	70	68
Rises & Sets	90°	86°	82°	78°	74°	71°	68°	66°

Hours from Noon	SEP 23 → / MAR 21	OCT 4 / MAR 11	OCT 14 / MAR 1	OCT 25 / FEB 18	NOV 3 / FEB 9	NOV 14 / JAN 29	NOV 27 / JAN 16	DEC 11 / JAN 2 ↓
0	180	180	180	180	180	180	180	180
1	134	141	146	150	153	155	157	159
2	114	120	126	131	134	137	140	142
3	105	110	114	119	122	125	128	130
4	98	103	107	111	114	117	120	122
5	94	98	102	106	109	112	114	116
6	90							
Rises & Sets	90°	94°	98°	102°	106°	109°	112°	114°

Before noon read all angles from North to East. *After* noon read all angles from North to West. Where an X appears the sun's direction is changing too rapidly to be of any practical value.

LATITUDE 22½° NORTH

Hours from Noon	MAR ↑21 SEP 23	MAR 31 SEP 13	APR 11 SEP 2	APR 22 AUG 22	MAY 1 AUG 12	MAY 12 AUG 2	MAY 26 JUL 19	JUN 10 JUL 3 ↓
0	180	180	180	180	180	180	180	0
1	145	140	133	124	115	105	93	85
2	124	118	112	105	100	94	87	83
3	111	106	101	96	86	88	83	80
4	102	98	94	90	86	83	79	77
5	96	92	88	84	81	78	75	73
6	90	86	83	79	76	73	70	69
Rises & Sets	90°	86°	81°	77°	74°	70°	67°	65°

Hours from Noon	SEP ↑23 MAR 21	OCT 4 MAR 11	OCT 14 MAR 1	OCT 25 FEB 18	NOV 3 FEB 9	NOV 14 JAN 29	NOV 27 JAN 16	DEC 11 JAN 2 ↓
0	180	180	180	180	180	180	180	180
1	145	149	153	155	157	159	160	161
2	124	128	133	137	139	142	144	145
3	111	115	120	123	126	129	131	133
4	102	106	110	114	117	120	122	124
5	96	100	103	107	110	112	115	117
6	90							
Rises & Sets	90°	94°	99°	103°	106°	110°	113°	115°

After noon read all angles from North to West.

LATITUDE 20° NORTH

Hours from Noon	MAR ↑21 SEP 23	MAR 31 SEP 13	APR 11 SEP 2	APR 22 AUG 22	MAY 1 AUG 12	MAY 12 AUG 2	MAY 26 JUL 19	JUN 10 JUL 3 ↓
0	180	180	180	180	180	180	x	x
1	142	136	127	117	107	95	83	75
2	121	115	108	101	95	89	83	78
3	109	104	99	93	89	85	80	77
4	101	97	93	88	85	81	78	75
5	95	91	87	83	80	77	74	72
6	90	86	82	79	76	73	70	68
Rises & Sets	90°	86°	82°	79°	76°	73°	70°	68°

Hours from Noon	SEP ↑23 MAR 21	OCT 4 MAR 11	OCT 14 MAR 1	OCT 25 FEB 18	NOV 3 FEB 9	NOV 14 JAN 29	NOV 27 JAN 16	DEC 11 JAN 2 ↓
0	180	180	180	180	180	180	180	180
1	142	147	151	154	156	158	159	160
2	121	126	131	135	138	140	143	144
3	109	113	118	122	125	128	130	132
4	101	105	109	113	116	119	122	123
5	95	99	103	107	109	112	115	117
6	90							
Rises & Sets	90°	94°	99°	103°	106°	109°	112°	115°

Before noon read all angles from North to East. After noon read all angles from North to West.

LATITUDE 27½° NORTH

Hours from Noon	MAR →21 SEP 23	MAR 31 SEP 13	APR 11 SEP 2	APR 22 AUG 22	MAY 1 AUG 12	MAY 12 AUG 2	MAY 26 JUL 19	JUN 10 JUL 3 ↓
0	180	180	180	180	180	180	180	180
1	150	146	141	135	129	121	112	105
2	129	124	119	113	108	103	97	93
3	115	110	106	101	97	93	89	86
4	105	101	97	93	90	86	83	80
5	97	93	90	86	83	80	77	75
6	90	86	83	79	77	74	71	69
Rises & Sets	90°	85°	81°	76°	73°	70°	66°	64°

Hours from Noon	SEP →23 MAR 21	OCT 4 MAR 11	OCT 14 MAR 1	OCT 25 FEB 18	NOV 3 FEB 9	NOV 14 JAN 29	NOV 27 JAN 16	DEC 11 JAN 2 ↓
0	180	180	180	180	180	180	180	180
1	150	153	156	158	159	161	162	163
2	129	133	136	140	142	144	146	147
3	115	119	123	126	129	131	133	135
4	105	109	112	116	118	121	123	125
5	97	101	104	108	110	113	115	117
Rises & Sets	90°	94°	99°	104°	107°	110°	114°	116°

After noon read all angles from North to West.

LATITUDE 25° NORTH

Hours from Noon	MAR →21 SEP 23	MAR 31 SEP 13	APR 11 SEP 2	APR 22 AUG 22	MAY 1 AUG 12	MAY 12 JUL 2	MAY 26 JUL 19	JUN 10 JUL 3 ↓
0	180	180	180	180	180	180	180	180
1	148	143	137	130	123	114	103	95
2	126	121	116	109	104	98	92	88
3	113	108	104	99	95	90	86	83
4	104	100	96	91	88	85	81	79
5	96	93	89	85	82	79	76	74
6	90	86	83	79	76	74	71	69
Rises & Sets	90°	86°	81°	77°	73°	70°	67°	64°

Hours from Noon	SEP →23 MAR 21	OCT 4 MAR 11	OCT 14 MAR 1	OCT 25 FEB 18	NOV 3 FEB 9	NOV 14 JAN 29	NOV 27 JAN 16	DEC 11 JAN 2 ↓
0	180	180	180	180	180	180	180	180
1	148	151	154	157	158	160	161	162
2	126	131	135	138	141	143	145	146
3	113	117	121	125	127	130	132	134
4	104	108	111	115	118	120	123	125
5	96	100	104	107	110	113	115	117
6	90							
Rises & Sets	90°	94°	99°	103°	107°	110°	113°	116°

Before noon read all angles from North to East. After noon read all angles from North to West.

LATITUDE 30° NORTH

Hours from Noon	MAR 21 → / SEP 23	MAR 31 / SEP 13	APR 11 / SEP 2	APR 22 / AUG 22	MAY 1 / AUG 12	MAY 12 / AUG 2	MAY 26 / JUL 19	JUN 10 / JUL 3 ↓
0	180	180	180	180	180	180	180	180
1	152	149	144	139	134	128	120	114
2	131	127	122	116	112	107	101	97
3	117	112	108	103	100	96	92	89
4	106	102	98	94	91	88	85	82
5	98	94	90	87	84	81	78	76
6	90	87	83	80	77	74	72	70
Rises & Sets	90°	85°	81°	76°	73°	69°	66°	63°

Hours from Noon	SEP 23 → / MAR 21	OCT 4 / MAR 11	OCT 14 / MAR 1	OCT 25 / FEB 18	NOV 3 / FEB 9	NOV 14 / JAN 29	NOV 27 / JAN 16	DEC 11 / JAN 2 ↓
0	180	180	180	180	180	180	180	180
1	152	155	157	159	160	161	162	163
2	131	135	138	141	143	145	147	148
3	117	120	124	127	130	132	134	136
4	106	110	113	117	119	122	124	125
5	98	101	105	108	111	113	116	117
6	90							
Rises & Sets	90°	95°	99°	104°	107°	111°	114°	117°

Before noon read all angles from North to East.

LATITUDE 32½° NORTH

Hours from Noon	MAR 21 → / SEP 23	MAR 31 / SEP 13	APR 11 / SEP 2	APR 22 / AUG 22	MAY 1 / AUG 12	MAY 12 / AUG 2	MAY 26 / JUL 19	JUN 10 / JUL 3 ↓
0	180	180	180	180	180	180	180	180
1	153	151	147	143	139	133	127	122
2	133	129	125	120	116	111	106	102
3	118	114	110	106	102	99	95	92
4	107	104	100	96	93	90	86	84
5	98	95	91	88	85	82	79	77
6	90	87	83	80	77	75	72	70
7								63
Rises & Sets	90°	85°	80°	76°	72°	68°	65°	62°

Hours from Noon	SEP 23 → / MAR 21	OCT 4 / MAR 11	OCT 14 / MAR 1	OCT 25 / FEB 18	NOV 3 / FEB 9	NOV 14 / JAN 29	NOV 27 / JAN 16	DEC 11 / JAN 2 ↓
0	180	180	180	180	180	180	180	180
1	153	156	158	160	161	162	163	164
2	133	136	139	142	144	146	148	149
3	118	122	125	128	131	133	135	136
4	107	111	114	117	120	122	124	126
5	98	102	105	108	111	113	116	118
Rises & Sets	90°	95°	99°	104°	108°	111°	116°	118°

After noon read all angles from North to West.

LATITUDE 37½° NORTH

Hours from Noon	MAR ↑21	MAR 31	APR 11	APR 22	MAY 1	MAY 12	MAY 26	JUN 10 ↓
	SEP 23	SEP 13	SEP 2	AUG 22	AUG 12	AUG 2	JUL 19	JUL 3
0	180	180	180	180	180	180	180	180
1	156	154	151	148	145	143	138	134
2	136	133	130	126	122	118	114	111
3	121	118	114	110	107	104	100	98
4	109	106	103	99	96	93	90	88
5	99	96	93	89	87	84	81	79
6	90	90	87	80	78	76	73	71
7							64	63
Rises & Sets	90°	85°	78°	75°	71°	67°	63°	60°

Hours from Noon	SEP ↑23	OCT 4	OCT 14	OCT 25	NOV 3	NOV 14	NOV 27	DEC 11 ↓
	MAR 21	MAR 11	MAR 1	FEB 18	FEB 9	JAN 29	JAN 16	JAN 2
0	180	180	180	180	180	180	180	180
1	156	158	160	161	162	163	164	164
2	136	139	142	144	146	147	149	150
3	121	124	127	130	132	134	136	137
4	109	113	116	119	121	123	125	127
5	99	102	106	109	111	113		
6	90							
Rises & Sets	90°	95°	100°	105°	109°	113°	117°	119°

After noon read all angles from North to West.

LATITUDE 35° NORTH

Hours from Noon	MAR ↑21	MAR 31	APR 11	APR 22	MAY 1	MAY 12	MAY 26	JUN 10 ↓
	SEP 23	SEP 13	SEP 2	AUG 22	AUG 12	AUG 2	JUL 19	JUL 3
0	180	180	180	180	180	180	180	180
1	155	152	149	146	142	138	133	129
2	135	131	127	123	119	115	110	107
3	120	116	112	108	105	101	97	95
4	108	105	101	97	94	91	88	86
5	99	95	92	88	86	83	80	78
6	90	87	83	80	78	75	73	71
7							64	63
Rises & Sets	90°	85°	80°	75°	72°	68°	64°	62°

Hours from Noon	SEP ↑23	OCT 4	OCT 14	OCT 25	NOV 3	NOV 14	NOV 27	DEC 11 ↓
	MAR 21	MAR 11	MAR 1	FEB 18	FEB 9	JAN 29	JAN 16	JAN 2
0	180	180	180	180	180	180	180	180
1	155	157	159	160	161	162	163	164
2	135	138	141	143	145	147	148	149
3	120	123	126	129	131	134	136	137
4	108	112	115	118	120	123	125	126
5	99	102	105	108	111	113		
6	90							
Rises & Sets	90°	95°	100°	105°	108°	112°	116°	118°

Before noon read all angles from North to East. After noon read all angles from North to West.

LATITUDE 40° NORTH

Hours from Noon	MAR 21 → / SEP 23	MAR 31 / SEP 13	APR 11 / SEP 2	APR 22 / AUG 22	MAY 1 / AUG 12	MAY 12 / AUG 2	MAY 26 / JUL 19	JUN 10 / JUL 3 ↓
0	180	180	180	180	180	180	180	180
1	157	155	153	151	148	145	142	139
2	138	135	132	128	125	122	118	115
3	123	120	116	112	109	106	103	100
4	110	107	104	100	98	95	92	90
5	100	97	93	90	88	85	82	81
6	90	87	84	81	78	76	74	72
7						67	65	63
Rises & Sets	90°	85°	80°	74°	70°	66°	62°	59°

Hours from Noon	SEP 23 → / MAR 21	OCT 4 / MAR 11	OCT 14 / MAR 1	OCT 25 / FEB 18	NOV 3 / FEB 9	NOV 14 / JAN 29	NOV 27 / JAN 16	DEC 11 / JAN 2 ↓
0	180	180	180	180	180	180	180	180
1	157	159	160	162	163	164	165	165
2	138	141	143	145	147	148	150	150
3	123	126	128	131	133	135	137	138
4	110	113	116	119	121	123	125	127
5	100	103	106	109	111			
6	90							
Rises & Sets	90°	95°	100°	106°	110°	114°	118°	121°

Before noon read all angles from North to East.

LATITUDE 42½° NORTH

Hours from Noon	MAR 21 → / SEP 23	MAR 31 / SEP 13	APR 11 / SEP 2	APR 22 / AUG 22	MAY 1 / AUG 12	MAY 12 / AUG 2	MAY 26 / JUL 19	JUN 10 / JUL 3 ↓
0	180	180	180	180	180	180	180	180
1	158	157	155	152	150	148	145	143
2	139	137	134	131	128	125	121	119
3	124	121	118	114	112	109	105	103
4	111	108	105	102	99	96	94	92
5	100	97	94	91	89	86	84	82
6	90	87	84	81	79	77	74	73
7						67	65	63
Rises & Sets	90°	85°	79°	74°	69°	65°	61°	58°

Hours from Noon	SEP 23 → / MAR 21	OCT 4 / MAR 11	OCT 14 / MAR 1	OCT 25 / FEB 18	NOV 3 / FEB 9	NOV 14 / JAN 29	NOV 27 / JAN 16	DEC 11 / JAN 2 ↓
0	180	180	180	180	180	180	180	180
1	158	160	161	162	163	164	165	165
2	139	142	144	146	147	149	150	151
3	124	127	129	132	134	135	137	138
4	111	114	117	120	122	124	126	127
5	100	103	106	109	111			
6	90							
Rises & Sets	90°	95°	101°	106°	111°	115°	119°	122°

After noon read all angles from North to West.

LATITUDE 45° NORTH

Hours from Noon	MAR →21 / SEP 23	MAR 31 / SEP 13	APR 11 / SEP 2	APR 22 / AUG 22	MAY 1 / AUG 12	MAY 12 / AUG 2	MAY 26 / JUL 19	JUN 10 / JUL 3 ↓
0	180	180	180	180	180	180	180	180
1	159	158	156	154	152	150	148	146
2	141	138	136	133	130	127	124	122
3	125	122	120	116	114	111	108	106
4	112	109	106	103	101	98	95	94
5	101	98	95	92	90	87	85	83
6	90	87	84	81	79	77	75	73
7					69	67	65	63
Rises & Sets 90°	84°	79°	73°	69°	64°	60°	56°	

Hours from Noon	SEP →23 / MAR 21	OCT 4 / MAR 11	OCT 14 / MAR 1	OCT 25 / FEB 18	NOV 3 / FEB 9	NOV 14 / JAN 29	NOV 27 / JAN 16	DEC 11 / JAN 2 ↓
0	180	180	180	180	180	180	180	180
1	159	161	162	163	163	164	165	165
2	141	143	145	147	148	149	150	151
3	125	128	130	133	134	136	137	139
4	112	115	118	120	122	124	126	127
5	101	104	106	109				
6	90							
Rises & Sets 90°	96°	101°	107°	111°	116°	120°	124°	

LATITUDE 47½° NORTH

Hours from Noon	MAR →21 / SEP 23	MAR 31 / SEP 13	APR 11 / SEP 2	APR 22 / AUG 22	MAY 1 / AUG 12	MAY 12 / AUG 2	MAY 26 / JUL 19	JUN 10 / JUL 3 ↓
0	180	180	180	180	180	180	180	180
1	160	159	157	156	154	152	150	149
2	142	140	137	135	132	130	127	125
3	126	124	121	118	116	113	110	108
4	113	110	108	105	102	100	97	95
5	101	98	96	93	91	88	86	84
6	90	87	85	82	80	78	75	74
7					69	67	65	64
Rises & Sets 90°	84°	78°	72°	67°	63°	58°	55°	

Hours from Noon	SEP →23 / MAR 21	OCT 4 / MAR 11	OCT 14 / MAR 1	OCT 25 / FEB 18	NOV 3 / FEB 9	NOV 14 / JAN 29	NOV 27 / JAN 16	DEC 11 / JAN 2 ↓
0	180	180	180	180	180	180	180	180
1	160	161	162	163	164	164	165	165
2	142	144	146	147	149	150	151	152
3	126	129	131	133	135	136	138	139
4	113	116	118	121	122	124	126	127
5	101	104	106	109				
6	90							
Rises & Sets 90°	96°	102°	108°	113°	117°	122°	125°	

Before noon read all angles from North to East. After noon read all angles from North to West.

LATITUDE 50° NORTH

Hours from Noon	→ MAR 21 / SEP 23	MAR 31 / SEP 13	APR 11 / SEP 2	APR 22 / AUG 22	MAY 1 / AUG 12	MAY 12 / AUG 2	MAY 26 / JUL 19	JUN 10 / JUL 3 ↓
0	180	180	180	180	180	180	180	180
1	161	160	158	157	155	154	152	151
2	143	141	139	136	134	132	130	128
3	127	125	123	120	118	115	113	111
4	114	111	109	106	104	101	99	97
5	102	99	96	94	92	89	87	86
6	90	87	85	82	80	78	76	75
7					69	67	65	64
Rises & Sets	90°	84°	77°	71°	66°	61°	56°	53°

Hours from Noon	→ SEP 23 / MAR 21	OCT 4 / MAR 11	OCT 14 / MAR 1	OCT 25 / FEB 18	NOV 3 / FEB 9	NOV 14 / JAN 29	NOV 27 / JAN 16	DEC 11 / JAN 2 ↓
0	180	180	180	180	180	180	180	180
1	161	162	163	164	164	165	165	166
2	143	145	146	148	149	150	151	152
3	127	130	132	134	135	137	138	139
4	114	116	119	121	123	124	126	
5	102	104	107	109				
6	90							
Rises & Sets	90°	96°	102°	109°	114°	119°	124°	127°

Before noon read all angles from North to East.

LATITUDE 52½° NORTH

Hours from Noon	→ MAR 21 / SEP 23	MAR 31 / SEP 13	APR 11 / SEP 2	APR 22 / AUG 22	MAY 1 / AUG 12	MAY 12 / AUG 2	MAY 26 / JUL 19	JUN 10 / JUL 3 ↓
0	180	180	180	180	180	180	180	180
1	161	160	159	158	157	155	154	153
2	144	142	140	138	136	134	132	131
3	128	126	124	121	119	117	115	113
4	115	112	110	107	105	103	101	99
5	102	99	97	94	92	90	88	87
6	90	88	85	83	81	79	77	75
7				71	69	67	66	64
8						54	54	53
Rises & Sets	90°	83°	77°	70°	65°	59°	54°	50°

Hours from Noon	→ SEP 23 / MAR 21	OCT 4 / MAR 11	OCT 14 / MAR 1	OCT 25 / FEB 18	NOV 3 / FEB 9	NOV 14 / JAN 29	NOV 27 / JAN 16	DEC 11 / JAN 2 ↓
0	180	180	180	180	180	180	180	180
1	161	162	163	164	164	165	165	166
2	144	146	147	149	150	151	151	152
3	128	130	132	134	136	137	138	139
4	115	117	119	121	123	124	126	
5	102	104	107					
6	90							
Rises & Sets	90°	97°	103°	110°	115°	121°	126°	130°

After noon read all angles from North to West.

LATITUDE 55° NORTH

Hours from Noon	MAR 21 → SEP 23	MAR 31 SEP 13	APR 11 SEP 2	APR 22 AUG 22	MAY 1 AUG 12	MAY 12 AUG 2	MAY 26 JUL 19	JUN 10 JUL 3 ↓
0	180	180	180	180	180	180	180	180
1	162	161	160	159	158	157	156	155
2	145	143	141	140	138	136	134	133
3	129	127	125	123	121	119	117	115
4	115	113	111	108	106	104	102	101
5	102	100	98	95	93	92	90	88
6	90	88	85	83	81	79	78	76
7				71	69	68	66	65
8							54	53
Rises & Sets	90°	83°	76°	69°	63°	57°	51°	47°

Hours from Noon	SEP 23 → MAR 21	OCT 4 MAR 11	OCT 14 MAR 1	OCT 25 FEB 18	NOV 3 FEB 9	NOV 14 JAN 29	NOV 27 JAN 16	DEC 11 JAN 2 ↓
0	180	180	180	180	180	180	180	180
1	162	163	163	164	165	165	166	166
2	145	146	148	149	150	151	152	152
3	129	131	133	135	136	137	138	139
4	115	117	120	122	123	125		
5	102	105	107					
Rises & Sets	90°	97°	104°	111°	117°	123°	129°	133°

LATITUDE 57½° NORTH

Hours from Noon	MAR 21 → SEP 23	MAR 31 SEP 13	APR 11 SEP 2	APR 22 AUG 22	MAY 1 AUG 12	MAY 12 AUG 2	MAY 26 JUL 19	JUN 10 JUL 3 ↓
0	180	180	180	180	180	180	180	180
1	162	162	161	160	159	158	157	156
2	146	144	142	141	140	138	136	135
3	130	128	126	124	123	121	119	117
4	116	114	112	110	108	106	104	103
5	103	101	98	96	94	93	91	89
6	90	88	86	83	82	80	78	77
7				71	69	68	66	65
8					55	55	54	53
Rises & Sets	90°	83°	75°	67°	61°	55°	48°	43°

Hours from Noon	SEP 23 → MAR 21	OCT 4 MAR 11	OCT 14 MAR 1	OCT 25 FEB 18	NOV 3 FEB 9	NOV 14 JAN 29	NOV 27 JAN 16	DEC 11 JAN 2 ↓
0	180	180	180	180	180	180	180	180
1	162	163	164	164	165	165	166	166
2	145	147	148	149	150	151	152	152
3	130	132	134	135	136	137	139	
4	116	118	120	122	123			
5	103	105	107					
6	90							
Rises & Sets	90°	97°	105°	113°	119°	125°	132°	137°

After noon read all angles from North to West.

Before noon read all angles from North to East.

LATITUDE 2½° SOUTH

Hours from Noon	MAR →21 / SEP 23	MAR 31 / SEP 13	APR 11 / SEP 2	APR 22 / AUG 22	MAY 1 / AUG 12	MAY 12 / AUG 2	MAY 26 / JUL 19	JUN 10 / JUL 3 ↓
0	180	180	180	180	180	180	180	180
1	99	113	125	135	140	145	149	151
2	94	102	110	117	121	126	130	133
3	93	98	104	109	113	117	120	123
4	91	96	101	105	108	112	115	117
5	91	95	99	103	106	109	112	114
6	90	94	98	102	105	108	111	113
Rises & Sets	90°	94°	98°	102°	105°	108°	111°	113°

Hours from Noon	SEP →23 / MAR 21	OCT 4 / MAR 11	OCT 14 / MAR 1	OCT 25 / FEB 18	NOV 3 / FEB 9	NOV 14 / JAN 29	NOV 27 / JAN 16	DEC 11 / JAN 2 ↓
0	180	0	0	0	0	0	0	0
1	99	84	69	57	49	43	37	34
2	94	86	78	71	65	60	55	52
3	93	87	81	76	71	67	63	61
4	92	87	82	78	75	72	69	67
5	91	87	82	78	75	72	69	67
6	90	86	82	78	75	72	69	67
Rises & Sets	90°	86°	82°	78°	75°	72°	69°	67°

Before noon read all angles from South to East.
After noon read all angles from South to West.

LATITUDE 60° NORTH

Hours from Noon	MAR →21 / SEP 23	MAR 31 / SEP 13	APR 11 / SEP 2	APR 22 / AUG 22	MAY 1 / AUG 12	MAY 12 / AUG 2	MAY 26 / JUL 19	JUN 10 / JUL 3 ↓
0	180	180	180	180	180	180	180	180
1	163	162	161	160	160	159	158	157
2	146	145	144	142	141	140	138	137
3	131	129	127	126	124	122	121	119
4	117	115	113	111	109	107	106	104
5	103	101	99	97	95	94	92	91
6	90	88	86	84	82	81	79	78
7				71	70	68	67	66
8						55	54	53
9								41
Rises & Sets	90°	82°	74°	65°	59°	52°	44°	39°

Hours from Noon	SEP →23 / MAR 21	OCT 4 / MAR 11	OCT 14 / MAR 1	OCT 25 / FEB 18	NOV 3 / FEB 9	NOV 14 / JAN 29	NOV 27 / JAN 16	DEC 11 / JAN 2 ↓
0	180	180	180	180	180	180	180	180
1	163	163	164	165	165	165	166	166
2	146	147	149	150	150	151	152	153
3	131	132	134	135	137	138	139	
4	117	118	120	122	123			
5	103	105	107					
Rises & Sets	90°	98°	106°	115°	121°	128°	136°	141°

Before noon read all angles from North to East.
After noon read all angles from North to West.

LATITUDE 5° SOUTH

Hours from Noon	MAR →21 / SEP 23	MAR 31 / SEP 13	APR 11 / SEP 2	APR 22 / AUG 22	MAY 1 / AUG 12	MAY 12 / AUG 2	MAY 26 / JUL 19	JUN 10 / JUL 3 ↓
0	180	180	180	180	180	180	180	180
1	108	121	131	139	144	148	151	153
2	99	106	113	120	124	129	132	135
3	95	101	106	111	115	119	122	124
4	93	97	102	106	110	113	116	118
5	91	95	100	104	107	110	113	115
6	90	94	98					
Rises & Sets	90°	94°	98°	102°	105°	108°	111°	113°

Hours from Noon	SEP →23 / MAR 21	OCT 4 / MAR 11	OCT 14 / MAR 1	OCT 25 / FEB 18	NOV 3 / FEB 9	NOV 14 / JAN 29	NOV 27 / JAN 16	DEC 11 / JAN 2 ↓
0	180	180	0	0	0	0	0	0
1	108	93	78	64	55	47	41	37
2	99	91	83	75	69	64	58	55
3	95	89	84	78	74	70	66	63
4	93	88	84	79	76	72	69	66
5	91	87	83	79	76	73	70	67
6	90	86	82	78	75	72	69	67
Rises & Sets	90°	86°	82°	78°	75°	72°	69°	67°

LATITUDE 7½° SOUTH

Hours from Noon	MAR →21 / SEP 23	MAR 31 / SEP 13	APR 11 / SEP 2	APR 22 / AUG 22	MAY 1 / AUG 12	MAY 12 / AUG 2	MAY 26 / JUL 19	JUN 10 / JUL 3 ↓
0	180	180	180	180	180	180	180	180
1	116	127	136	142	147	150	153	155
2	103	110	117	123	127	131	135	137
3	97	103	108	113	117	120	124	126
4	94	99	103	108	111	114	117	119
5	92	96	100	104	107	110	113	115
6	90							
Rises & Sets	90°	94°	98°	102°	105°	108°	111°	113°

Hours from Noon	SEP →23 / MAR 21	OCT 4 / MAR 11	OCT 14 / MAR 1	OCT 25 / FEB 18	NOV 3 / FEB 9	NOV 14 / JAN 29	NOV 27 / JAN 16	DEC 11 / JAN 2 ↓
0	180	180	0	0	0	0	0	0
1	116	102	87	72	62	53	45	41
2	103	95	87	79	73	67	62	58
3	97	92	86	80	76	72	68	65
4	94	90	85	80	77	73	70	68
5	92	88	84	78	76	73	72	68
6	90	86	82	78	75	72	69	67
Rises & Sets	90°	86°	82°	78°	75°	72°	69°	67°

Before noon read all angles from South to East. *After* noon read all angles from South to West.

LATITUDE 12½° SOUTH

Hours from Noon	MAR 21→ / SEP 23	MAR 31 / SEP 13	APR 11 / SEP 2	APR 22 / AUG 22	MAY 1 / AUG 12	MAY 12 / AUG 2	MAY 26 / JUL 19	JUN 10↓ / JUL 3
0	180	180	180	180	180	180	180	180
1	129	137	143	148	151	154	156	157
2	111	117	123	128	132	135	138	140
3	102	107	112	117	120	124	127	129
4	97	102	106	110	113	116	119	121
5	93	97	101	105	108	111	114	116
6	90							
Rises & Sets	90°	94°	98°	102°	105°	108°	112°	114°

Hours from Noon	SEP 23→ / MAR 21→	OCT 4 / MAR 11	OCT 14 / MAR 1	OCT 25 / FEB 18	NOV 3 / FEB 9	NOV 14 / JAN 29	NOV 27 / JAN 16	DEC 11 / JAN 2↓
0	180	180	180	180	0	0	0	0
1	129	119	105	90	79	67	57	52
2	111	103	96	88	82	75	69	66
3	102	97	91	86	81	77	73	70
4	97	93	88	83	80	76	73	71
5	93	89	85	81	78	75	72	70
6	90	86	82	78	75	72	69	67
Rises & Sets	90°	86°	82°	78°	75°	72°	68°	66°

After noon read all angles from South to West.

LATITUDE 10° SOUTH

Hours from Noon	MAR 21→ / SEP 23	MAR 31 / SEP 13	APR 11 / SEP 2	APR 22 / AUG 22	MAY 1 / AUG 12	MAY 12 / AUG 2	MAY 26 / JUL 19	JUN 10↓ / JUL 3
0	180	180	180	180	180	180	180	180
1	123	132	140	146	149	152	155	156
2	107	114	120	126	130	133	137	139
3	100	105	110	115	119	122	125	127
4	96	100	105	109	112	115	118	120
5	93	97	101	105	108	111	114	116
6	90							
Rises & Sets	90°	94°	98°	102°	105°	108°	111°	113°

Hours from Noon	SEP 23→ / MAR 21→	OCT 4 / MAR 11	OCT 14 / MAR 1	OCT 25 / FEB 18	NOV 3 / FEB 9	NOV 14 / JAN 29	NOV 27 / JAN 16	DEC 11 / JAN 2↓
0	180	180	180	180	0	0	0	0
1	123	111	96	81	70	60	51	46
2	107	99	91	83	77	71	66	62
3	100	94	89	83	79	74	70	67
4	96	91	87	82	78	75	71	69
5	93	89	84	80	77	74	71	69
6	90	86	82	78	75	72	69	67
Rises & Sets	90°	86°	82°	78°	75°	72°	69°	67°

Before noon read all angles from South to East. After noon read all angles from South to West.

LATITUDE 17½° SOUTH

Hours from Noon	MAR 21→ / SEP 23	MAR 31 / SEP 13	APR 11 / SEP 2	APR 22 / AUG 22	MAY 1 / AUG 12	MAY 12 / AUG 2	MAY 26 / JUL 19	JUN 10 / JUL 3 ↓
0	180	180	180	180	180	180	180	180
1	138	144	149	152	155	157	158	160
2	117	123	128	133	136	139	141	143
3	107	112	116	120	123	126	129	131
4	100	104	108	112	115	118	121	123
5	95	98	102	106	109	112	115	117
6	90							
Rises & Sets	90°	94°	98°	103°	106°	109°	112°	114°

Hours from Noon	SEP 23→ / MAR 21	OCT 4 / MAR 11	OCT 14 / MAR 1	OCT 25 / FEB 18	NOV 3 / FEB 9	NOV 14 / JAN 29	NOV 27 / JAN 16	DEC 11 / JAN 2 ↓
0	180	180	180	180	180	180	0	0
1	138	131	121	109	98	86	74	66
2	117	111	104	97	91	84	78	74
3	107	102	96	91	87	82	78	75
4	100	96	91	87	83	80	76	74
5	95	91	87	83	80	76	73	71
6	90	86	82	79	76	73	70	68
Rises & Sets	90°	86°	82°	77°	74°	71°	68°	66°

LATITUDE 15° SOUTH

Hours from Noon	MAR 21→ / SEP 23	MAR 31 / SEP 13	APR 11 / SEP 2	APR 22 / AUG 22	MAY 1 / AUG 12	MAY 12 / AUG 2	MAY 26 / JUL 19	JUN 10 / JUL 3 ↓
0	180	180	180	180	180	180	180	180
1	134	141	146	150	153	155	157	159
2	114	120	126	131	134	137	140	142
3	105	110	114	119	122	125	128	130
4	98	103	107	111	114	117	120	122
5	94	98	102	106	109	112	114	116
6	90							
Rises & Sets	90°	94°	98°	102°	106°	109°	112°	114°

Hours from Noon	SEP 23→ / MAR 21	OCT 4 / MAR 11	OCT 14 / MAR 1	OCT 25 / FEB 18	NOV 3 / FEB 9	NOV 14 / JAN 29	NOV 27 / JAN 16	DEC 11 / JAN 2 ↓
0	180	180	180	180	180	180	0	0
1	134	125	114	100	88	76	65	58
2	114	107	100	92	86	80	74	70
3	105	99	94	88	84	80	75	72
4	98	94	90	85	81	78	74	72
5	94	90	86	82	79	76	73	70
6	90	86	82	78	75	73	70	68
Rises & Sets	90°	86°	82°	78°	74°	71°	68°	66°

Before noon read all angles from South to East. After noon read all angles from South to West.

LATITUDE 20° SOUTH

Hours from Noon	MAR 21 →	MAR 31	APR 11	APR 22	MAY 1	MAY 12	MAY 26	JUN 10
	SEP 23	SEP 13	SEP 2	AUG 22	AUG 12	AUG 2	JUL 19	JUL 3 ↓
0	180	180	180	180	180	180	180	180
1	142	147	151	154	156	158	159	160
2	121	126	131	135	138	140	143	144
3	109	113	118	122	125	128	130	132
4	101	105	109	113	116	119	122	123
5	95	99	103	107	109	112	115	117
6	90							
Rises & Sets	90°	94°	99°	103°	106°	109°	112°	115°

Hours from Noon	SEP 23 →	OCT 4	OCT 14	OCT 25	NOV 3	NOV 14	NOV 27	DEC 11
	MAR 21	MAR 11	MAR 1	FEB 18	FEB 9	JAN 29	JAN 16	JAN 2 ↓
0	180	180	180	180	180	180	180	180
1	142	136	127	117	107	94	83	75
2	121	115	108	101	94	89	83	78
3	109	104	99	93	89	85	80	77
4	101	97	93	88	85	81	78	75
5	94	91	87	83	80	77	74	72
6	90	86	82	79	76	73	70	68
Rises & Sets	90°	86°	81°	77°	74°	71°	68°	65°

Before noon read all angles from South to East.

LATITUDE 22½° SOUTH

Hours from Noon	MAR 21 →	MAR 31	APR 11	APR 22	MAY 1	MAY 12	MAY 26	JUN 10
	SEP 23	SEP 13	SEP 2	AUG 22	AUG 12	AUG 2	JUL 19	JUL 3 ↓
0	180	180	180	180	180	180	180	180
1	145	149	153	155	157	159	160	161
2	124	128	133	137	139	142	144	145
3	111	115	120	123	126	129	131	133
4	102	106	110	114	117	120	122	124
5	96	100	103	107	110	112	115	117
6	90							
Rises & Sets	90°	94°	99°	103°	106°	110°	113°	115°

Hours from Noon	SEP 23 →	OCT 4	OCT 14	OCT 25	NOV 3	NOV 14	NOV 27	DEC 11
	MAR 21	MAR 11	MAR 1	FEB 18	FEB 9	JAN 29	JAN 16	JAN 2 ↓
0	180	180	180	180	180	180	180	0
1	145	140	133	124	115	105	93	85
2	124	118	112	105	100	94	87	83
3	111	106	101	96	92	88	83	80
4	102	98	94	90	86	83	79	77
5	96	92	88	84	81	78	75	73
6	90	86	83	79	76	73	70	69
Rises & Sets	90°	86°	81°	77°	74°	70°	67°	65°

After noon read all angles from South to West.

Before noon read all angles from South to East. *After* noon read all angles from South to West.

LATITUDE 25° SOUTH

Hours from Noon	MAR 21 / SEP 23	MAR 31 / SEP 13	APR 11 / SEP 2	APR 22 / AUG 22	MAY 1 / AUG 12	MAY 12 / AUG 2	MAY 26 / JUL 19	JUN 10 / JUL 3
0	180	180	180	180	180	180	180	180
1	148	151	154	157	158	160	161	162
2	126	131	135	138	141	143	145	146
3	113	117	121	125	127	130	132	134
4	104	108	111	115	118	120	123	125
5	96	100	104	107	110	113	115	117
6	90							
Rises & Sets	90°	94°	99°	103°	107°	110°	113°	116°

Hours from Noon	SEP 23 / MAR 21	OCT 4 / MAR 11	OCT 14 / MAR 1	OCT 25 / FEB 18	NOV 3 / FEB 9	NOV 14 / JAN 29	NOV 27 / JAN 16	DEC 11 / JAN 2
0	180	180	180	180	180	180	180	180
1	148	143	137	130	123	114	103	95
2	126	121	116	109	104	98	92	88
3	113	108	104	99	95	90	86	83
4	104	100	96	91	88	85	81	79
5	96	93	89	85	82	79	76	74
6	90	86	83	79	76	74	71	69
Rises & Sets	90°	86°	81°	77°	73°	70°	67°	64°

LATITUDE 27½° SOUTH

Hours from Noon	MAR 21 / SEP 23	MAR 31 / SEP 13	APR 11 / SEP 2	APR 22 / AUG 22	MAY 1 / AUG 12	MAY 12 / AUG 2	MAY 26 / JUL 19	JUN 10 / JUL 3
0	180	180	180	180	180	180	180	180
1	150	153	156	158	159	161	162	163
2	129	133	136	140	142	144	146	147
3	115	119	123	126	129	131	133	135
4	105	109	112	116	118	121	123	125
5	97	101	104	108	110	113	115	117
6	90							
Rises & Sets	90°	94°	99°	104°	107°	110°	114°	116°

Hours from Noon	SEP 23 / MAR 21	OCT 4 / MAR 11	OCT 14 / MAR 1	OCT 25 / FEB 18	NOV 3 / FEB 9	NOV 14 / JAN 29	NOV 27 / JAN 16	DEC 11 / JAN 2
0	180	180	180	180	180	180	180	180
1	150	146	141	135	129	121	112	105
2	129	124	119	113	108	103	97	93
3	115	110	106	101	97	93	89	86
4	105	101	97	93	90	86	83	80
5	97	93	90	86	83	80	77	75
6	90	86	83	79	77	74	71	69
Rises & Sets	90°	85°	81°	76°	73°	70°	66°	64°

Hours from Noon	MAR →21 SEP 23	MAR 31 SEP 13	APR 11 SEP 2	APR 22 AUG 22	MAY 1 AUG 12	MAY 12 AUG 2	MAY 26 JUL 19	JUN 10 JUL 3 ↓
0	180	180	180	180	180	180	180	180
1	153	156	158	160	161	162	163	164
2	133	136	139	142	144	146	148	149
3	118	122	125	128	131	133	135	136
4	107	111	114	117	120	122	124	126
5	98	102	105	108	111	113	116	
6	90							
Rises & Sets	90°	95°	99°	104°	108°	111°	115°	118°

Hours from Noon	SEP →23 MAR 21	OCT 4 MAR 11	OCT 14 MAR 1	OCT 25 FEB 18	NOV 3 FEB 9	NOV 14 JAN 29	NOV 27 JAN 16	DEC 11 JAN 2 ↓
0	180	180	180	180	180	180	180	180
1	153	151	147	143	139	133	127	122
2	133	129	125	120	116	111	106	102
3	118	114	110	106	102	99	95	92
4	107	104	100	96	93	90	86	84
5	98	95	91	88	85	82	79	77
6	90	87	83	80	77	75	72	70
7								63
Rises & Sets	90°	85°	80°	76°	72°	68°	65°	62°

After noon read all angles from South to West.

Hours from Noon	MAR →21 SEP 23	MAR 31 SEP 13	APR 11 SEP 2	APR 22 AUG 22	MAY 1 AUG 12	MAY 12 AUG 2	MAY 26 JUL 19	JUN 10 JUL 3 ↓
0	180	180	180	180	180	180	180	180
1	152	155	157	159	160	161	162	163
2	131	135	138	141	143	145	147	148
3	117	120	124	127	130	132	134	136
4	106	110	113	117	119	122	124	125
5	98	101	105	108	111	113	116	117
6	90							
Rises & Sets	90°	95°	99°	104°	107°	111°	114°	117°

Hours from Noon	SEP →23 MAR 21	OCT 4 MAR 11	OCT 14 MAR 1	OCT 25 FEB 18	NOV 3 FEB 9	NOV 14 JAN 29	NOV 27 JAN 16	DEC 11 JAN 2 ↓
0	180	180	180	180	180	180	180	180
1	152	149	144	139	134	128	120	114
2	131	127	122	116	112	107	101	97
3	117	112	108	103	100	96	92	89
4	106	102	98	94	91	88	85	82
5	98	94	90	87	84	81	78	76
6	90	87	83	80	77	74	72	70
Rises & Sets	90°	85°	81°	76°	73°	69°	66°	63°

Before noon read all angles from South to East. *After* noon read all angles from South to West.

LATITUDE 35° SOUTH

Hours from Noon	MAR 21 → SEP 23	MAR 31 SEP 13	APR 11 SEP 2	APR 22 AUG 22	MAY 1 AUG 12	MAY 12 AUG 2	MAY 26 JUL 19	JUN 10 ↓ JUL 3
0	180	180	180	180	180	180	180	180
1	155	157	159	160	161	162	163	164
2	135	138	141	143	145	147	148	149
3	110	123	126	129	131	134	136	137
4	108	112	115	118	120	123	125	126
5	99	102	105	108	111	113		
6	90							
Rises & Sets	90°	95°	100°	105°	108°	112°	116°	118°

Hours from Noon	SEP 23 → MAR 21	OCT 4 MAR 11	OCT 14 MAR 1	OCT 25 FEB 18	NOV 3 FEB 9	NOV 14 JAN 29	NOV 27 JAN 16	DEC 11 ↓ JAN 2
0	180	180	180	180	180	180	180	180
1	155	152	149	146	142	138	133	129
2	135	131	127	123	119	115	110	107
3	120	116	112	108	105	101	97	95
4	108	105	101	97	94	91	88	86
5	99	95	92	88	86	83	80	78
6	90	87	83	80	78	75	73	71
7							64	63
Rises & Sets	90°	85°	80°	75°	72°	68°	64°	62°

LATITUDE 37½° SOUTH

Hours from Noon	MAR 21 → SEP 23	MAR 31 SEP 13	APR 11 SEP 2	APR 22 AUG 22	MAY 1 AUG 12	MAY 12 AUG 2	MAY 26 JUL 19	JUN 10 ↓ JUL 3
0	180	180	180	180	180	180	180	180
1	156	158	160	161	162	163	164	164
2	136	139	142	144	146	147	149	150
3	121	124	127	130	132	134	136	137
4	109	113	116	119	120	123	125	127
5	99	102	106	109	111	113		
6	90	90						
Rises & Sets	90°	95°	100°	105°	109°	113°	117°	119°

Hours from Noon	SEP 23 → MAR 21	OCT 4 MAR 11	OCT 14 MAR 1	OCT 25 FEB 18	NOV 3 FEB 9	NOV 14 JAN 29	NOV 27 JAN 16	DEC 11 ↓ JAN 2
0	180	180	180	180	180	180	180	180
1	156	154	151	148	145	142	138	134
2	136	133	130	126	122	118	114	111
3	121	118	114	110	107	104	100	98
4	109	106	103	99	96	93	90	88
5	99	96	93	89	87	84	81	79
6	90	87	84	80	78	76	73	71
7							64	63
Rises & Sets	90°	85°	80°	75°	71°	67°	63°	60°

Before noon read all angles from South to East. *After* noon read all angles from South to West.

LATITUDE 40° SOUTH

Hours from Noon	→MAR 21 / SEP 23	MAR 31 / SEP 13	APR 11 / SEP 2	APR 22 / AUG 22	MAY 1 / AUG 12	MAY 12 / AUG 2	MAY 26 / JUL 19	JUN 10 / JUL 3 ↓
0	180	180	180	180	180	180	180	180
1	157	159	160	162	163	163	164	165
2	138	141	143	145	147	148	150	150
3	123	126	128	131	133	135	137	138
4	110	113	116	119	121	123	125	127
5	100	103	106	109	111			
6	90							
Rises & Sets	90°	95°	100°	106°	106°	110°	114°	118°	121°

Hours from Noon	→SEP 23 / MAR 21	OCT 4 / MAR 11	OCT 14 / MAR 1	OCT 25 / FEB 18	NOV 3 / FEB 9	NOV 14 / JAN 29	NOV 27 / JAN 16	DEC 11 / JAN 2 ↓
0	180	180	180	180	180	180	180	180
1	157	155	153	151	148	145	142	139
2	138	135	132	128	125	122	118	115
3	123	120	116	112	109	106	103	100
4	110	107	104	100	98	95	92	90
5	100	97	93	90	88	85	82	81
6	90	87	84	81	78	76	74	72
7						67	65	63
Rises & Sets	90°	85°	80°	74°	70°	66°	62°	59°

Before noon read all angles from South to East.

LATITUDE 42½° SOUTH

Hours from Noon	→MAR 21 / SEP 23	MAR 31 / SEP 13	APR 11 / SEP 2	APR 22 / AUG 22	MAY 1 / AUG 12	MAY 12 / AUG 2	MAY 26 / JUL 19	JUN 10 / JUL 3 ↓
0	180	180	180	180	180	180	180	180
1	158	160	161	162	163	164	165	165
2	139	142	144	146	147	149	150	151
3	124	127	129	132	134	135	137	138
4	111	114	117	120	122	124	126	127
5	100	103	106	109	111			
6	90							
Rises & Sets	90°	95°	101°	106°	106°	111°	115°	119°	122°

Hours from Noon	→SEP 23 / MAR 21	OCT 4 / MAR 11	OCT 14 / MAR 1	OCT 25 / FEB 18	NOV 3 / FEB 9	NOV 14 / JAN 29	NOV 27 / JAN 16	DEC 11 / JAN 2 ↓
0	180	180	180	180	180	180	180	180
1	158	157	155	152	150	148	145	143
2	139	137	134	131	128	125	121	119
3	124	121	118	114	112	109	105	103
4	111	108	105	102	99	96	94	92
5	100	97	94	91	89	86	84	82
6	90	87	84	81	79	77	74	73
7						67	65	63
Rises & Sets	90°	85°	79°	74°	69°	65°	61°	58°

After noon read all angles from South to West.

LATITUDE 45° SOUTH

Hours from Noon	MAR → 21 / SEP 23	MAR 31 / SEP 13	APR 11 / SEP 2	APR 22 / AUG 22	MAY 1 / AUG 12	MAY 12 / AUG 2	MAY 26 / JUL 19	JUN 10 / JUL 3 ↓
0	180	180	180	180	180	180	180	180
1	159	161	162	163	163	164	165	165
2	141	143	145	147	148	149	150	151
3	125	128	130	133	134	136	137	139
4	112	115	118	120	122	124	126	127
5	101	104	106	109				
6	90							
Rises & Sets	90°	96°	101°	107°	111°	116°	120°	124°

Hours from Noon	SEP → 23 / MAR 21	OCT 4 / MAR 11	OCT 14 / MAR 1	OCT 25 / FEB 18	NOV 3 / FEB 9	NOV 14 / JAN 29	NOV 27 / JAN 16	DEC 11 / JAN 2 ↓
0	180	180	180	180	180	180	180	180
1	159	158	156	154	152	150	148	146
2	141	138	136	133	130	127	124	122
3	125	122	120	116	114	111	108	106
4	112	109	106	103	101	98	95	94
5	101	98	95	92	90	87	85	83
6	90	87	84	81	79	77	75	73
7				69	69	67	65	63
Rises & Sets	90°	84°	79°	73°	69°	64°	60°	56°

LATITUDE 47½° SOUTH

Hours from Noon	MAR → 21 / SEP 23	MAR 31 / SEP 13	APR 11 / SEP 2	APR 22 / AUG 22	MAY 1 / AUG 12	MAY 12 / AUG 2	MAY 26 / JUL 19	JUN 10 / JUL 3 ↓
0	180	180	180	180	180	180	180	180
1	160	161	162	163	164	164	165	165
2	142	144	146	147	149	150	151	152
3	126	129	131	133	135	136	138	139
4	113	116	118	121	122	124	126	127
5	101	104	106	109				
6	90							
Rises & Sets	90°	96°	102°	108°	113°	117°	122°	125°

Hours from Noon	SEP → 23 / MAR 21	OCT 4 / MAR 11	OCT 14 / MAR 1	OCT 25 / FEB 18	NOV 3 / FEB 9	NOV 14 / JAN 29	NOV 27 / JAN 16	DEC 11 / JAN 2 ↓
0	180	180	180	180	180	180	180	180
1	160	159	157	156	154	152	150	149
2	142	140	137	135	132	130	127	125
3	126	124	121	118	116	113	110	108
4	113	110	108	105	102	100	97	95
5	101	98	96	93	91	88	86	84
6	90	87	85	82	80	78	75	74
7					69	67	65	64
Rises & Sets	90°	84°	78°	72°	67°	63°	58°	55°

Hours from Noon	MAR 21 / SEP 23 →	MAR 31 / SEP 13	APR 11 / SEP 2	APR 22 / AUG 22	MAY 1 / AUG 12	MAY 12 / AUG 2	MAY 26 / JUL 19	JUN 10 / JUL 3 ↓
0	180	180	180	180	180	180	180	180
1	161	162	163	164	164	165	165	166
2	143	145	146	148	149	150	151	152
3	127	130	132	134	135	137	138	139
4	114	116	119	121	123	124	126	
5	102	104	107	109				
6	90							
Rises & Sets	90°	84°	77°	71°	66°	61°	56°	53°

Hours from Noon	SEP 23 / MAR 21 →	OCT 4 / MAR 11	OCT 14 / MAR 1	OCT 25 / FEB 18	NOV 3 / FEB 9	NOV 14 / JAN 29	NOV 27 / JAN 16	DEC 11 / JAN 2 ↓
0	180	180	180	180	180	180	180	180
1	161	160	158	157	155	154	152	151
2	143	141	139	136	134	132	130	128
3	127	125	123	120	118	115	113	111
4	114	111	109	106	104	101	99	97
5	102	99	96	94	92	89	87	86
6	90	87	85	82	80	78	76	75
7					69	67	65	64
8								53
Rises & Sets	90°	84°	77°	71°	66°	61°	56°	53°

Before noon read all angles from South to East. *After* noon read all angles from South to West.